Titled Trains of The Western

Cecil J. Allen

LONDON

IAN ALLAN LTD

first published 1974

ISBN 07110 0513 3

The "Bristolian" at 100 m.p.h.—4-6-0 No. 6018 *King Henry VI* hurtles down Dauntsey bank on 28 July 1955.

Published by Ian Allan Ltd, Shepperton, Surrey and printed and bound in the United Kingdom by R. J. Acford Ltd, Chichester, Sussex

Contents

△ The first Western Pullman—the short-lived "Torquay Pullman" of 1929-30 passes Twyford on its way westward behind a "King" 4-6-0.

◁ The down afternoon "Birmingham Pullman" diesel multiple-unit comes off the Bicester line at Aynho Junction in August 1962, passing a "King" 4-6-0 heading for London with the up "Inter-City".

Photo by M. Mensing

The Birmingham Pullman

The former Great Western Railway had no particular love for Pullman cars. It is true that in May, 1929, an experiment was tried with the introduction of Pullmans on the Transatlantic boat trains from Plymouth to Paddington, run in connection with the French Line steamers, and that in July of the same year an all-Pullman train began to run between Paddington and Paignton—The " Torquay Pullman ". Going down, it left Paddington at 11.0 a.m., covered the 193.9 miles to Newton Abbot non-stop in 205 minutes, and reached Torquay at 2.40 and Paignton at 2.50 p.m. On the up journey, starting from Paignton at 4.30 and Torquay at 4.40 p.m., it was back into Paddington by 8.30 p.m. But it had to compete with the forerunner of the " Torbay Express ", which ran at more convenient times for the patrons of this route and which required no supplementary fare. In consequence the Pullman never received adequate patronage, and was withdrawn in 1930, as also were the cars from the boat trains. All the cars involved moved to the Southern Railway, some from then on working in Transatlantic boat trains between Southampton and Waterloo, and others finding employment in the " Bournemouth Belle ".

Regular Pullman services did not reappear on the Western until after nationalisation. By the early 1950s British Railways had grasped the potential of trainboard luxury as a selling-point in competition with motorways and expanding domestic air services. Pullman travel was making a new impression on the business market north of the Thames and a spread of the Pullman network was planned. First fruits on the Western emerged in 1955 as a new Pullman service between Paddington and South Wales, described later in this book.

In the second half of the 1950s, a successor to Pullmans was born on the Continent—the " Trans-Europ Express ", an international network of first-class-only, limited-accommodation, high-speed trains specifically timed for a business clientele. In the 1959-60 winter British Railways unveiled their copy, the " Blue Pullman " multiple-unit, fully air-conditioned (an innovation for Britain) and with saloons lavishly equipped for a new level of passenger comfort. Power plant comprised two 1,500 rpm, MAN 1,000 h.p. engines, one in each 67½ ton end power car, with electric transmission to eight traction motors spread throughout the unit. A six-car, all-first-class version was the first to take the track, as the London-Manchester " Midland Pullman ". In 1960 an eight-car variant, including second-class saloons, followed and three sets were allocated to the Western, where one of the services the new units inaugurated was the first West Midlands Pullman—the " Birmingham Pullman."

On most of their peak-hour runs the " Blue Pullmans " pulled in satisfying business, but the conception of the units themselves was seriously flawed. A streamlined multiple-unit format seems to have been chosen primarily because it was thought to have some indefinable popular appeal, as witness the success of the first Continental European " Trans-Europ Express " sets. But abroad the double-ended idea had operating point, since many of the TEE itineraries involved quick reversal at intermediate stops where back in history stations had been laid out as termini (e.g. Frankfurt, Munich and Florence). BR had no such problems.

To offset this fancied glamour of multiple-units, BR lumbered themselves with very inflexible tools. A defect on one Pullman put a whole unit out of action, because of intricate main and auxiliary power and control cables linking the vehicles, and also because traction power was not confined to one car. For nearly the whole first two years of its " Blue Pullman " operation the Western Region felt impelled to keep one whole costly set idle to cover possible failures. When it took the plunge in late 1961 and scheduled all three sets in daily revenue service, it was forced to maintain a locomotive-hauled train of old-style Pullmans as a reserve (a stopgap, incidentally, which the regular business customers regarded as a very poor substitute for the air-conditioned, extra-fare comfort of the " Blue Pullman " saloons).

Additionally BR suffered from another inherent failing of multiple-units at that time. No one had then mastered the art of designing a multiple-unit bogie to ride as smoothly as a hauled coach. Although BR chose for the " Blue Pullmans " the Swiss-designed Schlieren bogie which had a fine reputation on the Continent, it did not suit the shorter British coach bodies and British permanent way. Exhaustive and expensive research cured some of the units' most traumatic excesses, but to the end of their days they could still give one an unrelaxingly lively ride.

The comfortable timings mapped out for the Western's " Blue Pullmans " initially were disappointing, The new " Birmingham Pullman " of 1961 was generously given 5 minutes over 2 hours to run up to Paddington with no more than two intermediate stops—one at Solihull to pick up residents living on the south side of the city, and the other at Leamington Spa. Wolverhampton patrons had to make an early start, at 7 a.m.; Birmingham Snow Hill was left at 7.30 a.m., and with no less than 95 minutes allowed for the 87.3 miles from Leamington the London terminus was reached at 9.35 a.m., or at exactly the same time as the new " Bristol Pullman ". Indeed, on the first day of the new service the two trains most artistically dead-heated up the length of two adjacent arrival platforms at Paddington and came to a stand at precisely the same moment.

As with the Bristol train, the " Birmingham Pullman " made a midday excursion as far as Snow Hill and back, and on the fastest timing scheduled up to that date over the former G.W.R. route, 1 hour 55 minutes, but with only one intermediate stop, at Leamington. Leaving Paddington at 12.10 p.m. the train reached Birmingham at 2.5 p.m., and with a quick turn round it was on its way back to London by 2.30 p.m., arriving at 4.25 p.m. Here there was an equally brief turn-around time, for the final journey was begun at 4.50 p.m., Birmingham being reached at 6.55 and Wolverhampton at 7.20 p.m.

The only subsequent alteration in the working of the train was to change the mid-morning departure from Paddington from 12.10 to 10.10 a.m., and the start of the return trip from 2.30 to 1 p.m. out of Snow Hill, possibly in the hope of doing a little more luncheon business in the up direction than had been the case going down. But the " Birmingham Pullman " had no more than a short life. During the electrification of London Midland main line between Euston and Birmingham the Western Region had been carrying practically the whole of this traffic, but with the bringing into operation in March, 1967, of the full L.M.R. electric service, that of the Western Region was very severely pruned, and among the casualties was the " Birmingham Pullman ".

The Bristol Pullman

First of the new diesel-powered " Blue Pullman " train sets to take up service in 1960 was the " Bristol Pullman ". This left Temple Meads at 7.45 a.m., and ran non-stop to London over the Badminton route, 117.65 miles in 110 minutes. Instead, of standing idle during the day, it then returned at 10.5 a.m. *via* Bath, running the 106.85 miles to Bath in 95 minutes, and reaching Bristol at 12 noon. Thirty minutes later it was starting back to London, again making the run in 115 minutes, and the final journey was from Paddington at 4.55 p.m., non-stop to Bristol *via* Badminton in 110 minutes. Bath, however, was too important to be missed out on the up morning and down evening trips, and from mid-October the up Pullman started its day 5 minutes earlier and finished it 5 minutes later, by reason of the diversion to the Bath route and a call there. It was again a disappointment to many that the new Bristol service took longer on the journey than the 105 minutes of

▷ When a "Blue Pullman" dmu was incapacitated, a substitute train of locomotive-hauled steam-age Pullmans was put on. Here a rake of cars *Athene, Thetis, Melandra, Ceteia, Thalia, Juana, Hebe* and *Fortuna* forms the midday Birmingham-London service on 2 April 1963, passing High Wycombe behind "Western" class diesel-hydraulic No. D1004 *Western Crusader*, then in maroon livery.

Photo by H. K. Harman

▽ The westbound "Bristol Pullman", seen shortly after its inauguration, passes St. Annes Park on its way into Bristol.

Photo by G. F. Heiron

" King " class 4-6-0 No. 6013 *King Henry VIII* heads the pre-war " Bristolian " out of London over Hanwell Viaduct.

the steam-hauled " Bristolian ", which by 1954 had been restored to its pre-war schedule; the latter was certainly non-stop, but its point-to-point times were as fast as those of the Pullman.

In the middle 1960s the down midday " Bristol Pullman " working was changed, first from 10.5 to 10.45 a.m. out of Paddington; next came an alteration in the starting time to 12.45 p.m., with the introduction of a stop at Chippenham, and a fast time of 84 minutes over this 94-mile stretch; the return from Bristol was at 3.15 p.m., and the Paddington arrival at 5.15 p.m., 30 minutes before departure on the last down trip of the day. Later still, Reading was added as an intermediate stop.

Finally, in March, 1967, yet another alteration took place in the midday working. The Paddington start went back to 10.45 a.m., the Chippenham stop was cut out, and with Reading and Bath stops the booked time to Bristol became 2 hours exactly. In the reverse direction, this way with a stop at Swindon as well as at Bath and Reading, the time went up to a rather indifferent 2 hours 5 minutes, though it may be added that all the main line times in the 1967 timetable were increased by an average of 5 minutes or so because of delays likely to be experienced in the resignalling of Paddington station and its approaches.

Another change of note in 1967 concerned the morning and evening Paddington-Bristol " Blue Pullman " workings. To such an extent had their patronage increased that with the help of the released " Birmingham Pullmans " two six-car trains were made up, which were coupled to form a 12-car train on the 8.15 a.m. from Bristol, still stopping only at Bath and taking 1 hour 50 minutes to London. On arrival at Paddington the train split into its two sections. One of these formed the 10.45 a.m. to Bristol; the other left at 12.15 p.m. on an entirely new 60-minute run to Oxford—an experiment designed in particular to attract American visitors to the University city. Returning at 4.15 p.m., the " Oxford Pullman " reached Paddington with a 30-minute margin for reunion with the other Bristol set, and a 12-car working back at 5.45 p.m. to Bath and Bristol. But the Oxford working attracted little patronage, and was soon abandoned. Incidentally, there had been some hopes of using the displaced Birmingham Pullman set of cars to form the " Golden Hind " between Paddington and Plymouth, but the motive power authorities could not sanction this because the South Devon gradients would have caused difficulties with the train's power plant.

In its final years the " Bristol Pullman " had to maintain higher speeds than when it was first introduced. The growing importance of Chippenham became recognised by a stop there in both directions; and with a start from Temple Meads at 8.15 a.m. the working departure of 8.43 a.m. from Chippenham left 77 minutes to cover the 94 miles to Paddington, for an arrival at precisely 10 a.m., at the end of a journey of 105 minutes. Going down, after leaving Paddington at 4.45 p.m. the " Bristol Pullman " was booked to pass Swindon, 77.3 miles, in 60½ minutes and to reach Chippenham in 73 miles, at a booked average of 77.3 m.p.h.

start to stop. Then followed the Bath stop, and the $1\frac{3}{4}$-hour journey finished in Bristol Temple Meads at 6.30 p.m.

But in 1973 the decision has been reached to withdraw all Pullman services on the Western Region, the " Bristol Pullman " among them.

The Bristolian

To mark the centenary of the opening in 1835 of the Great Western main line between Paddington and Bristol, it was decided by the G.W.R. management to put on a new express which would link the two cities in a shorter time than ever previously. There had been hopes that a schedule of 90 minutes might have been tried, but eventually, in order that excessively high speed might not be necessary, a booking of 105 minutes in each direction was brought into operation, 15 minutes less than the previous best.

This required a slightly higher average speed on the down journey than on the up, for the down and the up trains took different routes. Brunel's original main line, 118.3 miles in length from Paddington to Temple Meads Station, Bristol, was used in the westbound direction, and the end-to-end average was thus 67.6 m.p.h.; but on the up journey the train left Temple Meads by way of Stapleton Road, climbed the 1 in 75 of Ashley Hill bank ($2\frac{1}{4}$ miles long), and from Filton Junction used the Badminton-cut-off, which was opened in 1901, rejoining the older main line at Wootton Bassett. This reduced the distance to 117.6 miles, and the overall speed to 67.2 m.p.h. But because of the Ashley Hill bank, the slowing through Filton, and the long 1 in 300 climb to Badminton, the up journey was probably the harder of the two.

A seven-coach train sufficed for normal " Bristolian " needs. This formation included two third-class brakes, three composites, one third, and in the centre one of the latest buffet cars, with a counter along its full length, and pedestal seats for passengers taking refreshments. The coaches were of the latest wide type, with recessed end doors, and the weight of the seven-coach formation was 221 tons empty, or 235 tons with the normal passenger complement. In the first months of the " Bristolian's " running, a " King " class 4-6-0 was thought to be necessary, but it was soon found that the speed was well within the capacity of a " Castle ", and the working was turned over to the highly competent link of engines and crews at Old Oak Common shed that were responsible also for the working of the " Cheltenham Flyer ".

Departure from Paddington was at 10 a.m., and Bristol was reached at 11.45 a.m. In the reverse direction, the " Bristolian " left Temple Meads at 4.30 p.m., and was due in London at 6.15 p.m. This was probably the only express on Great Western metals which served two stations only—the starting point and the destination—without any intermediate stop. The down " Bristolian " also could claim to have the most level main line in Britain on which to maintain its high speed.

When Brunel engineered his original line between Paddington and Bristol, by using the Thames Valley as far as Didcot, and curving across the flat country between there and Wootton Bassett, he contrived to keep his maximum steepness of gradient down to 1 in 754, and for the major part of the distance to work to nothing steeper than 1 in 1320. West of Wootton Bassett he dropped down Dauntsey bank with $1\frac{1}{2}$ miles at 1 in 100; and from Corsham he cut through to the Avon Valley by means of the Box tunnel, with $1\frac{3}{4}$ miles down at 1 in 100 and $\frac{3}{4}$ mile at 1 in 120; but both these gradients are in favour of down trains, so that the down " Bristolian " had no hindrance to speed whatever, other than the severe service slack through Bath. It was booked to pass Swindon, 77.3 miles, in $66\frac{1}{2}$ minutes. The fastest part of the journey was between Slough and Chippenham, a distance of 75.5 miles for which the timetable allowed only 61 minutes; this entailed an average speed of 74.3 m.p.h.

On the up journey, after negotiating the gradients and slacks of the Badminton route to which reference has been made earlier, the train was allowed 62 minutes from passing Swindon to Paddington, which called for roughly the same speeds as those of the "Cheltenham Flyer". Coming up, the fastest stretch was from Badminton to Southall, 91 miles allowed only 71 minutes for an average of all but 77 m.p.h. The "Bristolian" was withdrawn on the outbreak of war, and up to the winter of 1952-1953 no faster timing than 2 hours 10 minutes between Paddington and Bristol had reappeared in the Western Region timetable.

But acceleration back to the old standards soon began, and by 1954 the 105-minute schedule in both directions between Paddington and Bristol had been restored. Once more "King" 4-6-0s were rostered to the train, as the operating authorities at first deemed the extra weight of the new BR standard coaching stock allocated to the "Bristolian"—all but 250 tons tare for seven coaches Monday to Thursday, and over 280 tons when an eighth coach was added at weekends—to be overmuch for a "Castle". But as the "Castles" became rejuvenated with four-row superheaters and double blastpipes and chimneys they took over and proved easy masters of the schedule. In fact, the fastest "Bristolian" run ever recorded with steam is credited to *Drysllwyn Castle*, which on an April day in 1958 hurried up from Bristol to Paddington in 93 minutes 50 seconds. On this memorable trip the 7.2 miles from Hullavington to Brinkworth were eaten up at an average of 98.2 m.p.h. and a maximum of 102 m.p.h. was recorded.

But the North Eastern Region was exploiting its Darlington-York speedway to nibble at the Western's British speed title. So, in the summer of 1959, came a Western counterblast: the "Bristolian" time was to be cut to 100 minutes both ways, requiring a start-to-stop average of 71.0 m.p.h. going down and 70.6 m.p.h. on the return journey—the first post-war British schedules at 70 m.p.h.-plus. By this time the Western Region's "Warship" diesel-hydraulic locomotives were available, and on the opening day of the summer service No. D805 *Benbow*, with an 8-coach train of 300 tons gross, whirled us down to Bristol in 93 minutes 48 seconds, or in 91 minutes net, the latter representing a net average speed of 78.0 m.p.h. from start to stop. The "Warships"

△ " Britannia " Pacific on the down " Bristolian "—No. 70023 *Venus* leaves Bath in the mid-1950s. *Photo by G. F. Heiron*

◁ When the " Bristolian " was accelerated back to a 105-minute London-Bristol schedule in 1954 the operators at first regarded it as essentially a " King " task. In this August 1954 shot No. 6009 *King Charles II* is storming up the 1 in 75 from Stapleton Road to Filton Junction, outside Bristol, with the up train. At this date Western coaches of Hawksworth pattern made up the train. *Photo by G. F. Heiron*

were frequently logged at 100 m.p.h., not merely at the foot of Dauntsey and Hullavington banks, but also on nearly level track between Swindon and Didcot. On one outstanding trip No. D804 *Avenger* touched 102 m.p.h. at both Little Somerford and Wantage Road in cutting the Bristol-Paddington time to 92 minutes 52 seconds, or 87 minutes net (overall average 81.1 m.p.h.) if the effects of three permanent way slowings were taken into account. But by the autumn the civil engineers were nervous and had a ceiling of 90 m.p.h. rigorously imposed. This plus insertion of added allowances for engineering works saw the " Bristolian's " timing eased out once more to 105 minutes, though with recovery margins deducted the net allowance was only 94 minutes.

So matters continued until the Western Region timetable revolution of 1961. In the summer of that year the Paddington-Bristol service was put on to an even-interval basis, in which all trains without exception, the " Bristolian " among their number, called at Bath. As the loading of the train from now on might be increased to ten or eleven coaches, it was unhappily ordered that the schedule be increased by no less than 14 minutes in each direction, to 119 minutes. With the advent of the 2,700 h.p. " Western " diesels, however, time-cutting began afresh, and by 1966 the former " Bristolian ", now nameless, was running once again on a 105-minute schedule, and with the Bath stop permanently included. Going down it was leaving Paddington at 8.45 a.m., and the return from Bristol was 4.15 p.m. Moreover, by now it had become far

473

heavier than formerly, in particular coming up, when the diesel had to handle a 12-coach load of 425 tons tare and 450 tons or so gross. In the summer of 1967 the times were eased by 5 minutes both ways, but it was explained that this was a temporary measure, to allow for delays that might be caused during resignalling work at Paddington and in the Bristol area.

The 1972 timetable brought further changes. A new Bristol station was opened on the outskirts of the city at Parkway on the Badminton line, to serve as a motorists' railhead and compete with the new M4 motorway by eliminating the laborious trek into the congested city to pick up a train at Temple Meads. Parkway, just short of the divergence of the Filton spur from the South Wales main line, is 111.8 miles from Paddington. This stop now

◁ The " Castles " take over—a gleaming No. 7034 *Ince Castle* climbs out of Bristol through Ashley Hill with the up " Bristolian " made up of B.R. stock in chocolate-and-cream livery, in March 1958. *Photo by G. F. Heiron*

▽ " Warship " era on the " Bristolian "—No. D806 *Avenger* sets out on the 100 minute schedule to Paddington past Dr Day's Bridge Junction, Bristol, with the up express in June 1959.

Photo by G. F. Heiron

replaced Bath as the only intermediate call for the " Bristolian ". Until April, 1973, the express, limited in weight to 350 tons (ten coaches), was allowed $92\frac{1}{2}$ minutes from Paddington to Parkway for a start-to-stop average of 72.5 m.p.h. and 105 minutes to Temple Meads; coming up the times were 4.40 p.m. from Temple Meads and 4.51 p.m. from Parkway, with a London arrival at 6.25 p.m.

But in May, 1973, in common with most other Western Region expresses, the " Bristolian " had 5 minutes added to these times, to allow for permanent way work in preparation for introduction of the future High Speed Diesel trains. The 8.40 a.m. was now due in Temple Meads at 10.30 a.m., and the 4.40 p.m. up into Paddington by 6.30 p.m.; the new 110 minutes timing was thus 5 minutes longer than the 105 minutes of the " Bristolian " when the train was first introduced in 1935, though it may be granted that it was then non-stop.

The summer of 1973 also saw the Paddington-Bristol services re-equipped with BR's new MkIID air-conditioned, electrically-heated coaching stock. That meant exclusive haulage by the 2,750 h.p. Class 47 Brush/Sulzer diesels, since the 2,700 h.p. " Western " diesel-hydraulics are not equipped to provide such vehicles with the electric power for their auxiliaries.

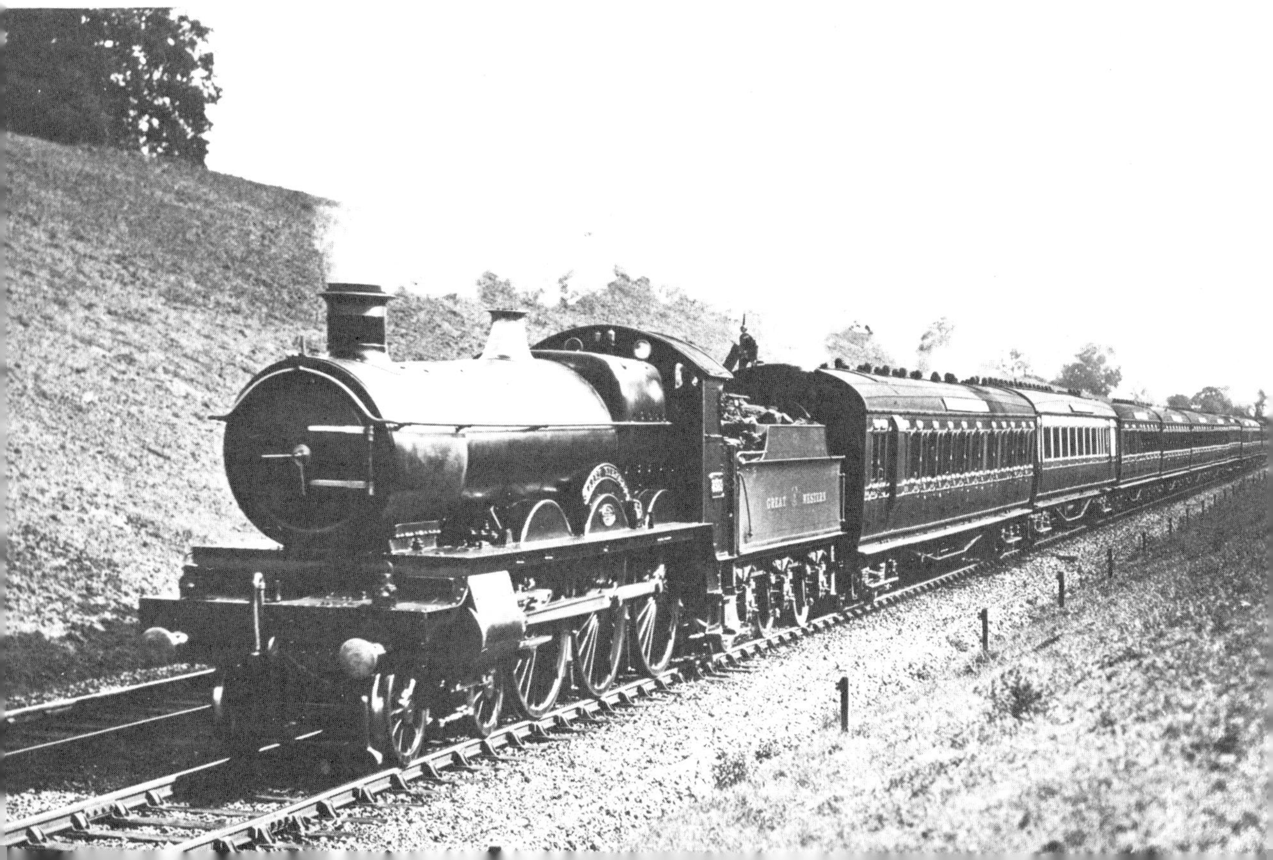
GREAT WESTERN

△ " Bristolian "—Class 47 diesel-electric No. 1937 emerges from Box Tunnel in April 1973, with the 8.45 a.m. Paddington-Bristol. Apart from the leading brake, the train is composed of Mk IID air-conditioned, electrically-heated coaches.

Photo by J. H. Cooper-Smith

◁ Forerunner of the " Cambrian Coast Express " in the first quarter of this century, with " Saint " 4-6-0 No. 2929 *Saint Stephen* in charge.

△ " Bristolian " of the future—the High Speed Diesel Train (HSDT), with Mk. III coaches powered front and rear by 2250 h.p. Paxman Valenta-engined diesel-electric locomotives, due to enter Bristol line service in 1975 and expected to cut the London-Bristol time eventually to 83 minutes. The prototype HSDT has already set up a world's diesel traction speed record of 141 m.p.h. on test between Darlington and York; it is seen at Newcastle in July 1973.

Photo by I. S. Carr

At the time of writing a Paddington-Bristol schedule of 100 minutes is expected back in the books by 1975, when the first of BR's High Speed Trains (HST) of MkIII coaches with new Class 41 2,250 h.p. diesels at each end enters revenue-earning service. In the following year enough of these new units, already tested up to a world record for diesel traction of 141 m.p.h., should be available for the whole Paddington-Bristol Temple Meads timetable to be rewritten on the basis of a best and fastest ever timing of 82 minutes.

Substantial track improvements and realignments have been put in hand to allow the HSTs to exploit their maximum speed potential of 125 m.p.h. They will hoist the *average* speed between Paddington and Bristol Parkway up to 96 m.p.h. and cut the fastest timings from London to Swindon down to 50 minutes, to Bristol Parkway to 70 minutes, and to Bath to 71 minutes.

The Cambrian Coast Express and the William Shakespeare

In the summer of 1910 the Great Western Railway brought to completion the last of four important cut-off routes by which the worst circuits made by the original main lines from Paddington were eliminated. This was the main line from Paddington to the North. The original route, *via* Didcot and Oxford, following the Thames Valley, was almost perfect in its absence of gradients as far as Leamington Spa; but a distance of $129\frac{1}{4}$ miles from Paddington to Birmingham hampered the G.W.R. considerably in competing with the then London & North Western Railway, with its 113-mile route, for the traffic from London to Birmingham and beyond. It was planned, therefore, to make a much more direct line from London to Banbury, and in the task the Great Western found an unexpected ally.

The Great Central Railway in 1899 had opened its London Extension into Marylebone terminus, to which access was obtained by using the then Metropolitan line from Quainton Road Junction, north of Aylesbury, to Harrow; from Harrow into Marylebone the G.C.R. built its own independent tracks. But the Great Central soon found itself hampered both by the extremely heavy gradients and the dense occupation of the Metropolitan line; the latter affected chiefly the express passenger services, whereas the former severely limited the freight train loads. Consequently the Great Western and Great Central companies combined to build a new joint line, the former to shorten its distance and the latter to ease its gradients to the North.

The project involved the construction of no less than 59 route miles of new line. No existing route was used other than that of the G.W.R. single line branch from Maidenhead to Oxford *via* Thame; the course of this was followed roughly from High Wycombe to Princes Risborough, but actually complete reconstruction and realignment with doubling of the track were needed to adapt the earlier branch for high speed passenger work, so that to all intents and purposes this 8 miles formed part of the new construction.

Of the whole line the portion actually joint—later, of course, between the Great Western and London & North Eastern Railways—was the $32\frac{3}{4}$ miles from Northolt Junction through High Wycombe and Princes Risborough to Ashendon

Junction. Connecting with this the G.C.R. built a spur $6\frac{1}{2}$ miles long from Neasden to Northolt, with the down line making a burrowing junction at Northolt, and another line 6 miles long from Ashendon to their existing main line at Grendon Underwood Junction, 9 miles north of Aylesbury. The new Great Western connections were from Old Oak Common West Junction, 3 miles out of Paddington to Northolt (7 miles), with a spur from West Ealing to Greenford, and from Ashendon for $18\frac{1}{4}$ miles through Bicester to Aynho Junction, 5 miles south of Banbury. There was a fly-over for the up G.W.R. Bicester line at Ashendon, and for the down line at Aynho.

Until the opening of the Wycombe and Bicester route to Birmingham and the North in July, 1910, the G.W.R. had never ventured a tighter time than 2 hours 17 minutes for their $129\frac{1}{4}$ miles between Paddington and Birmingham, and no more than four trains made the journey in 2 hours 20 minutes or less. But with the distance cut to $110\frac{1}{4}$ miles, the G.W.R. immediately put into operation a series of two-hour trains in each direction, equalling the current London & North Western times, and over a considerably more difficult route. Considerable use was made of slip coaches, in order to avoid as many intermediate stops as possible; at different periods Princes Risborough, Bichester, Banbury, Leamington and Knowle were all served by various " slips " going north, the last-mentioned in order to set down

7811

residents in the southern suburbs of Birmingham.

The principal destination of northbound trains from Paddington was Birkenhead, though some of the Birmingham two-hour trains stopped short at Shrewsbury, and portions of them were detached at Wolverhampton. But the Bicester cut-off was also of considerable value to the Welsh coast resorts on Cardigan Bay, and in particular to Aberystwyth, reached by way of Shrewsbury, the then G.W. & L.N.W.R. joint line to Buttington, and what was the Cambrian Railway from there onwards through Welshpool and Machynlleth. From the beginning of 1923 the Cambrian became the property of the Great Western, and development of this seaside traffic soon began.

But before that date, in July, 1921, the precursor of the "Cambrian Coast Express" had been put into operation, as a restaurant car train from Paddington at 9.50 a.m. from Aberystwyth, and Pwllheli—the two portions were separated at Dovey Junction—on every weekday during the summer season. By 1922 the start had been altered to 10.15 a.m., and the train was travelling by way of Ealing, to pick up passengers at Ealing Broadway, and rejoining the Birmingham main line at Greenford. In 1923, when the G.W.R. was fighting the L.M.S.R. strongly for the traffic between London, Shrewbury, Chester and Birkenhead, the 10.20 a.m. from Paddington, as it was now, had become a Birkenhead express, non-stop to Birmingham in two hours, with an Aberystwyth portion detached at Snow Hill. The year 1924 saw the introduction of systematic departure times from Paddington, and the starting time of the Welsh train was changed to 10.10 a.m., thus splitting up the interval between the 9.10 and 11.10 a.m. Birkenhead departures. During these years departure of the up train from Aberystwyth had been at or about 12 noon.

The name "Cambrian Coast Express" was adopted in 1927 as the official title of the train. By now the express, still leaving Paddington at 10.10 a.m. during the summer months, had become a Friday and Saturday working only. In the last summer before the outbreak of the 1939-1945 war the starting time from London had moved back to the 10.20 a.m. of 1923, while the working was restricted to Saturdays only. The 87.3 miles to Leamington were run in the fast time of 90½ minutes, and after a stop of 3 minutes there, 26½ minutes were allowed for the 23.3 miles on to Birmingham, where the arrival at Snow Hill was at 12.20 p.m. The usual 19 minutes for the difficult 12.4 miles to Wolverhampton saw the "Cambrian Coast Express" into that town at 12.44 p.m.

Here the "Castle" 4-6-0, which had brought the train from London, was exchanged for motive power more suited to the light track and bridges of the Cambrian line—either one or two "Duke" 4-4-0 locomotives, or latterly one of the "Manor" 5 ft. 8 in. 4-6-0 engines, which were now permitted to run over the route. This arrangement was necessary as the train avoided Shrewsbury, and used the Abbey Foregate curve in order to make a non-stop run from Wolverhampton to Welshpool, covering the 49.7 miles in 71½ minutes. The remaining stops were at Machynlleth, Dovey Junction and Borth, and Aberystwyth was reached at 3.55 p.m. The up train now left the Welsh resort at 10 a.m., made the same stops as on the down journey, with a conditional halt in addition at Newtown, and reached Wolverhampton, for the change of engines, at 1.28 p.m. After 7 minutes there, and a 19-minute run to Birmingham, the "Cambrian Coast Express" was ready to take its place at 2 p.m. as one of the hourly departures for Paddington, calling at Leamington from 2.25 to 2.28 p.m., and due in London at 4 p.m. The up run thus took 25 minutes longer than the down. The total journey was one of 234¾ miles.

There is little need to stress the difficulty of the running west of Welshpool. Much of the route is single track, and the gradients are very trying, especially on the climb to Talerddig summit, between Moat Lane and Machynlleth, where the

◁ The WR devised its own style of titled train headboard, embellished with an emblem appropriate to the train name, during the 1950s. One is carried here by 4-6-0 No. 7811 *Dunley Manor* leaving Aberystwyth with the up "Cambrian Coast Express" in July 1958.
Photo by R. O. Tuck

◁ A "Cambrian Coast Express" headboard is sported by 2-6-2T No. 5541, working the Pwllheli portion of the train along the coast from Aberdovey to Dovey Junction in March 1959. *Photo by G. W. Morrison*

△ The short-lived "William Shakespeare", the 10.10 Paddington-Wolverhampton with a three-coach through portion for Stratford-upon-Avon at the rear, was one of the first expresses to display BR standard coaching stock. It is headed over Aynho troughs in September 1951 by 4-6-0 No. 7025 *Sudeley Castle*. *Photo by G. J. Jefferson*

▽ Heyday of the "Cambrian Coast Express"—No. 6010 *King Charles I* storms Hatton Bank with the down train on the two-hour London-Birmingham schedule.

Photo by T. E. Williams

▷ "Western" class 2,700 h.p. diesel-hydraulic No. D1002 *Western Explorer* passes Denham with the up "Cambrian Coast Express" in August 1962. *Photo by G. J. Jefferson*

line is 693 ft. above sea level. From the Aberystwyth direction the ascent begins 3 miles from Machynlleth, and is unbroken for $10\frac{1}{2}$ miles, finishing with $3\frac{1}{4}$ miles at 1 in 52 from Llanbrynmair to the top. From the east the difficulty is not so great, and is confined to short stretches at 1 in 71 and 1 in 80. There are also $6\frac{1}{4}$ miles of 1 in 75 ups-and-downs between Borth and Aberystwyth. The locomotive or locomotives hauling the " Cambrian Coast Express " over the $111\frac{1}{2}$ miles between Wolverhampton and Aberystwyth thus had quite a tough task before them.

In the first summer after the 1939-1945 war there was a revival of the Saturday " Cambrian Coast " working, though without any distinctive name; the train left Paddington on Saturdays at its former 10.10 a.m. time, and made the only non-stop run of the day to Birmingham, taking $2\frac{1}{4}$ hours. From Wolverhampton the stops were the same as before, with the addition of Newtown, and Aberystwyth was reached at 4.35 p.m. In the reverse direction, leaving Aberystwyth at 9.30 a.m., and calling additionally at Leamington Spa, the express was into Paddington by 4.10 p.m. In 1950 the down train was starting at 10.50 a.m., and reaching Aberystwyth at 5.15 p.m., but in the up direction the times were unchanged.

In 1951 the Festival of Britain touched the Paddington–West Midlands route. To captivate—it was hoped—the foreign tourists forecast to swarm over Stratford-upon-Avon, the 10.10 summer Saturday path of another Welsh coastal train from Paddington was appropriated for the " William Shakespeare. " This was one of five shop-window titled trains BR announced that year to parade the first standard main-line coaching stock. The main part of the 10.10 was a daily working to Birmingham (12.30 p.m.) and Wolverhampton (12.53 p.m.),

but it also conveyed a three-coach section for Stratford-upon-Avon. The up through "William Shakespeare" coaches were attached to the 7.50 p.m. from Birmingham, due into Paddington at 10.10 p.m.

But the venture was a commercial flop. The "William Shakespeare" title vanished at the end of the 1951 summer service, never to reappear. So did the outward through coaches from Paddington, though the return evening working resumed an anonymous existence in 1952.

By 1951 the name "Cambrian Coast Express" was back in currency on the summer Saturday working mentioned. Not until 1954, though, did it became really significant in the post-war timetables. In that year's summer the train became daily, on a 2 hour schedule each way between Paddington and

◁ Deputy for a failed "King", "Hall" 4-6-0 No. 4947 *Nanhoran Hall* battles for lost time south of Leamington with the up "Cambrian Coast Express" in August 1961.

Photo by R. J. Blenkinsop

▽ Finale, March 4, 1967—the last up "Cambrian Coast Express" near Commins Coch, on the Cambrian line, behind Class 4 4-6-0 No. 75033. *Photo by K. Hale*

Birmingham, and 45 minutes quicker outwards and 60 minutes faster inwards than any previous service between London and Aberystwyth. For a time the train had " King " haulage throughout between Paddington and Shrewsbury. Banbury was now the only stop before Birmingham; beyond Wolverhampton, instead of a non-stop run to Welshpool, the express ran into Shrewsbury and reversed there, reaching Aberystwyth at 4.5 p.m., in 5 hours 55 minutes from London. A restaurant car was included as far as Shrewsbury, and through coaches for Barmouth and Pwllheli were detached at Machynlleth. The up journey, beginning at 11.15 a.m., was less speedy by $\frac{3}{4}$ hour, for the train stopped at all stations to Weshpool; but from Snow Hill, Birmingham, it took its place at 4 p.m. in the sequence of hourly departures for Paddington, where it was due at 6 p.m.

In 1961 the advent of the midday " Birmingham Pullman " displaced the " Cambrian Coast " from its 10.10 a.m. Paddington departure; this now became 12.10 p.m. Leamington was added to its stops, and the time from Paddington to Aberystwyth was increased to 6 hours. Coming up, after an Aberystwyth start at 9.45 a.m., the express reached Birmingham in time to take up the 2 p.m. two-hour working to Paddington. That this time could be achieved with stops at both Leamington and Banbury included was due to the fact that diesel power had now taken over from steam. Moreover, the assignment had been made more difficult not only because of the attachment at Wolverhampton of the restaurant car that had worked down on the 10.10, but also by enlargement of load to 14 coaches, of some 500 tons gross weight, in readiness for the return working, out of Paddington at 5.10 p.m.; this had become the most popular of all the down evening trains at that period, when L.M.R. traffic was transferred to the W.R. route during electrification from Euston to the North-West.

So matters continued until the complete transformation that took place with the completion of the Euston-Wolverhampton electrification in March, 1967. Paddington was no longer the terminus for North Wales traffic, and the " Cambrian Coast Express " ceased to exist, despite a vociferous outcry. From now on the traveller had to leave Euston for Aberystwyth, and, moreover, if he desired a through train he could only have one on Saturdays. On Saturdays only, an electrically-hauled express whisked him from Euston to Birmingham New Street in 95 minutes; at Wolverhampton electric was changed to diesel power, and after reversal at Shrewesbury Aberystwyth was reached at 2.55 p.m., in $5\frac{1}{4}$ hours from London—the fastest time yet. The return journey was of almost identical duration; 10.5 a.m. from Aberystwyth and 3.21 p.m. into Euston. On other weekdays the through journey involved changes at both Wolverhampton and Shrewsbury. Moreover, the entire journey between London and Aberystwyth was now on the metals of the London Midland Region.

The Capitals United Express and the Red Dragon

Until comparatively recent years the train service between Paddington and South Wales was hardly renowned for its high speed. Originally, of course, the South Wales trains followed the roundabout course dictated by the Severn estuary, making the circuit from Swindon via Gloucester to reach its north bank. The opening in 1886 of the Severn Tunnel cut the distance by 15 miles, and with the completion in 1901 of the Badminton cut-off not only were Newport and all stations beyond 25 miles nearer London, but on the whole by a route with easier gradients. The one major handicap, however, was and still is the steep descents from both directions to carry the main line under the waters of the Severn.

Westbound, the line descends for 2 miles at 1 in 90-68 from beyond Patchway to Pilning—though in later years this stretch was eased for up trains by the construction of a new up line inclined for 3 miles at 1 in 100—and then there is a 3-mile

" Britannia " Pacific No. 70018 *Flying Dutchman* pounds past Patchway Tunnel Box on the climb out of the Severn Tunnel with the up " Red Dragon " in June 1960.

Photo by E. T. Gill

fall at 1 in 100 from Pilning to the centre of the tunnel. Out of the tunnel the trains must climb 3 miles at 1 in 90 to Severn Tunnel Junction, so that in the eastbound direction there is a total of 6 miles up at 1 in 100 from the tunnel to Patchway. The Badminton cut-off, however, was magnificently engineered with sweeping 1 in 300 grades, $8\frac{3}{4}$ miles continuously from Little Somerford to Badminton and 11 miles continuously down at the same inclination from here to Stoke Gifford. At the beginning of the latter is the $2\frac{1}{2}$ mile Sodbury Tunnel, which the uninitiated westbound traveller sometimes imagines to be the Severn Tunnel—not realising that he is at the highest and not the lowest point on the line.

In the very first issue of the *Railway Magazine*, in July 1897, there appeared an article headed " The Flying Welshman ", describing in sensational terms a footplate journey from Newport to Paddington on the 10 a.m. train from Cardiff. A Dean 4-2-2 succeeded in working a seven-coach formation, restaurant car included, up over the 143.5 miles from Newport to Paddington via Bristol non-stop in 6 minutes under the schedule allowance of 177 minutes, at an average of just over 50 m.p.h.—not a bad effort for the period but hardly deserving of the epithet " flying ". This, however, was the footplate traveller's description, and was not an official title. In these days the fastest down South Wales train was the 3.35 p.m. from Paddington, which covered the 106.9 miles to Bath in 2 hours, and after a halt there reached Newport at 6.33 p.m. and Cardiff at 6.54 p.m. The overall time of 4 hours 50 minutes to Swansea compared with the $4\frac{3}{4}$ hours of the up express already mentioned.

For many years after the opening of the shortened Badminton route, which brought the best times

EXPRESS
171

between Paddington and Cardiff down to about 3 hours and to and from Swansea to 4½ hours, there was little in the way of acceleration, although of course the weight of the trains was constantly on the increase, and eventually " Castle " class 4-6-0s might have to work loads of up to 400 tons and more up the steep inclines from the Severn Tunnel. Also in steam days the arduous Severn Tunnel climb hampered freight train working, of heavy coal trains in particular, and no doubt the lack of enterprise in many of the passenger timings may have been to allow some margin for delays from this cause.

In the 1950s, the then General Manager of the Western Region was seeking pretexts to repaint set trains in the former Western Railway chocolate-and-cream colours. To name a train seemed a sound excuse, and the South Wales route got its share of new titled trains. One was the 5.55 p.m. from Paddington, which in 1950 acquired the title " Red Dragon ". This was a distinctly lethargic beast, for in the down direction, with numerous stops, it was not until ten minutes before midnight that the last of its tail dragged its weary way into Carmarthen. The up journey was rather better; although the Carmarthen section had to be away by 7.30 a.m., the main train did not leave Swansea until 8.45 a.m., and was a very popular service from Cardiff and Newport, running up non-stop from the latter in 165 minutes and reaching Paddington at 1.5 p.m.

Another new named train was the " Capitals United "—the capitals, of course, being London and Cardiff. The title was conferred in 1956 on the descendent of the former 3.35 p.m. down, by now leaving Paddington at 3.55 p.m. The somewhat less than euphonious name was reportedly the brainchild of Lord Mancroft, a Junior Minister with responsibility for Welsh affairs in the Tory Government of the day. The train had a conditional stop at Badminton, and reached Newport in 2 hours 21 minutes and Cardiff 20 minutes later; the time to Swansea, after the usual Bridgend, Port Talbot and Neath stops, was 3 hours 57 minutes. In the up direction the express carrying the title was the 8 a.m. from Cardiff, calling at Newport and with a time of 147 minutes from there non-stop to Paddington except on Mondays, when Badminton was honoured with a call. Both names were among the number erased in the Western Region time table reorganisations of the 1960s.

The Cathedrals Express

◁ The westbound " Capitals United Express " in May 1956, soon after its titling, passing Wapley Common Sidings behind " Britannia " Pacific No. 70025 *Western Star*.
Photo by G. F. Heiron

◁ A " County " 4-6-0 was a rarity on a Western named train. In this unusual scene No. 1012 *County of Denbigh* makes for London in the mid-1950s with the up " Capitals United Express ", overtaking " Grange " 4-6-0 No. 6871 *Bourton Grange* at Iver.

Another short-lived Western train name was that of the " Cathedrals Express ". This was a post-World War II train running between London, Oxford, Worcester and Hereford—four cathedral cities, hence the title, which also prompted Paddington to deck the engine headboard with "Olde English" type and a bishop's mitre device.

The Worcester main line of the former Great Western Railway is one over which overall times have scarcely improved since the beginning of the century. As early as 1904, it was possible to leave Paddington at 4.45 p.m. and to be hurried non-stop

"Kings" take on the South Wales service—in March 1961, No. 6019 *King Henry V*, newly reallocated to Cardiff Canton depot, accelerates the down "Capitals United Express" through West Ealing. *Photo by M. Pope*

▷ The diesel age "Capitals United Express", with coaching stock now in all-maroon livery, heads for London through Bishton (Mon.) in August 1963 behind 2,700 h.p. diesel-hydraulic No. D1064 *Western Regent*.
Photo by S. Rickard

over the 120 miles to Worcester in $2\frac{1}{4}$ hours, and to come up from Worcester at 8.55 a.m. in the same time. These are the two trains on which in September, 1957 the title " Cathedrals Express " was conferred.

Long before then Oxford's industrial expansion had forced the city into scheduled stop reckoning. Moreover, the opening of the Bicester cut-off had cut Oxford out of the itinerary of principal expresses to and from Birmingham and the North, making the city totally reliant on the Worcester service. Intermediate towns like Kingham, Moreton-in-Marsh and Evesham were also demanding attention. In 1939 the 12.45 p.m. from Paddington, though stopping at Oxford, was still reaching Worcester in 2 hours 10 minutes, but the 4.45 p.m. was stopping also at Moreton-in-Marsh and Evesham and taking 2 hours 21 minutes. The 8.55 a.m. up, however, with the help of a 60-minute sprint over the 63.4 miles from Oxford to Paddington, was making the same three stops but running up from Worcester in $2\frac{1}{4}$ hours.

Initially, the " Cathedrals Express " began its journey as a four-car portion from Hereford, making four intermediate stops to Worcester Shrub Hill, where the restaurant car and three more vehicles were added. After intermediate stops at Evesham, Moreton-in-Marsh, Oxford and Reading, the train was into Paddington at 1.30. In the reverse direction, the title was in the 1959–60 winter timetable switched to the 2.45 p.m. from Paddington, one of two additional expresses added to the route that year to provide a better spread of departures throughout the day. The 2.45 was non-stop to Oxford in 71 minutes for the 63.5 miles, and with further stops at Kingham, Moreton-in-Marsh and Evesham, made Worcester in $2\frac{1}{2}$ hours.

By the time that 2,750 h.p. Brush-Sulzer diesels had taken over the service, in 1965, four stops—Oxford, Kingham, Moreton-in-Marsh and Evesham—were being included in the schedule of the down train, now leaving Paddington at 5.15 p.m.; while the up train, now at 9 a.m. from Worcester, needing 2 hours 25 minutes, with additional halts at Charlbury and Reading.

Not until 1967 was Paddington–Worcester at last pared to 2 hours 5 minutes by new trains at 6.15 p.m. down and 7.50 a.m. up, calling at Oxford and Kingham in the former case and Evesham and Oxford in the latter. But in the early 1970s the logical successor to the former " Cathedrals Express " was taking 2 hours 24 minutes. Starting

at 5.15 p.m. it made stops at Didcot, Oxford, Charlbury, Kingham, Moreton-in-Marsh and Evesham, so that, despite tight point-to-point times and speed at various points reaching 90 m.p.h., Worcester was not reached until 7.39 p.m., a journey 9 minutes longer than that of some 70 years previously. In the up direction, however, the 7.00 a.m. from Hereford, 7.47 (working time) from Worcester, with the same intermediate stops less Didcot was a little faster; until 1973 timetable changes it had the fastest time of the day from Oxford to Paddington, 58 minutes for the 63.4 miles, and reached London at 9.56 a.m., but the arrival time then edged back to 10.3 a.m. This made the aggregate 2 hours 16 minutes from Worcester, or one minute more than its time in 1939—when, however, there were two intermediate stops only as compared with the latter-day five.

The calibre of motive power on the Worcester trains has declined latterly. The 2,750 h.p. Brush Class 47s have been switched to heavier work, following the decision to phase out the high-power Western diesel-hydraulics. Most Worcester services were thereafter handled by 1,700 h.p. Hymek diesel-hydraulics. Then the axe was taken to these and at the time of writing Brush 1,350 h.p. diesel-electrics transferred from the Eastern Region are seen on Worcester expresses with growing frequency.

It may be added that in recent years the 14 miles of this main line from Wolvercot Junction, Oxford, to Ascott-under-Wychwood and the 25¾ miles from Moreton-in-Marsh to Norton Junction, Oxford, have been reduced from double to single track, involving reduced speeds for tablet exchange at various points. The latter section includes the one steep gradient of the route, where up trains have to face a climb of 4½ miles at 1 in 100 from Honeybourne to the summit at Campden, in the Cotswold Hills. But the times of the Paddington–Worcester expresses are framed for loads not exceeding 315 tons (nine coaches), so that this gradient presents no difficulty.

The Cheltenham Flyer

It was as a very ordinary train that the "Cheltenham Flyer" began its course. After the First World War an afternoon service was put on from Cheltenham and Gloucester to Paddington, due shortly after 5 p.m. But in 1923 the Great Western Railway, which had been steadily speeding up its long-distance services, decided to lay claim to the blue riband of railway speed in Great Britain, held until then by the North Eastern Railway—and later the London and North Eastern—with its 43-minute run over the 44.1 miles from Darlington to York. The almost perfectly level and well-aligned stretch from Swindon to Paddington was ideal for the purpose and the Cheltenham train was selected to make the new record. Its timing over the 77.3 miles from Swindon was cut to 75 minutes, and now required a start-to-stop average of 61.8 m.p.h.

The first step had thus been taken to turn what until then had been called the "Cheltenham Spa Express" into the "Cheltenham Flyer"—the nickname by which this train was always known in later years, though it never came into official use. Railway speeds all over the world were advancing rapidly, and the 75-minute schedule was not destined to remain in force for long. Six years later, in July, 1929, the timing was cut to 70 minutes, and the booked speed rose to 66.2 m.p.h.; at the time this was the fastest regular railway run in the world. Then the supremacy was challenged from an unexpected quarter. In 1931 the Canadian Pacific and Canadian National Railways were fighting for the traffic between Montreal and Toronto, and the competition grew so vigorous that the C.P.R. cut the time of its fastest service to 108 minutes for the 124 miles from Montreal West to Smith's Falls, which called for an average of 68.9 m.p.h. from start to stop. In September,

△ The "Cathedrals Express" threads Wolvercote Junction, Oxford, en route for London behind 4-6-0 No. 7011 *Banbury Castle* in June 1961. *Photo by G. Smith*

▽ Close-up of the elaborate "Cathedrals Express" headboard.

▽ The contemporary Worcester line—an ex-Eastern Region Class 31 diesel-electric, No. 5655, on the singled stretch past the site of Fladbury station with the 11.50 Worcester-Paddington in May 1973. *Photo by A. A. Vickers*

1931, therefore, the G.W.R. accelerated the "Cheltenham Flyer" to a 67-minute run from Swindon, so bringing the average speed up to 69.2 m.p.h. Finally, in order to reduce the schedule to a round figure, there came, in September, 1932, the cut to 65 minutes, and the raising of the start-to-stop average to 71.4 m.p.h.

After this final acceleration, the "Cheltenham Flyer" was still the fastest train in the world. Daily it carried a headboard to this effect, and as this was mounted on the locomotive before it left Old Oak Common for Gloucester, on the down

△ The "Cheltenham Flyer" of 1931, its "Castle" carrying the headboard proclaiming it as the "World's Fastest Train".

▷ The record-breaking No. 5006 *Tregenna Castle* starts the "Cheltenham Flyer" out of Swindon in the 1930s.

journey the 10.45 a.m. semi-fast from London also made this somewhat startling claim! But from then onwards the march in world railway speed became so extraordinarily rapid that the " Cheltenham Flyer ", though still running on its 71.4 m.p.h. schedule, by 1939 had to be content with a place well below the one-hundredth among the world's fastest runs, largely, of course, owing to the introduction of diesel-electric streamline trains in Germany and the United States. In Great Britain the " Cheltenham Flyer's " speed was just beaten by the 71.9 m.p.h. of the L.N.E.R. " Coronation " streamliner between London and York.

The best recorded journey of the " Cheltenham Flyer " was made on June 6th, 1932, when the 77.3 miles from Swindon to Paddington were covered in 56 minutes 47 seconds, at an average of 81.7 m.p.h.—the fastest start-to-stop speed achieved in Great Britain up till then and for a good many years afterwards. For 70 miles on end, between mileposts 72 and 2, an average rate of 87.5 m.p.h. was maintained, though this feat was beaten by the 70 miles covered at 91.8 m.p.h. on September 27th 1935 by the L.N.E.R. " Silver Jubilee " streamliner. On the G.W.R. run the engine was No. 5006, *Tregenna Castle*, a 4-cylinder 4-6-0 " Castle " of the class which was always responsible for working the train; the load was one of six bogie vehicles, weighing 186 tons empty, and 195 tons gross.

It was only between Swindon and Paddington that the " Cheltenham Flyer " developed any turn of speed, and over this section the schedule demanded a sustained 80 m.p.h., or something closely approaching that figure, for most of the distance. The main train, which consisted usually of a six-coach set, was made up of third-class brake, corridor composite, restaurant car, corridor composite, third class, and third-class brake. Leaving St. James station at Cheltenham Spa at 2.40 p.m., and calling at Malvern Road, it ran down to Gloucester, 7½ miles, in 13 minutes. Here reversal was necessary; the engine for the run to London was attached to what had been the rear of the train, and at the other end a through composite brake coach which left Hereford at 1.15 p.m., and had come across to Gloucester *via* Ross, calling at all stations. Previously, for some years, the main train avoided Gloucester, running direct from Engine Shed Junction to Gloucester South Junction, where the Hereford coach was attached.

Departure from Gloucester was at 2.58 p.m., and between there and Swindon stops were made at Stroud and Kemble; also on this length the " Castle " had to tackle the stiff climb up 4 miles at 1 in 60–90 from Brimscombe to the summit at the east end of Sapperton tunnel. The 44¼ miles

CHELTENHAM SPA EXPRESS
T09

from Cheltenham to Swindon thus took 71 minutes, by contrast with the high speed from Swindon onwards. Swindon was left at 3.55 p.m. and Paddington was reached at 5 p.m. There was no corresponding down service.

On the day of the record 1932 run referred to earlier, arrangements were made for an extremely fast run in the opposite direction on the 5 p.m. down " Cheltenham Spa Express ", which normally was non-stop to Kemble; on this trip, " Castle " class 4-6-0 No. 5005, *Manorbier Castle*, with a load of 205 tons, worked the train to a special stop at Swindon in one second over the hour. The 5.15 p.m. non-stop two-hour express from Bristol to Paddington was then stopped specially at Swindon to pick up those who had been recording the test journeys, and brought them back to Paddington in 66½ minutes. Between 3.48 and 7.12 p.m., these recorders made *three* journeys over this 77.3 miles of line, so covering 232 miles in 3 hours 24 minutes, and in an actual running time of 3 minutes over 3 hours.

After the 1939–1945 war the " Cheltenham Flyer " never reappeared. Until April 1973, however, expresses daily were booked to cover the 77.3 miles from Swindon to Paddington in a working time of 64½ minutes start to stop, and faster times still were made pass-to-stop by expresses not calling at Swindon. But in 1973 these times were temporarily increased because of work in preparation for future high-speed services.

The Cheltenham Spa Express

In earlier years a number of trains between Paddington and Cheltenham were so indicated in the public timetables, including the one which as just described became the " Cheltenham Flyer ", but more recently the title has been applied to and officially retained by two expresses only. In steam days, up to the 1939–1945 war, these were the 8 a.m. up from Cheltenham and the 5 p.m. down from Paddington. Both were non-stop between Kemble and Paddington, and the up express, with its allowance of no more than 86½ minutes for the 91 miles up from Kemble, was fairly high on the list of the fastest Great Western runs. The 5 p.m. down, allowed 90 minutes, was also within the mile-a-minute orbit. Both trains had to reverse in Gloucester, and their other stops were at Stroud in both directions and also Stonehouse coming up, in addition to Kemble, where connections were made with the Circencester and Tetbury branches.

△ The GWR's unique Pacific, No. 111 *The Great Bear*, heads the afternoon Cheltenham tea car express out of Paddington around 1920.

◁ The down " Cheltenham Spa Express " emerges from Sapperton Tunnel in July 1960 behind No. 7035 *Ogmore Castle*.

◁ The " Cheltenham Spa Express " completes its journey after reversal at Gloucester behind a 2-6-2T; the down train passes Churchdown in April 1964 behind No. 5518.

Photo by B. J. Ashworth

A good deal has happened to the trains concerned since then. As with the Worcester main line, 12¾ miles of the Swindon–Gloucester line, from Swindon Locomotive Yard to Kemble, have been reduced to single track. The only stations remaining open between Swindon and Gloucester are Kemble, Stroud and Stonehouse. More important, by means of a new connection laid in at Standish Junction in 1964 between the Swindon–Gloucester line and the former Midland West of England main line, trains from Paddington now run direct into the Midland Eastgate station at Gloucester, and reversal there to proceed to Cheltenham is no longer necessary. Also the former Great Western St. James terminus at Cheltenham is no more, and the " Cheltenham Spa Express " is now accommodated in the former Midland Lansdown station.

As to the trains themselves, in 1973 the up express left Cheltenham at 8.10 a.m. and after calls at Stroud, Kemble and Swindon was booked up to Paddington in 68 minutes arriving at 10.17 a.m. Despite the additional stops, this overall time of 2 hours 7 minutes from Cheltenham was 23 minutes shorter than in 1939. But going down it was a different story; the departure from Paddington had been advanced to 4.48 p.m., and with additional stops at Didcot and Swindon it was not until 7.15 p.m. that Cheltenham Lansdown was reached, a journey only 3 minutes faster than in steam days.

The Cornish Riviera Limited

Easily the most famous train in the history of the Great Western Railway and its successor, the Western Region of British Railways, is the " Cornish Riviera Express ". In the first decade of the present century, competition was keen between the Great Western and London & South Western Railways for the traffic between London, Exeter and Plymouth. The L.S.W.R. had a substantial advantage in distance to Exeter—171¾ as compared with 194 miles—and to Plymouth also the 231 miles to North Road by the L.S.W.R. compared with 246 miles by G.W.R.; and though the South Western was hampered by what, on the whole, were the longer and more severe gradients of the two routes, with increasingly powerful locomotives the shorter route could boast the shorter overall times.

By 1904 the Great Western was well on the way towards a substantial shortening of its main line; in 1901 the Patney to Westbury cut-off had been brought into use and the Berks. & Hants line had been brought up to fast running standards, while work had begun on the Castle Cary to Langport line, the two together promising a cut in distance of 20 miles from Paddington to Taunton and all stations west of that point. Actually it was 1906 before the latter was completed, but meantime the Great Western, now with the first of Churchward's locomotives available and capable of efficient high speed running over long distances continuously, decided to take time by the forelock. So there came about the introduction of the first regular non-stop run between Paddington and Plymouth on July 1, 1904.

Already the G.W.R. had begun non-stop running over the 193.9 miles between Paddington and Exeter via Bristol, avoiding Temple Meads station by the Pylle Hill loop, and was making the very creditable time of 3½ hours each way. But to add 52.0 miles to that distance, including the fearsome gradients between Newton Abbot and Plymouth, was a startling development indeed for those early years, and enabled the Great Western to claim what was easily the longest regular non-stop run in the world at that period. The new train was scheduled to leave Paddington at 10.10 a.m., and to run to Plymouth in 4 hours 25 minutes, 28 minutes less than the 10.50 a.m. down, which up till then had made the best time; calling at Truro, Gwinear Road and St. Erth in Cornwall, the new express reached Penzance at 5.10 p.m. On the up run departure from Penzance was at 10 a.m. and from Plymouth at 12.35 p.m., and the London arrival was at 5.0 p.m., the up non-stop time being the same 265 minutes as on the down journey.

The load was one of seven coaches, five of former G.W.R. clerestory-roofed stock and a new 68 ft. dining car with elliptical roof for Penzance, with a tri-composite for Falmouth, detached at Truro (there being still, of course, first second and third class accommodation in Great Western trains). This load of a little more than 200 tons was entrusted generally to one of Churchward's new " City " class 4-4-0s, but the French compound Atlantic *La France* also took a share in the working and did well. It is interesting to recall that a competition was promoted by one of the railway papers to provide a name for the new service, and that among the names submitted were " Cornish Riviera Limited " and " Royal Duchy Express ".

△ Begrimed 2-6-2T No. 5514 rests at Gloucester after titled train duty, with the " Cheltenham Spa Express " headboard on its running plate, in July 1956.

Photo by P. J. Sharpe

▽ Usual power for the " Cornish Riviera " at its inception: a Churchward " City " class 4-4-0.

Many of the entries included the word " Riviera " and out of them all Mr. J. C. Inglis, then G.W.R. General Manager, selected " Riviera Express ". But it was not long before " Cornish " became added to the title, and officially the train was being shown in the timetables as " ' Cornish Riviera ' Limited Express ", which the railway staff very soon shortened to " The Limited ".

July, 1906, was the long-awaited opening throughout of the Westbury route to the West, and to it, needless to say, the " Cornish Riviera " was immediately transferred. The starting time from Paddington was altered to 10.30 a.m., and when the winter timetables of 1906-1907 were published, it was seen that this was now to become an all-the-year-round service to and from the west, summer and winter alike. The arrival at North Road was fixed at 2.37 p.m., 2 minutes later, but the Cornish arrivals remained much the same, except that Penzance was reached 5 minutes earlier, at 5.5 p.m., an acceleration of 25 minutes from London. With times unaltered in Cornwall, the up " Limited " now was into Paddington by 4.45 instead of 5.0 p.m.

By now the " Cornish Riviera " was composed of the new Great Western 70 ft. stock, with elliptical-roofed coaches of " clipper " outline, and so had increased in weight. Moreover, it had increased in another way, for with the diversion to the Westbury route the train began to set down passengers at intermediate stations by means of slip coaches. Before long the express was leaving

△ " Star " class 4-6-0 No. 4019 *Knight Templar* parades a " Cornish Riviera " rake of 70 ft. coaches in the new chocolate and cream livery of 1922.

Paddington with three of these slip portions on its tail—at Westbury, for Weymouth; at Taunton, for both Minehead and Ilfracombe; and at Exeter, this section at first running through to the Torquay line and in later years to Brent and Kingsbridge. Passengers in the slip coaches, needless to say, had no access to the restaurant car, but those in the through portions of the main train—to Falmouth, St. Ives and Penzance—were more fortunate.

On the up journey the last-mentioned through coaches were run but not, of course, those from Ilfracombe, Minehead and Weymouth; Exeter was served by stopping at St. Davids, whence the 173.7 miles to Paddington were run in 179 minutes. These substantial increases of train weight posed no traction problems, for Churchward's new 4-6-0s were now available—at first the two-cylinder " Saints ", but from 1907 onwards the four-cylinder " Stars".

The effect of the slipping was nicely to proportion the load to the increasing severity of the gradients, as the train worked its way westwards.

△ The " Cornish Riviera " stock of 1929, with recessed doors, headed by 4-6-0 No. 4087 *Cardigan Castle.*

It would be difficult to find a single run anywhere else in the country with so great a variety of gradients within its length; from Paddington to Reading the course is virtually level; from there to Taunton the inclinations on the westbound journey are no more than moderate. But beyond Tauton there is first the 3-mile climb at 1 in 80-90-127 through the Blackdown Hills to Whiteball summit; and then, after Newton Abbot, there are the formidable ascents to Dainton summit, and from Totnes up to Brent, the former including a short strip as steep as 1 in 36, and the latter $1\frac{1}{2}$ miles averaging 1 in 50, followed by the $2\frac{1}{4}$ mile descent at 1 in 42 from Hemerdon to Plympton.

Space does not permit a detailed description of the way in which the load of the " Limited " had developed to the standard prevailing immediately before the Second World War. By that time the traffic to Exeter, and the desirability of picking up passengers at Exeter for Cornwall, had resulted in the substitution of a stop at Exeter for the previous slip, leaving only the Westbury and Taunton slip portions, though these had expanded to two coaches each. In all, the " Limited " now consisted of no fewer than eight through portions daily, except in the height of the summer; these were the main train, with the restaurant cars, for Penzance; a through coach for St. Ives, detached at St. Erth; one for Falmouth, detached at Truro; one for Newquay, detached at Par; one for Kingsbridge, detached at Exeter and worked forward by a stopping train; the Taunton slip,

▽ By January 1936, date of this picture, the " Limited " has been re-equipped with the new recessed door " Centenary " stock of 1935; No. 6025 *King Henry III* is near Somerton on the up train. *Photo by F. J. Arthur*

consisting of though coaches for both Ilfracombe and Minehead; and the two Weymouth coaches slipped at Westbury. At times of week-end pressure, an additional coach might be included for Plymouth, making a ninth portion.

Many different types of stock appeared in succession on the "Cornish Riviera Limited" in the intervening years. The original 70-ft. coaches, with recessed end doors only, were succeeded by flush-sided 70-ft. cars with side doors, then by 60-ft. vehicles, and finally by some new and luxurious stock, introduced shortly before the war, again of maximum width and with recessed end doors. The original composite restaurant

◁ The "Cornish Riviera Limited" in September 1933: "Bulldog" 4-4-0 No. 3401 *Vancouver* assists No. 6003 *King George IV* up Hemerdon bank with the London-bound train. The first vehicle of the train is a bullion van.

Photo by G. C. Allen

▽ The early post-war "Riviera" west of Plymouth—the up train near Bodmin Road, at the foot of the climb up the Fowey valley to Doublebois, behind 4-6-0 No. 5095 *Barbury Castle* in August 1949.

Photo by R. J. Doran

6013

◁ In the mid-1950s the summer Saturday "Limited" provided indirectly a fine spectacle, since its "King" 4-6-0 from London, after detachment at Newton Abbot, was worked forward piloting another "King" on the following 10.35 Paddington-Plymouth; the pair seen climbing Dainton bank in June 1957, are Nos. 6013 *King Henry VIII* and 6028 *King George VI*. *Photo by D. S. Fish*

△ Dieselisation—in May 1961 the up "Riviera" leaves Penzance for Plymouth behind N.B.L. diesel-hydraulic Type 4 No. D603 *Conquest*. *Photo by C. J. Blay*

◁ The early post-war "Cornish Riviera"—with ex-G.W.R. coaching stock newly repainted in B.R. crimson and cream livery the train ascends Dainton bank in June 1949 double-headed by 4-6-0s Nos. 6022 *King Edward III* and 6813 *Eastbury Grange*.

Photo by J. G. Hubback

car and kitchen also had given place to an independent kitchen and first-class car coupled to a third-class open car, of very modern design. Again, the " Star " class 4-cylinder 4–6–0s had been succeeded, first by the " Castles " in 1923, and then by the more powerful " Kings " in 1927. At this period the empty weight of the 14-coach train out of Paddington had mounted to 498 tons, which meant a loaded weight of at least 530 tons. So far from " limited " had the train become that it was now officially known as the " Cornish Riviera Express ", though still always called the " Limited " by staff.

By 1939 the winter weight of the down " Limited " with lighter coaches had diminished to 468 tons empty and nearly 500 tons with a normal complement of passengers and luggage, but on its accelerated schedule the haulage had become one of the most exacting locomotive tasks in the country. New cut-off routes had been built to avoid both Westbury and Frome, so cutting out the service speed restrictions through both stations (incidentally, the Westbury cut-off now made it necessary to detach the Weymouth slip portion at Heywood Road Junction, and to work it over the mile from there into Westbury with a shunting engine), thus slightly reducing the Paddington-Exeter distance to 173.5 miles, but this was scheduled in the working timetable to be covered in 169 minutes start-to-stop, so involving an average speed of 61.6 m.p.h. throughout. For the 52 miles from Exeter to Plymouth 72 minutes were allowed, and at North Road station, where engines were changed, the booked arrival was 2.35 p.m. Stopping after that at Par, Truro, Gwinear Road and St. Erth, the " Limited " reached Penzance at 5 p.m. Through Cornwall the train was usually worked by a " Castle " class 4–6–0, as this was the heaviest type permitted to work over Saltash bridge. Later the high pressure " Counties " became available for the run through Cornwall.

During the currency of the summer timetable, the " Limited " reverted to a nominal non-stop

run between Paddington and Plymouth, covering the distance in 4 hours 2 minutes, and reaching Penzance at 4.55 p.m. In the working timetable, however, a stop was shown at Newton Abbot from 1.43 to 1.47 p.m. to take an assisting engine between there and Plymouth. The summer formation consisted only of sections for Penzance, St. Ives, Falmouth, Newquay and Weymouth; the other through portions of the normal winter load were run on additional trains which operated during the summer season only. The summer load of the " Limited " was normally twelve to fifteen bogies to Westbury and two less from there.

For most of its history the " Cornish Riviera Limited " was an easier working in the up direction than in the down; the up schedule was not quite so fast, and the absence of Ilfracombe, Minehead and Weymouth portions to some degree lightened the load. On its pre-1939 schedule, for many years the departure from Penzance was at 10 a.m., and from North Road, Plymouth, at 12.30 p.m.; in the summer the train ran non-stop from here to Paddington, with an allowance of $4\frac{1}{4}$ hours, but during the remaining nine months a stop at Exeter was included, and the train was booked to run up from there in 2 hours 55 minutes, arriving at 4.45 p.m.

One of the more remarkable happenings in the history of this famous train occurred for a week in May, 1925, when on the Monday, Wednesday and Friday in the down direction and the Tuesday, Thursday and Saturday in the up, it was worked by the L.N.E.R. Class " A1 " Pacific No. 4474, *Victor Wild*, turn-and-turn about with the G.W.R. 4-6-0 No. 4074, *Caldicot Castle*. In this exchange trial, which was not without its effect on later

On summer Saturdays at the time of this July 1958 photo the " Cornish Riviera Limited " complete was a through train between Paddington and St. Ives, to which it is heading near Carbis Bay, double-headed down the branch from the main line at Par by 2-6-2Ts Nos. 4563 and 4570. *Photo by B. A. Butt*

L.N.E.R. locomotive design, the " Castle " made the better times, and did so on a lower fuel consumption. ("Foreign Pacifics" again worked the down train in February, 1956, when the "Kings" were hurriedly withdrawn from service for a period because of bogie fractures and Stanier 4-6-2s Nos. 46207, 46210, 46254 and 46257 were borrowed from the London Midland to help fill the gap.)

When the Second World War broke out, the 10.30 a.m. down at first was altered to travel *via* Bath and Bristol, combining the work of the previous 10 a.m., 10.30 a.m., 11.15 a.m. and 12 noon trains, but it was soon found impossible to accommodate all these passengers in a single service. So a combined " Cornish Riviera " and " Torbay " service *via* Westbury reappeared at 10.30 a.m., and soon the "Torbay" was split off as a separate train at 10.40 a.m., leaving the 10.30 a.m. as a recognisable wartime edition of its peacetime self, non-stop between Paddington and Exeter, even to the extent of being one of the very few trains in the country still to carry its name on the carriage headboards.

There were no through portions other than the main train from Paddington to Penzance, but as many additional coaches for Plymouth were run on the rear as required, and because of the number of Servicemen travelling, a formation of 14 coaches was usually needed over this stage. The allowance to Exeter was 3½ hours (a slowing of 41 minutes); Plymouth was reached at 3.25 p.m., and Penzance at 6.25 p.m. In the up direction departure from Penzance was at 9.30 a.m., from Plymouth 12.30 p.m., and from Exeter 1.55 p.m., and Paddington was reached at 5.30 p.m. After the war a cut of 15 minutes each way between Paddington and Exeter was made from October 1st, 1945. The allowance over the 173.5 miles from Paddington to Exeter came down to 195 minutes (53.4 m.p.h.), and Penzance was reached 35 minutes earlier, at 5.50 p.m., in 7 hours 20 minutes from London. Restaurant cars, of an entirely new internal design, reappeared on the last day of 1945.

The summer of 1946 saw a further improvement, with a non-stop run in each direction between Paddington and Plymouth (4½ hours down and 4 hours 40 minutes up), and the London-Penzance time cut to 6 hours 55 minutes down and 7¼ hours up. With the winter timetables of 1950-51, the Westbury slip portion was restored to the train.

The summer timetables of 1952 showed another substantial speed-up of the " Cornish Riviera Express ", with 4¼ hours now allowed in both directions for the 225.5 miles between Paddington and Plymouth, and no stop other than that required for attaching and detaching the assisting locomotive at Newton Abbot. (At weekends, incidentally, the timetables at this time showed much longer " non-stop " runs; in 1951 the summer Saturday " Riviera " had no publicly booked stop between Paddington and Truro, 279 miles, though operationally the train paused at Newton Abbot to take on a pilot for the South Devon banks and again at Devonport Junction to replace the " King " with something lighter before the Cornish main line was reached.) In the 1952-1953 winter timetables the Exeter stop was not reinstated; from then on the time of 6 hours 40 minutes from London to Penzance was only 10 minutes slower than that of pre-war winters, while the Penzance to London time of 6¾ hours (the arrival in Paddington was now 4.30 p.m.) was right back to the pre-war figure. But the train was lighter in weight, for none of the old through portions were carried, other than the Weymouth slip on the down journey. For a time the 4-hour booking from Paddington to Plymouth was restored, but a gradual falling off of traffic made it necessary to increase the usefulness of the train by stopping once again at Exeter.

Then, in 1961, there came a complete recasting of the Western Region timetable which affected the " Cornish Riviera Express " considerably. Between 1958 and 1960 diesel-hydraulic locomotives had replaced the " King " 4-6-0s on these workings; first there were the 2,200 h.p. " Warships ", but no acceleration of any note had taken place as yet. In the new timetable every West of England express combined portions both for Torbay and for Plymouth and beyond, and these included the " Cornish Riviera Limited "; also a stop at Taunton as well as Exeter was to be made by each express. Instead of the non-stop run to Plymouth, therefore, the " Riviera " now had to stop twice *en route* in each direction, and its allowance from Paddington to Plymouth accordingly was increased to 4¼ hours; as had always been customary, though for no understandable reason, the journey up from

△ By 1952 " Britannia " Pacifics were working west of Plymouth: here is No. 70019 *Lightning* on the down " Riviera " at St. Erth in April 1952. *Photo by B. A. Butt*

▽ The Great Western lives again—with coaches in chocolate and cream and engine decked out with Western-style headboard, the up " Cornish Riviera Limited " of December 1958 passes Rattery box behind double-chimney 4-6-0 No. 6028 *King George VI*.
Photo by D. S. Fish

Plymouth was allowed 10 minutes more. But better times lay ahead. In this same year there appeared from Swindon Works the first of the 2,700 h.p. "Western" diesels.

Initially the Paddington–Plymouth time was tightened to an even 4 hours, with an allowance of only 124 minutes (average 69.0 m.p.h.) for the first 142.7 miles to Taunton. By 1967 the train was into Penzance by 5 p.m., after detachment of the Torbay section at Exeter and the restaurant cars at Plymouth (thus depriving passengers of refreshment for the final stage of all but $2\frac{1}{2}$ hours and ten intermediate stops through Cornwall). But in 1968 drastic improvement was made west of Plymouth.

In a marketing bid to create travel the Western Region re-cast and accelerated the whole Paddington–Plymouth service in the summer of 1968. The timetable was regularised on a near hourly-interval basis and intermediate stop patterns reshaped, so as to speed up off-peak trains and promote travel to and from some of the railheads with growing traffic potential, particularly Exeter. The operation was based on standard 10- or 12-coach train-sets, each making at least one Paddington–Plymouth or–Penzance round trip daily and in one or two cases beginning a third leg within each 24 hours. Only portions of each train-set—and none with a refreshment car—were run west of Plymouth. Only one train each way daily was timed at more than $4\frac{1}{4}$ hours overall between London and Plymouth.

A lavish element of the scheme was the creation of four pairs of "Warship" diesels to work as 4,400 h.p. multiple-units and permit sharp timing of the crack trains—among them, of course, the "Riviera". This and the "Golden Hind" were now quickened to a $3\frac{3}{4}$ hour schedule for the 225.5 miles, better than a mile a minute despite intermediate stops at Taunton and Exeter (Newton Abbot as well in the case of the "Hind") and negotiation of the South Devon banks. Between Paddington and Taunton the "Riviera" was now booked at 118 minutes for the 142.75 miles, an average of 72.6 m.p.h. West of Plymouth, stops were pruned to enhance the justification of the train's "Limited" appellation, so that Penzance was now reached a whole half-hour earlier at 4.30 p.m.; in the reverse direction the cut was 5 minutes greater.

The "Warships", however, were in the twilight of their careers, doomed by unreliability, their high

◁ In 1968 the "Cornish Riviera" was given a pair of 2,200 h.p. "Warship" diesel-hydraulics to allow a 3¾ hr. Paddington-Plymouth timing; on a June afternoon in 1969 Nos. 822 *Hercules* and 869 *Zest* wheel the up train past Royal Oak into Paddington. *Photo by J. H. Cooper-Smith*

▽ By September 1972, the "Riviera" had been re-equipped with B.R. Mk. II coaches; Class 52 diesel-hydraulic No. 1034 *Western Dragoon* completes the run from London at Penzance. *Photo by G. Gillham*

" Western " diesel-hydraulic on the latter-day restricted load " Riviera ", climbing from Totnes to Dainton in August 1971.

Photo by J. H. Cooper-Smith

costs of maintenance and the mere fact of their hydraulic transmissions in a diesel-electric BR world. The next stage of " Riviera " development would lie entirely with single-unit "Western" Class 52 diesel-hydraulics or Class 47 diesel-electrics.

It came in 1972, when the entire West Country service was put on a full hourly interval pattern of limited loads. Departures from Paddington were evenly balanced between Torbay and Plymouth–Penzance, always on the half-hour. And since the Plymouth departures were established at 30 minutes past the odd hours, the 66 years-old 10.30 a.m. Paddington time of the " Riviera " was abolished; it was now the 11.30 a.m. In the new order it was officially re-christened the " Cornish Riviera Limited ", for its make-up was strictly limited to 300 tons (nine coaches), and seat reservation was made compulsory. The formation consisted of five coaches running through to Penzance, and two restaurant and buffet cars with a composite brake detached at Plymouth. At times of extreme pressure an additional second might be run between Paddington and Plymouth, even though this meant infringement of the 300 tons maximum. The train-set, incidentally, made its first run of the day as the up " Golden Hind ", due into Paddington at 10.41.

As to schedule, Plymouth was brought within $3\frac{1}{2}$ hours of London, at an average speed of 64.4 m.p.h. On the down journey this meant covering the 173.5 miles from Paddington to Exeter, now a non-stop run, in 143 minutes, at 72.8 m.p.h. average. Over the steep gradients between Exeter and Plymouth the 51.0 miles took 64 minutes, the working arrival at North Road being at 2.59 p.m., or in 3 hours 29 minutes from Paddington. In Cornwall the stops now were at Liskeard, Bodmin Road, St. Austell, Truro, Redruth and St. Erth (to

which Camborne subsequently was added), and journey's end was at 4.53 p.m. in Penzance. So the 6 hours 35 minutes from Paddington to Penzance in 1904 had shrunk to 5 hours 27 minutes in 1972, the major part of this substantial cut having been effected in Cornwall. But the small 1973 decelerations already referred to added 2 minutes to the Paddington–Exeter time, and Penzance was not reached till 5.0 p.m.

The up "Cornish Riviera Limited" was now despatched from Penzance at 11 a.m. and with the same stops as in the down direction reached Plymouth at 12.49 p.m. Here 10 minutes were allowed to attach the restaurant cars—for the one serious shortcoming in the present-day amenities on this train was the absence of any refreshment facilities in either direction over nearly two hours through Cornwall, and no possibility of serving lunch in the up direction before 1 p.m., which means a very late meal for the second relay of passengers. Finally, at 1 p.m. the accelerated "Limited" left Plymouth, and with a tight 62 minutes thence to Exeter and 151 minutes up from there, the train was at rest in Paddington by 4.35 p.m., the overall journey from Penzance having occupied 5 hours 35 minutes. Conversely, this train-set then formed the evening "Golden Hind" back to Plymouth.

Another slashing improvement in Paddington-Plymouth times is unlikely until 1977 or 1978, when the 125 m.p.h. HST diesel trains take over the principal services. Although it will be too expensive to improve the track for speeds generally higher than 100 m.p.h. west of Taunton, the HSTs are forecast to cut the best journey time from Paddington to Exeter to 1 hour 57 minutes, to Plymouth to 2 hours 50 minutes, and to Penzance to 4 hours 36 minutes.

The Cornishman

Among well-known titled trains of the past, the "Cornishman" of the G.W.R., though this title was never official enough to appear in timetables or other railway literature of the period, certainly was of sufficient note to deserve a place. It began its career in the days when the main line from Paddington to Penzance was still being operated on Brunel's 7 ft. gauge, and on May 20th, 1892, it had the distinction of being the last broad gauge express to leave London for stations in Cornwall before the final change of gauge from 7 ft. to 4 ft. 8½ in. was made.

When the "Cornishman" came into operation in the summer of 1890, it was the fastest train between London and the West of England, and one of the fastest in the country. Leaving Paddington at 10.15 a.m., it reached Bristol at 12.45 p.m., Exeter at 2.20 p.m., Plymouth at 3.50 p.m., and Penzance at 6.57 p.m., but contrary to later practice the up run was faster, and with departure from Penzance at 11.15 a.m. and arrival in Paddington at 7.50 p.m. the overall time was reduced to 8 hours 35 minutes. This, of course, was *via* Bristol, and over a total distance of 325¼ miles, as compared with the present 305 miles *via* Westbury. A popular feature of this express was that it deigned to carry third-class passengers, at a time when not a few important trains were still first and second only.

In those days the agreement between the G.W.R. and the company controlling the hotel and refreshment rooms at Swindon station made it compulsory to stop every express at Swindon for at least 10 minutes to give passengers time to obtain refreshments. It was not until 1895 that the railway, by paying the large sum of £100,000, obtained release from their engagement, and until 1895, therefore, the "Cornishman" stopped at Swindon in both directions. The time allowed for the 77.3 miles from Paddington to Swindon was 87 minutes, calling for an average speed of 53.3 m.p.h. from start to stop over this length.

By 1895 the G.W.R., now on the standard 4 ft. 8½ in. gauge throughout from Paddington to Penzance, had laid down water-troughs near Goring and at Keynsham, between Bath and Bristol, so that with the abolition of the Swindon stop from October 1st, 1895, the "Cornishman" was able to make the first regular non-stop runs between Paddington and Bristol. Departure from London was altered from 10.15 to 10.30 a.m., and the time allowed for the 118.3 miles was cut to 135 minutes, calling for an average speed of 52.6 m.p.h. By a further cut of 15 minutes in 1903 the down "Cornishman" became the first train on record to put Bristol within 2 hours of Paddington daily; the average of 59.2 m.p.h. start-to-stop still kept this express in the front rank of the fastest British trains.

Well before this date a division into two parts of the "Cornishman" in each direction, during the height of the summer season, had earned a new record. A relief section for Newquay, timed to leave Paddington at 10.25 a.m., was booked to run the 193.6 miles from Paddington to Exeter without a stop, from July 20th, 1896. The running times as far as Bath were unchanged; the train avoided Temple Meads station at Bristol by the relief line, and was due in Exeter at 2.10 p.m., in 3¾ hours from London. Average speed for the run was thus 51.6 m.p.h., but the load was five bogie vehicles only. The 10.25 a.m. from Paddington reached Plymouth at 3.37 p.m., and stood there 5 minutes; the next stop was at Par at 4.45 p.m., and arrival in Newquay was at 5.47 p.m. In the reverse direction, leaving Newquay at 11.5 a.m., calling at all stations up to Par and after that at Liskeard, Devonport, Plymouth, Exeter and Bristol, the up express was due in Paddington at 6.48 p.m.

By an easy margin the run between Paddington and Exeter at that time was the longest in the world without intermediate stop. From 1899 non-stop running in the up direction became regular

△ The original London-West of England " Cornishman " of the 19th Century takes the sea wall curve near Teignmouth on May 20, 1892, just before conversion of the G.W.R. broad gauge, behind " Convertible " 2-4-0 No. 3501.

▽ The 1935 revival of the " Cornishman ", when the title was applied to the summer relief " Riviera ", the 10.35 Paddington-Penzance and 10.20 St. Erth-Paddington. The down train skirts the sea wall at Teignmouth behind 4-6-0 No. 6012 *King Edward VI.*

throughout the year, and from 1902 in the down direction also; then, from July 1st, 1904, came the complete eclipse of the " Cornishman " by the new " Cornish Riviera Limited " express, with its daily non-stop runs of 245.6 miles in each direction between Paddington and North Road station at Plymouth.

With that the " Cornishman " title was pigeon-holed until the mid-1930s. By then booming holiday traffic was overtaxing the " Cornish Riviera Limited's " accommodation in the summer peak, and hence in the summer timetable of 1935 the " Cornishman " was officially exhumed as a complement to the " Riviera ". The " CRE " throughout the summer was made an exclusively reserved seat service, from Mondays to Fridays publicly non-stop to and from Truro (though, of course, pausing officially at both Newton Abbot and Devonport respectively, for help over the South Devon banks and to change engines at the entrance to Cornwall), and accepting passengers to or from Truro, Falmouth, St. Ives and Penzance only. On Saturdays the " CRE's " first public stop was not until St. Erth (299½ miles from London). Accordingly, the 10.35 a.m. from Paddington, publicly non-stop to Plymouth, was glamourised as the " Cornishman ", to cater for the intermediate traffic turned off the " Riviera ". Running every weekday it conveyed traffic for Plymouth, Newquay (a separate portion), St.

Erth, Helston and Penzance, where it was due at 5.7 p.m.; it also took the " Riveria's " Weymouth slip coach. In the reverse direction the " Cornishman " started from St. Erth at 10.20 a.m. and served Gwinear Road, Truro and Par to Plymouth, whence it was publicly non-stop to Paddington, reached at 4.50 p.m. Evidently receipts did not justify the munificence, for the " Cornishman " lasted the 1935 summer only; by 1936 the 10.35 had become an anonymous Saturdays only train.

In the summer of 1952, the name " Cornishman " was revived once more and applied to an entirely different service—that running daily between Wolverhampton, Birmingham, Plymouth and Penzance by way of Stratford-on-Avon and Cheltenham. In the earlier years of Great Western history, G.W.R. communication between the Midlands and the West of England had to be made circuitously by Oxford and the west curve at Didcot on to the Bristol main line. Then, in 1908, the G.W.R. opened a new and costly direct route which enabled this company to compete much more effectively than before with the Midland Birmingham–Bristol route through Cheltenham. The new Great Western line took off from the London main line at Tyseley 3 miles south of Birmingham (Snow Hill), cut in a south-westerly direction through Stratford-on-Avon to the northern fringes of the Cotswolds, connecting with the Oxford–Worcester main line at Honeybourne, and then continued through Broadway to a new station at Cheltenham called Malvern Road.

The post-war Penzance-Wolverhampton " Cornishman " on its original West Midlands route, passing under the Worcester-London main line at Honeybourne Junction in May 1957 behind 4-6-0 No. 4083 *Abbotsbury Castle.* *Photo by R. J. Blenkinsop*

The express next took the joint Midland–Great Western line from Cheltenham to Gloucester, but left it just short of Gloucester to join the G.W.R. Gloucester–London line, so by-passing Gloucester to the east. At Standish Junction the trains of the Great Western Birmingham–Bristol service crossed over to the parallel Midland line, and with the aid of running powers made use of the latter as far south as Yate. There they branched off, to run up a short spur to the Swindon–South Wales main line of the G.W.R., which they followed to Stoke Gifford, then branching eastwards down through Filton and Stapleton Road into Temple Meads station at Bristol.

At first, several through services in each direction daily were established, but in the course of years their number diminished, until by 1939 only one through service continued to run throughout the year, at 10.40 a.m. from Wolverhampton and 11.20 a.m. from Birmingham, reaching Bristol at 1.35 p.m., Plymouth at 4.52 p.m. and Penzance at 7.45 p.m. It returned from Penzance at 10.45 a.m., Plymouth at 1.40 p.m. and Bristol at 4.45 p.m., reaching Birmingham at 7 p.m. and Wolverhampton at 7.30 p.m.

This train was suspended during the Second World War, but subsequently reappeared, running in much the same times until the summer of 1952, when its timing was altered completely and, as previously mentioned, it received the title of " Cornishman ". The new " Cornishman " left Wolverhampton at 9.15 a.m. and Birmingham

(Snow Hill) at 9.50 a.m. Calling after that at Stratford-on-Avon and Cheltenham (Malvern Road), it diverged from the previous Gloucester by-pass to stop in the one-time Midland station, before resuming its journey to Bristol, which was reached at 12.28 p.m. Restarting 7 minutes later, it served Taunton by means of a slip-coach, and ran into Exeter at 2.8 p.m. The next stop was Plymouth (3.30-3.35 p.m.), and after calls at principal stations in Cornwall, Penzance was reached at 5.55 p.m.

The return journey began from Penzance at 10.30 a.m.; stops were made at St. Erth, Truro, St. Austell and Par (not at Bodmin Road or Liskeard in this direction), and Plymouth was left at 12.58 p.m. The Exeter stop was at 2.19-2.22 p.m. and that at Bristol at 3.56-4.2 p.m., and with the same stops beyond as on the reverse run, Birmingham was reached at 6.38 p.m. and Wolverhampton at 7.28 p.m. Refreshment facilities were available for the entire journey, and through coaches, detached and attached at Exeter, were run between Wolverhampton, Torquay and Kingswear.

Since then the " Cornishman " has undergone a number of changes. When almost all the passenger traffic was withdrawn from the Honeybourne–Cheltenham line, it was decided to transfer the " Cornishman " to the former Midland line between Birmingham and Cheltenham, which meant using New Street instead of Snow Hill station at Birmingham. It could have been run on, of course, to the High Level instead of the Low Level station at Wolverhampton, but it was decided instead greatly to increase the train's usefulness by continuing it over the former Midland line to Derby and Sheffield. The final stage has been a further extension to Leeds and Bradford, so that the " Cornishman " now provides a daily through service between Bradford and Penzance.

Until the end of April, 1967, Forster Square station at Bradford was the starting-point, and the former Midland line was used, not merely from there into the City station at Leeds, but after reversal at Leeds on over the Midland route through Normanton to Sheffield. At the beginning of May, 1967, however a considerable change in the working was ordered. The Bradford start was transferred to the Exchange station, and the " Cornishman " now took the former Great Northern line to Leeds, calling *en route* at New Pudsey. Then, after reversal at Leeds City, and in common by now with almost all the Midland trains to the south, it continued over the former G.N. line as far as Moorthorpe, where it ran up the spur to the Swinton & Knottingley line, rejoining the Midland main line at Swinton. Departure from Bradford was at 7.6 a.m. and from Leeds at 7.36 a.m; Birmingham was left at 10.25 a.m. and at the other end of the journey Plymouth was reached at 3.8 p.m. and Penzance at 5.55 p.m. In the reverse direction departure from Penzance was at 11.0 a.m. and from Plymouth at 1.30 p.m., Leeds City being reached at 9.32 p.m. and Bradford Exchange at 10.7 p.m. A beneficiary of the new route was Wakefield, where the " Cornishman " now stopped in each direction.

◁ Sporting new W.R.-style headboard 4-6-0 No. 5024 *Carew Castle* eases the up " Cornishman ", re-equipped with B.R. stock in chocolate and cream livery, up the Teign estuary to Teignmouth in June 1959. *Photo by S. Creer*

▽ The Penzance section of the up " Cornishman " enters Truro behind double-chimney 4-6-0 No. 1007 *County of Brecknock* in October 1958. *Photo by B. A. Butt*

Subsequently there were further changes. Engineering work on the line between Birmingham and Bristol, all of which south of Blackwell had become part of the Western Region, now permitted speeds up to 90 m.p.h. over suitable sections, and so a considerable acceleration became possible. Only on Saturdays did the " Cornishman " begin its southbound journey at Bradford; on other days the start was from Leeds City. Until April, 1973 this was at 7.35 a.m., and after stops at Wakefield, Sheffield and Derby the " Cornishman " fitted into the even-interval departures southwards from Birmingham New Street by leaving there at 10.15 a.m. on one of the only two daily non-stop runs from Birmingham to Bristol, taking the avoiding line to bypass Gloucester.

From Yate onwards the only line now available for passenger trains is what was formerly the spur

up to the Western Region South Wales main line at Westerleigh, and thence through Filton and Stapleton Road into Temple Meads; this was reached at 11.44 a.m. The next stop was at Exeter, at 1.1 p.m., and from here a non-stop run brought the " Cornishman " into Plymouth by 2.12 p.m. The remainder of the journey was less speedy, and after nine intermediate stops Penzance was not reached until 4.30 p.m., though this meant a trip from Leeds shorter by 1 hour 24 minutes than in 1967. In the northbound direction there were additional stops at Taunton and Cheltenham, and with a Penzance start at 10.25 a.m. and a Leeds arrival at 7.35 p.m. the overall time in this direction had become 9 hours 10 minutes.

Since then the " Cornishman " has been subjected to yet another change of route. By arrangement with the NCB the former Midland main line from Leeds through Normanton and Cudworth to Rotherham and Sheffield has been sufficiently cured of the pitfalls that troubled it to make possible a reversion to it from the Swinton & Knottingley route, which threads another key mining area. So, from the beginning of May, 1973 the " Cornishman " was diverted to the former. Not for the whole distance, however, as this would have deprived Wakefield of a valuable through service; so the train continued to serve Wakefield, and then switched up by the spur at Oakenshaw to the Midland line just where the latter crosses the former Great Northern main line at a point 2½ miles beyond Wakefield Westgate. Departure from Leeds City was now at 7.41 a.m.; that from Birmingham was unchanged at 10.15 a.m., but Plymouth was reached 3 minutes earlier, at 2.12 p.m. The Penzance arrival was 7 minutes later, however, at 4.37 p.m. Northbound, the " Cornishman " was away from Penzance at 10.25 a.m. and from Plymouth at 12.40 p.m., but Leeds was reached at 7.20 p.m., 15 minutes earlier and in 8 hours 55 minutes from Penzance. Restaurant cars were included in the train in both directions, but as with the London trains they did not operate west of Plymouth, and at the northern end of the journey they did not work beyond Sheffield.

The Devonian

Strictly speaking, for more than half of each year " Devonian ", when first introduced, was rather a misnomer for the train to which it was attached as a title. For the express proper ran over L.M.S.R. metals between Bradford and Bristol, and did not actually touch Devonshire. A set of three coaches, however, was handed over to the Great Western Railway at Temple Meads station, Bristol, and run through by that company to Torquay and Paignton, and it was this through coach working that gave the necessary " Devonian " flavour to the service.

Nationalisation, however, brought about a considerable change, for as we have seen already the whole of the former Midland main line from Blackwell, 12 miles south of Birmingham New Street and at the top of the celebrated Lickey incline, came under the control of the Western Region—that is, more than half the distance covered by the " Devonian ". Also at the northern end of the route, from Chesterfield onwards, the Eastern and not the London Midland Region was the controlling authority.

The trains on which the through Bradford–Paignton coaches worked were of long standing, and had seen little change up to the time when the title " Devonian " was conferred in 1927. After that they participated in the general Midland Division accelerations of 1937, and became very fast over the Birmingham–Bristol section.

The southbound " Devonian " was due to leave Bradford at 10.25 a.m., to reverse in Leeds City station and leave at 10.52 a.m. on a 50-minute run to Sheffield. After 5 minutes there, the express made a non-stop run to Derby in 52 minutes. Here the train dropped a through coach from Bradford to Bournemouth and acquired a Newcastle–Bristol coach which had come south on the 10.20

The modern "Cornishman"—Class 47 No. 1952 heads away from Dawlish with the up train in June 1971. *Photo by P. D. Hawkins*

431
6023

25

a.m. from York. For the 41.3 miles from Derby to Birmingham the allowance was 47 minutes, and a wait of 6 minutes was enjoined at the great Midland city.

Within the compass of 53 minutes allowed from Birmingham to Cheltenham, 45.5 miles, the " Devonian " had to climb to Barnt Green and make a service stop at Blackwell before descending the Lickey incline, after which it travelled at over a mile a minute all the way to Cheltenham. The stops here and at the closely adjacent town of Gloucester, with the short run between, took up

◁ The pre-war " Devonian ", formed of L.M.S. stock, near Brent Knoll, with 4-6-0 No. 6023 *King Edward II* in charge.
Photo by W. Vaughan-Jenkins

▽ " Castle " class 4-6-0 No. 5055 *Earl of Eldon* pulls out of Newton Abbot with the up " Devonian " in September 1959: although by now formed mostly of B.R. standard stock, the formation still includes an L.M.S. 12-wheeled restaurant-kitchen car (sixth vehicle).
Photo by D. S. Fish

16 minutes, and the concluding run on L.M.S.R. metals was over the 37 miles from Gloucester to Bristol in 44 minutes. For cross-country running of this description over a hard road, with numerous stops, the time of 4 hours 40 minutes for the 206 miles from Leeds to Bristol was an excellent one; it was the best of the day. The through Paignton coaches waited at Temple Meads from 3.32 to 3.50 p.m., and then left on a Great Western express of no special distinction, making numerous intermediate stops and reaching Torquay at 6.44 and Paignton at 6.51 p.m. The entire journey of 323 miles from Bradford to Paignton thus took 8 hours 26 minutes, but the G.W.R. section lowered the average speed considerably.

Northbound, the through coaches of the " Devonian " left Paignton at 9.15 and Torquay at 9.22 a.m. for a similarly leisurely run to Bristol, reached at 12.13 p.m. From here the " Devonian ", with its restaurant cars, was timed to start at 12.35 p.m. First came a 43-minute run to Gloucester, beginning with the tremendous pull up to Fishponds, 2 miles at between 1 in 69 and 1 in 90, so that highspeed travelling was necessary from Yate onwards to maintain this timing over a 37-mile run. After Cheltenham, too, this train was one of those booked to cover the 31.1 miles from Cheltenham to Bromsgrove in 31 minutes, start-to-stop, before attaching the " banker " required for assistance up the Lickey incline. Yet the 45.5 miles from Cheltenham to Birmingham were run in 54 minutes.

The rest of the journey needs little description. There was an additional stop at Burton-on-Trent, and leaving Birmingham New Street at 2.37 p.m. the " Devonian " was in Derby at 3.25 p.m., Sheffield at 4.25 p.m., Leeds at 5.24 p.m. and Bradford at 5.54 p.m., 8 hours, 39 minutes after leaving Paignton. Between Leeds and Bristol the engines used were almost invariably of the " Jubilee " 3-cylinder 4-6-0 type, though a Class 5 4-6-0 might appear at times and would prove an adequate substitute. From May to September inclusive the entire train, including L.M.S.R. stock and restaurant cars, ran through between Bradford and Kingswear. On Saturdays it divided into several parts. The through service came to an end on the outbreak of war in 1939, but was restored in October, 1946, with a time of $8\frac{3}{4}$ hours

from Bradford to Torquay and 8 hours 57 minutes back.

After that a considerable deterioration set in. In 1947 the overall time increased to 9 hours 48 minutes from Bradford to Kingswear and 9 hours 57 minutes in the reverse direction, while during the winter the train operated to and from Bristol only and was nameless. In the succeeding years it was subject to numerous changes. As with the " Cornishman " one of the last of these, in May 1967, was the transfer of the northern starting-point from Forster Square to the Exchange station at Bradford, and, after reversal in Leeds City, a change of course from the Normanton to the Wakefield route (with a stop at Wakefield Westgate), and thence by the Moorthorpe spur to the Swinton & Knottingley line, rejoining the former Midland main line at Swinton. By now the express had been considerably accelerated, particularly between Birmingham and Bristol, with the time over this 88.9 miles cut finally to 93 minutes southbound and 92 minutes northbound. With diesel power, almost exclusively Class 45 and 46 diesel electrics, of 2,500 h.p., the Lickey incline no longer presents any problems, and with realignment of the track through Bromsgrove it was now possible to pass that station at full speed and to take a run at the bank, which has helped the acceleration.

The final improvement, taking effect from May, 1973, moved the " Devonian ", like the " Cornishman ", to the Oakenshaw spur after Wakefield on to the former Midland main line, so that it proceeded through Cudworth to Swinton instead of via Moorthorpe. Departure from Leeds was now at 10.40 a.m., and Sheffield at 11.40 a.m.; Derby was the only stop between there and Birmingham, from which departure in the even-interval sequence was at 1.15 p.m., Bristol being reached at 2.48 p.m. The Western Region was still in no great hurry over the remainder of the journey, as the " Devonian " had to call at Weston-super-Mare, Taunton, Exeter, Dawlish, Teignmouth and Newton Abbot before ending its journey at Torquay at 5.13 p.m.

The 1971 " Devonian " at Newton Abbot: Class 45 diesel No. 66 leaves on the last leg of the journey to Paignton.

Photo by J. H. Cooper-Smith

and Paignton at 5.20 p.m. As compared with steam days, in 1939, the Leeds–Paignton time was reduced from 7 hours 59 minutes to 6 hours 40 minutes.

The northbound train was expedited similarly. Away from Paignton at 10.50 a.m. and Torquay at 10.56 a.m. the " Devonian ", with the same stops as southbound except Weston-super-Mare, was into Bristol by 1.03 p.m. Then, restarting at 1.13 p.m., there followed a fast 92-minute non-stop run to Birmingham; from there as before the stops were at Derby, Sheffield and Wakefield, and the arrival in Leeds City was at 5.16 p.m., in 6 hours 26 minutes overall.

The Flying Dutchman

No doubt there are many who have wondered how one of the best-known expresses in the earlier years of the Great Western Railway came to acquire the title of " Flying Dutchman ". For the reason we probably have to go back to the seventeenth century, when the famous Dutch admiral Tromp achieved such resounding victories at sea that he is reputed to have fastened a broom to the main-

mast of his flagship to signify his ability to " sweep the seas ". With little doubt Tromp was the inspiration of the third opera composed by Wagner, which the latter called *Der Fliegende Holänder*; this became so widely renowned, that the name " Flying Dutchman " was bestowed on a racehorse which in 1849 won both the Derby and the St. Leger.

In the previous year the morning express from Paddington to the west had been speeded up to cover the 53.1 miles from London to Didcot in 55 minutes, at a world record start-to-stop speed of 57.9 m.p.h. It is even claimed that on May 11, 1848, the locomotive *Great Britain* made the run in 47½ minutes, but there is no validating evidence. Anyway, there is no question that in the late 1840s the " Flying Dutchman " was the fastest train in the country, and so it is not surprising that, anticipating by many years what was to be the practice of the L.N.E.R. in naming express engines after racehorses, the name " Flying Dutchman " was fastened on to the 9.50 a.m. from Paddington.

Actually this express began to run in 1845. Leaving Paddington at 9.30 a.m. and calling at Didcot, Swindon and Bath, it took 3 hours to Bristol; here the Bristol & Exeter Railway took over, and with one intermediate stop, at Taunton, brought passengers into Exeter by 2.30 p.m., in 5 hours from London. The corresponding up service left Exeter at 11.45 a.m. and Bristol at 1.40 p.m., reaching Paddington at 4.45 p.m. The first runs were in March, 1845; two months later the time in each direction had been cut to 4½ hours, at which level it remained for several years. It was in 1848 that the starting time in the down direction was altered to 9.50 a.m., introducing the 55-minute run to Didcot, and despite the 10-minute halt at Swindon for refreshments that Bristol was reached in 2½ hours from Paddington, making this by an easy margin the fastest train in the world at that time. In 1849 a stop was introduced at Chippenham, adding 5 minutes to the down journey, but in the up direction this was balanced by cutting the Didcot–Paddington time from 65 to 60 minutes. By now the up " Flying Dutchman " was leaving Exeter at 12.30 p.m. and reaching London at 5 p.m.

From 1852 onwards Great Western speed was in the doldrums, but in 1862, under the spur of competition from the London & South Western Railway, which had begun a service from Waterloo to Exeter in 4¾ hours, the down " Flying Dutchman " was altered to leave Paddington at 11.45 a.m., to run to Didcot in 57 minutes, and reach Bristol and Exeter in 2 hours 40 minutes and 4½ hours from London respectively. In the up direction

◁ The down " Flying Dutchman " passes Acton at the turn of the century, headed by Dean Class 3031 4-4-2 No. 3050 *Royal Sovereign.*

◁ A Paddington-Bristol-Plymouth express passing Uphill Junction, convergence with the Weston-super-Mare line, early in this century headed by another Dean Class 3031 4-4-2, No. 3037 *Corsair.*

departure from Exeter was now at 10.30 a.m., and despite an additional stop, at Chippenham, the 4½-hour timing up from Exeter was maintained. Then in 1864 the Didcot stop in the down direction was cut out, and the 77.3 miles from Paddington to Swindon were booked to be covered in 90 minutes start to stop. In the same year an innovation in the up direction, also non-stop from Swindon in 90 minutes, was the slipping of a coach at Reading.

But once again, after this fast interlude, speed was allowed to deteriorate, until once again Bristol was 3 hours distant from Paddington, and Exeter 5 hours 5 minutes away. There was some tacit agreement with the London & South Western Railway as to avoiding unnecessary competition, for the latter also had decelerated its trains and was allowing the Great Western to keep just ahead in the matter of time. The " Flying Dutchman " was, or course, running on the 7-ft. broad gauge, and was a light train; its normal formation was seven six-wheel coaches between Paddington and Swindon, where two were detached, one for Weymouth and the other for Cheltenham; five only continued to Newton Abbot, where there was a second division, two coaches running to Torquay and the remaining three to Plymouth.

In 1867 the Great Western Railway was in very low water financially, and expenditure had to be cut in all directions. One casualty was the "Flying Dutchman ", which was cancelled in October of that year and not reinstated until 18 months later, though still on the poor timing of 3 hours to Bristol and 4¾ hours to Exeter. It continued to leave Paddington at 11.45 a.m., and on its down journey also had now acquired slip coaches, like the up train, the latter at Reading and the former at Chippenham and Bridgwater. Then in 1871 a speed-up took place, and once again it was the London & South Western Railway that provided the spur, by a new time of 4½ hours over their 171.8 miles from Waterloo to Exeter. So the " Flying Dutchman " was accelerated to run the 77.3 miles to Swindon in 87 minutes; with the usual 10-minute refreshment stop there and 3 minutes at Bath, Bristol was reached in 2 hours 36 minutes; then followed a fast run over the 44.8 miles from Bristol to Taunton in 51 minutes; and Exeter was brought within 4¼ hours of London, the fastest time yet. The down " Flying Dutchman " continued to Plymouth, reaching there at 6 p.m. after calling at Dawlish, Teignmouth and Newton Abbot, and in summer it ran through to Penzance, though a wearisome 3 hours was needed through Cornwall to reach this far western terminal.

Until now, all trains for the west other than the " Flying Dutchman " had been painfully slow, but in 1876, the year that the Great Western Railway absorbed the Bristol & Exeter, the opening by the London & South Western Railway of the continuation of its main line from Exeter to Plymouth jolted the bigger company. A new 2.30 p.m. express from Waterloo was put on to reach Plymouth in 6 hours 55 minutes, and by 1882 had been accelerated to a 4-hour timing to Exeter—15 minutes faster than the " Flying Dutchman " and 6 hours 38 minutes to Plymouth North Road. Moreover, the new L.S.W.R. express carried third-class passengers, whereas the " Flying Dutchman ", like all the faster G.W.R. trains, was designed to convey first-and second, class passengers only. To compete with this rival the Great Western in 1879 put on a new 3 p.m. from Paddington, reaching Exeter at 7.14 p.m. and Plymouth at 8.55 p.m., with a complementary up working at 2.8 p.m. from Plymouth and 3.55 p.m. from Exeter, which was into Paddington by 8.10 p.m. So the " Flying Dutchman " now had an equal in time, and which moreover opened its doors to the humble third-class passenger. The " Dutchman " was still operating on the 7 ft. broad gauge, but the new train ran on the 4 ft. 8½ in. standard gauge.

Not until 1890 did the " Flying Dutchman " at last carry passengers of all three classes, and in that year it was eclipsed by the inauguration of a new West of England express at 10.15 a.m. from Paddington; this was the " Cornishman " forerunner of the " Cornish Riveria Limited ". Under the agreement with the Swindon Refreshment Rooms Company, which the Great Western Railway was compelled to observe until it obtained its freedom at considerable expense in 1895, the new train had to spend the customary 10 minutes at Swindon, which was reached from Paddington in the old time of 87 minutes. The next stop was Bristol, at 12.45 p.m., in 2½ hours from London; then followed a non-stop run to Exeter, reached in 4 hours 5 minutes from Paddington, while the time to Plymouth was 5 hours 35 minutes, and to Penzance, still with desperately slow running through Cornwall, in 8 hours 42 minutes. The new up train left Penzance at 11.15 a.m., Plymouth at 2.10 p.m., Exeter at 3.45 p.m. and Bristol at 5.18 p.m., with a Paddington arrival at 7.50 p.m.

The final broad gauge run of the " Flying Dutchman " was made on May 29th, 1892, and on the following day it left Paddington at 11.45 a.m. as usual, but on the standard 4 ft. 8½ in. gauge. From now on the former " Flying Dutchman " was an express of no great distinction. It continued to start at 11.45 a.m. until July, 1904, when the starting time was altered to 12.25 p.m., but by acceleration the Plymouth arrival remained unchanged and Penzance was reached at 8.30 p.m.; by 1906 the start had become 1 p.m. and Bristol was being reached non-stop in 2 hours. But in 1911 the " Flying Dutchman " was cut short at Bristol, and sank into oblivion.

The Golden Hind

Erosion of gilt-edged business traffic by internal air services and spreading motorways forced BR in the early 1960s to schedule new and fast early morning trains from provincial cities to London, and fast return workings in the evening, so as to give executives ample time to attend to their affairs in the capital without the necessity to stay away overnight. So it was that the summer of 1964 saw the introduction by the Western Region of a new express from Plymouth to Paddington and back—the " Golden Hind ". The name, like that of the " Mayflower ", which ran for a time in the post-war years, was derived from Plymouth's maritime history. But whereas the " Mayflower " was an existing train of no great distinction, as described later, the " Golden Hind " was an entirely new service, and, moreover, in a faster time than any previously scheduled between Paddington and Plymouth. This was 3 hours 50 minutes up and 3 hours 55 minutes down; the latter was 5 minutes longer owing to the difficulty in finding a suitable high-speed path out of Paddington in the early evening.

It was decided to start the morning " Golden Hind" from Plymouth at 7.5 a.m., to call at Newton Abbot for the benefit of passengers from the Torbay branch (with a record 3 hours 20 minutes time from Torquay to London), and after that at Exeter and Taunton; the final timing was 127 minutes for the 142.7 miles from Taunton to the Paddington arrival at 10.55 a.m. Going down, the start was fixed at 5.20 p.m., and with 131 minutes to Taunton and 2 hours 42 minutes to Exeter and the Newton Abbot stop, Plymouth passengers were back in their home town by 9.15 p.m. Little effort was spared to give the train a memorable launch: the limited seven-coach load was of specially prepared stock, the restaurant car crew was hand-picked, and a so-called " Golden Stud " of six " Western " class 2,700 h.p. diesels was kept in special nick for the job. All seats were reserved. Within three months the train had built up a load factor of 70 per cent-plus.

Eventually, to align the " Hind " with an even-interval, 30 minutes past the hour framework of West of England departures from Paddington, its London start was moved on to 5.30 p.m. Overall time to Plymouth was first pared to 3 hours 50 minutes and then, in the major reorganisation of the 1968 summer, to 3 hours 45 minutes along with the " Riviera "—but with a Newton Abbot stop in addition to the " Riviera's " calls at Taunton and Exeter.

In 1972, the " Golden Hind " was not merely accelerated to reach Plymouth in 3 hours 37 minutes from Paddington, but also extended to Penzance, offering a two hours later departure than ever before from London to principal stations in Cornwall, Penzance included. Taunton was now reached in 119 minutes (71.9 m.p.h.), Torquay (by connection at Newton Abbot) in 3 hours 10 minutes, and Penzance in 5 hours 28 minutes. In the morning, passengers from Penzance for the " Golden Hind " had to start bright and early at 5.10 a.m., and with no chance of breakfast or light refreshments until they joined the main train on its 7.0 a.m. departure from Plymouth; by 10.38 a.m. the express was at rest in Paddington. From May, 1973, the " Golden Hind " has had to share in the slight general deceleration due to the engineering work previously referred to; the down " Golden Hind " now needed 122 minutes to reach Taunton, 3 hours 44 minutes to Plymouth and 5 hours 40 minutes; coming up the Penzance start was made even earlier at 5.5 a.m., while with the Plymouth start unchanged at 7.0 a.m. Paddington was not reached until 10.41 a.m.

At the start a maximum formation of seven coaches, including restaurant cars, was laid down for the " Golden Hind ", but latterly the working timetable has permitted a 2,700 h.p. " Western " or a 2,750 h.p. Brush diesel to take 300 tare tons, or up to 8 coaches of the latest stock, on this timing. As previously described, the " Golden Hind " and " Cornish Riviera Limited " were sharing train-sets in 1973.

Class 52 diesel-hydraulic No. 1064 *Western Regent* heads the " Golden Hind " out of London past Acton in April 1969.
Photo by J. H. Cooper-Smith

In the 125 m.p.h. HST diesel train era to come—on the West of England line in 1977/8—the "Golden Hind" timetable path will accommodate the route's crack train. The 5.30 p.m. from Paddington will run non-stop to Plymouth in 2 hours 50 minutes; the 7.45 a.m. up from Plymouth (6.30 a.m. from Penzance, giving Cornish folk well over an hour longer in bed than today), will be similarly non-stop to London in 2 hours 50 minutes.

The Inter-City

In October, 1950, a second " titled train " made its appearance on the Paddington–Birmingham main line, running daily. Since the 1939–1945 war the 9.10 a.m. down Birkenhead express had become so popular that a regular relief train was run from Paddington at 9 a.m., except on Saturdays, for Birmingham and Wolverhampton. This express, titled the " Inter-city ", could afford to miss Leamington, as the 9.10 a.m. down carried the Leamington traffic; though like the 9.10 a.m., the 9 a.m. halted at High Wycombe to pick up passengers. It was due in Snow Hill, Birmingham, at 11.10 a.m.—this 130 minutes was the nearest to the pre-war two hours reached up till then—and in Wolverhampton at 11.35 a.m. The stock, title included, returned from Wolverhampton at 4.25 p.m. and Birmingham at 4.50 p.m.; in this direction stops were made at both Leamington and High Wycombe, and the " Inter-City " was back in Paddington at 7.5 p.m.

By 1954 the down " Inter-City " had become a two-hour train to Birmingham. Some of the most brilliant locomotive work on the entire Great Western system was done on these services, the " Inter-City " included. When it began in 1910 the most powerful locomotives available were 2-cylinder " Saint " and 4-cylinder " Star " class 4–6–0s; from 1923 onwards the " Castles " began to give much-needed relief, and it was not long after the introduction in 1927 of the " Kings " that these, the most powerful express passenger class on the G.W.R., were drafted to the Birmingham route. From then on a number of these engines were stationed at Stafford Road shed, Wolverhampton, for this purpose, and shared the trains with " Kings " stationed at Old Oak Common, and with occasional " Castles ".

As compared with the L.M.S.R., which had little or no difficulty other than the start out of Euston, G.W.R. drivers *en route* to Birmingham had to reduce speed at Old Oak Common West Junction, High Wycombe and Leamington, and less severely at Ashendon and Aynho Junctions, and to master some long climbs, such as 7 miles at 1 in 175 to 1 in 264 from Denham almost to Beaconsfield; 5 miles at 1 in 179 to 1 in 164 past West Wycombe and Saunderton, and, worst of all, a bank which includes 3½ miles averaging 1 in 110 past Warwick up to Hatton. There were correspondingly arduous grades on the up journey, all of which had to be covered at the high average speeds required by the two-hour schedules. Except for Hatton bank, most of the long inclines were surmounted regularly by the two-hour trains at speeds of over 50 m.p.h., even with loads up to 400 tons; and maximum speeds of 80 to 90 m.p.h. were common north of Princes Risborough on the down journey, and past Bicester and Denham coming up.

In the year 1963 the Paddington–Birmingham–Wolverhampton service underwent a complete revolution. This was due to the diversion of practically the whole of the London Midland Region Birmingham service to the Western Region, in order to relieve the former's main line to the utmost degree possible during the work of electrification. From that date, therefore, the W.R. for four years was to operate an hourly service of express trains throughout the day, loading in many cases up to 12, 13 and even 14 vehicles—a haulage proposition that this route had never had to face previously. At first the trains were still entrusted to " Kings ", and with intermediate stops two-hour schedules between Paddington and Birmingham were very difficult to arrange; not until the advent of the 2,700 h.p. " Western " diesel-hydraulic locomotives and the 2,750 h.p. Brush-Sulzer diesel-electric units did two-hour bookings reappear on an extensive scale, and some even in under two hours. The 2.10 p.m. from Paddington, indeed, for a short period was booked non-stop over the 110.6 miles to Snow Hill in 110 minutes—the shortest time between London and Birmingham tabled by either route up until then. By this time, however, the " Inter-City " had lost its name.

But the 1963 revolution was overthrown with inauguration of the London Midland electric service between Euston, Birmingham and Wolverhampton in the spring of 1967. From now on there was no more purpose in the Western Region competing for the through traffic, though intermediate towns, such as High Wycombe, Banbury and Leamington, still needed service, and residents on the south side of Birmingham could still make faster journeys to and from London if the remaining Western Region expresses were to call at Solihull. So a service of only seven trains in each direction survived, all calling at High Wycombe, Bicester, Banbury, Leamington and Solihull, and some in addition at Princes Risborough. Work soon begun on reduction to single track of the line between Princes Risborough and Aynho Junction, and the only assistance to fast running was a realignment to do away with the speed restriction over Ashendon Junction.

Since then there have been even more revolutionary changes. Snow Hill station in Birmingham of the former Great Western Railway has been closed, and the trains from Paddington diverted over a sinuous stretch of line, demanding severely reduced speed, into the rival New Street station of the former London Midland & Scottish Railway. In the 1972 timetable four of the seven workings in each direction were switched to the original main line via Oxford; the 1973 timetable went even further and left only one morning Paddington–Birmingham train in each direction via Bicester. To compensate intermediate stations for these withdrawals, an hourly diesel multiple-unit service was put on between Marylebone and Banbury, calling at Gerrards Cross, Beaconsfield, High Wycombe, Princes Risborough and Banbury, and connecting there with the expresses via Oxford. The principal loser by these arrangements was Leamington, whose connections with London became considerably inferior to those of Great Western days.

While the Bicester route was still used by the Paddington–Birmingham expresses the point-to-point times were extremely tight, and maximum speeds up to 90 m.p.h. between stops were common, even over the single line; indeed, the 4.40 p.m. from New Street contrived to complete the journey to Paddington in no more than 2 hours 10 minutes with five intermediate stops. But this is all now in the past. The new main line which was opened with such a flourish of trumpets in 1910 has come to a humdrum end.

A September 1954 shot of the up " Inter-City " near Leamington Spa, headed by 4-6-0 No. 5031 *Totnes Castle*.

Photo by T. E. Williams

The Irish Mail via Fishguard

It was in 1906, after immense expenditure in blasting away a rocky hillside to make the necessary shelf on which to lay out the station, as well as a long breakwater extending well out into the bay to form an ocean quay, that the Great Western Railway brought into use their new port of Fishguard, in West Wales. The aim was to operate direct services between England and Southern Ireland, and from 1906 G.W.R. steamers began to run by both day and night between Fishguard and another new port which had been created at Rosslare, just across the St. George's Channel. Connecting restaurant car trains were put on between Rosslare, Waterford and Cork, and another connecting service was introduced between Rosslare and Wexford. Direct steamers ran also between Fishguard and both Waterford and Cork, largely in the interests of cattle shipments.

The prospects of Fishguard grew still brighter when the Cunard Steamship Company decided to make this a port of call for their steamers coming across the Atlantic from New York to Liverpool. Disembarkation at Fishguard, with fast travel over the G.W.R. from there to Paddington, made possible a far earlier arrival in London than was possible after the normal steaming up the Irish Sea into the Mersey. The possibilities of this traffic were so great that G.W.R. bestirred itself into making a costly new line to avoid the traffic handicaps in the vicinity of Swansea; the " Swansea District Lines ", as they are called, leave the South Wales main line at Court Sart, east of Neath, cross the Neath River south of that place, then tunnel under the main line and strike due west through Felin Fran to Morlais East Junction, where a turn is made due south to rejoin the main line near Llanelli. Actually this line saved only ½-mile, but it avoided some severe gradients and congestion on the old main line.

Originally, the plan was to continue westwards from Morlais to Pembrey, on the main line beyond Llanelli, which would have made a wonderfully direct route to Fishguard. But meantime the claims of the great port of Southampton on all the leading Transatlantic services had become so strong—partly because the use of Southampton made possible also a call at Cherbourg, across the English Channel, for the traffic to and from the mainland of Europe—that Cunard decided to transfer its liners from Liverpool to Southampton. This transfer put Fishguard completely out of the picture, and as a result the remainder of the Swansea District Lines scheme was never completed. So Fishguard was left with its Irish services; these never grew beyond relatively moderate passenger dimensions, though freight traffic, chiefly agricultural, was on a large scale.

At first the boat trains left Paddington at 8.45 both morning and evening, and each was allowed 5½ hours to make the journey of 261.4 miles from Paddington to Fishguard Harbour. With various special trains, at different times, the G.W.R. has run the entire distance non-stop, but in ordinary daily working the largest intermediate towns were of too great importance to be missed out in this way. So both trains called at Newport and Cardiff; in order to obtain a direct run past Swansea without reversal, the stop here was made at Landore, 1¼ miles away. In addition, the morning boat train called at Reading and the evening one at Swindon. Engines were changed once only, at Cardiff. Restaurant cars were run on both services, and the evening train in addition carried a first-class sleeping car, from the warmth and comfort of which its occupants were required to turn out at the uninviting hour of 2.15 a.m., on arrival at Fishguard.

During the 1914–1918 war the night boat service between Fishguard and Rosslare survived, but not the day service, and the latter was not reinstated until 1965, so that the morning express from Paddington became a train to Pembroke Dock and

△ The " Irish Mail via Fishguard " in the early 1920s, passing Acton behind 4-6-0 No. 2917 *Saint Bernard;* the last coach is a slip for Bristol, detached at Stoke Gifford.

▽ The day mail train from Fishguard to London, headed by 4-6-0 No. 7917 *North Aston Hall,* climbs from Neyland to Johnston in July 1963. *Photo by P. J. Esau*

Neyland, and no longer an " Irish Mail *via* Fishguard ". In the recovery period after the 1914–1918 war, the Great Western Railway decided to standardise its main line departures out of Paddington, and as the South Wales starting times were fixed at 5 minutes to the hour, the exit of the evening boat train was advanced to 7.55 p.m. The original stop at Swindon was exchanged for one at Didcot, and eventually the latter gave place to a stop at Reading. By now Swansea had become too important to bypass, and the train was running into Swansea and out again, instead of taking the direct spur from Landore; a further nightly stop had been added at Llanelli, and the train was prepared also to stop at both Severn Tunnel Junction and Neath if passengers wished to alight.

Up to 1939, therefore, the " Irish Mail *via* Fishguard ", leaving Paddington at 7.55 p.m., ran the 36 miles to Reading in the then standard allowance of 40 minutes, and was booked to stand there 6 minutes, dealing with a considerable volume of luggage, parcels and mails. Away again at 8.41 p.m., it continued through Didcot and Swindon to Wootton Bassett, where the finely engineered junction made it possible to take the diverging line to Badminton at a speed of 50 m.p.h. For most of the distance between here and the summit at Badminton the line rises at 1 in 300, and it then passes through the $2\frac{1}{2}$ miles of Sodbury Tunnel before descending at the same inclination to the junction with the Bristol–South Wales main line at Patchway.

At Stoke Gifford East Box, just before Patchway, two slip coaches were detached, to be worked by a waiting tank engine into Bristol, thus providing a late evening service from London to that city. From Patchway the descent steepens to 1 in 68, and then, after a level strip, to the 3 miles at 1 in 100 which lead to the middle of the Severn Tunnel. In the opposite direction this is the worst bank on the route, for although the 1 in 68 is flattened on the up line to 1 in 100, up trains are faced with 6 miles at 1 in 100 between the middle of the tunnel and Pilning, and with a further 12 miles at 1 in 300 before the summit is breasted at Badminton—an arduous task.

Including the conditional stop at Severn Tunnel Junction, the down " Irish Mail *via* Fishguard " was allowed 106 minutes to run the 97.4 miles from Reading to Newport. Here a stop of 4 minutes was scheduled, and a short run of 16 minutes brought the train into Cardiff at 10.47 p.m., for a wait of 8 minutes and a change of engine. There are awkward grades between Cardiff and Swansea, and these 45.8 miles were allowed exactly one hour, bringing the train into Swansea at 11.55 p.m. Here reversal took place, and on the stroke of midnight the train, after a second change of engine, was due out westwards. From Swansea for $1\frac{3}{4}$ miles the line climbs at 1 in 60 and 1 in 52 to Cockett tunnel, so that an assistant engine was provided either to the summit or to Llanelli, where a stop of one minute was made from 12.22 to 12.23 a.m. Then came a schedule of 77 minutes over the remaining 60.3 miles, including some heavy grades, to Fishguard Harbour, reached at 1.40 a.m.

In the reverse direction the start on the up journey of the " Irish Mail *via* Fishguard " was made $2\frac{1}{4}$ hours later, at 3.55 a.m. Banking assistance was needed from the start, for the single-track line out of Fishguard climbs at 1 in 50 for $1\frac{3}{4}$ miles past Manorowen halt. The first scheduled stop was at Gowerton, 67 miles from Fishguard, at 5.18 a.m., to take on another assisting engine for the $2\frac{1}{4}$ mile-climb at 1 in 50 to Cockett. Fifteen minutes later the train was in Swansea. Departure from Swansea was at 5.37 a.m., and as in the reverse direction there was an allowance of exactly an hour to Cardiff; the start from there was at 6.45 a.m., and from Newport at 7.5 a.m. An easy allowance followed of 113 minutes to a 5-minute stop at Reading and after that the schedule was as long as 44 minutes to Paddington, for the boat train had to be fitted in between other morning arrivals. Into London at 9.47 a.m., the up " Irish Mail " had thus taken 5 hours 52 minutes for the 263.6 miles from Fishguard *via* Swansea, as compared with $5\frac{3}{4}$ hours in the opposite direction.

The make-up of the train included composite sleeping car, composite restaurant car, corridor first, about three corridor thirds and a third brake, two or three long brake-vans, and the Bristol slip coaches in the down direction, eleven or twelve bogies in all out of Paddington, and two less in the reverse direction. Between London and Cardiff a " Castle " 4–6–0 was the invariable rule; west of Cardiff either 4-cylinder or 2-cylinder 4–6–0s might be used. The Fishguard–

Rosslare service did not long survive the outbreak of the 1939–1945 war, and with its withdrawal the boat trains in each direction were cancelled also, though the 8.55 a.m. from Paddington continued to run to Pembroke Dock.

From October 1st, 1945, however, the 7.55 p.m. down was restored as far as Swansea, and the 8.55 a.m. down had a through portion for Fishguard reinstated on Tuesdays, Thursdays and Saturdays. For a time the latter was relieved as far as Swansea by an 8.50 a.m. breakfast car train, which called only at Newport and Cardiff, and reached Swansea at 1 p.m., but this was withdrawn in the coal crisis, and after its reinstatement ran only on Saturdays and during the summer season. Irish boat passengers *via* Fishguard from then on left Paddington on the 6.55 p.m. express, but the boat portion was provided on Mondays, Wednesdays, and Fridays only; on other days the express terminated its journey at Swansea at 11.25 p.m., after having called at Reading, Newport and Cardiff. The time to Swansea thus exceeded that of pre-war days by 30 minutes.

When the boat portion was run, it left Swansea at 11.30 p.m., and with one intermediate halt, at Llanelli, made its way into Fishguard Harbour at 1.15 a.m., as compared with the pre-war 1.40 a.m. At Fishguard, the train had a turn-around time of $3\frac{3}{4}$ hours, and then was away on Tuesdays, Thursdays and Saturdays, back to Paddington at 4.55 a.m. In this direction, after leaving Llanelli, the train avoided Swansea altogether by taking the direct line through Morlais and Felin Fran, already mentioned. Cardiff was reached at 8.7 a.m. in time for attachment to the daily 8.15 a.m. for Paddington, but this made so many stops that the boat passengers were not into London until 11.40 a.m.—a run slower by 53 minutes than in pre-war days.

In 1964 the day service between Fishguard and Rosslare was reinstated during the summer months, and in subsequent years diesel traction accelerated certain of the connecting trains. But such has been the effect of air competition, and later still the troubles in Ireland, that during the winter months the sailings between Fishguard and Rosslare have been completely suspended. Until this suspension took place, night sailings were three times a week only; passengers from London travelled in through coaches on the 8.0 p.m., from Paddington, which after a halt of 15 minutes in Swansea proceeded at 11.55 p.m., and stopping only at Llanelli reached Fishguard Harbour at 1.35 a.m. The crossing to Rosslare, starting at 2.0 a.m., took $3\frac{1}{4}$ hours. In the opposite direction the service was similar; the ship left Rosslare Harbour at 11.30 p.m. and anchored at Fishguard at 2.45 a.m.; the connecting train was away at 4.45 a.m., but the through coaches were not due in Paddington until 10.32 a.m. Even in favourable conditions, the change from train to ship and vice versa in the very small hours must have been daunting.

It was a different matter, however, with the day service, which continued operation daily between May and October. During the height of the season a special boat express has latterly left Paddington at 8.26 a.m., calling only at Cardiff (the only down train of the day to miss Newport), Landore, Llanelli and Whitland, and reaching Fishguard by 1.32 p.m., in no more than 5 hours 6 minutes from London. In the weeks immediately preceding and following this special working, passengers from London travelled by the 8.0 a.m. from Paddington to Swansea, and thence by a special connection due in Fishguard at 1.18 p.m. At 2.0 p.m. the Rosslare ship was away on its $3\frac{1}{4}$-hour crossing, and despite waits at Rosslare Harbour of 45 and 60 minutes respectively, through passengers could be in Dublin Pearse by 9.25 p.m. and Cork by 9.35 p.m.

The return journey has become even faster. A start from Cork at 7.0 a.m. and from Dublin at 8.25 a.m. catches the 11.45 a.m. steamer from Rosslare Harbour; after a Fishguard arrival at 3.0 p.m., 45 minutes are needed for customs and other formalities, and the 3.45 p.m. boat train, with Clarbeston Road, Llanelli and Cardiff stops only, has been making the fine time of 4 hours 45 minutes to Paddington, at an average of all but 60 m.p.h., and the fastest ever tabled. The explanation of the quicker journey than that in the down direction is that the up express bypasses Swansea by the Felin Fran line; from Cardiff to Paddington the 145.3 miles are allowed 140 minutes only.

Unusual titled train power—2-8-0 No. 4706 passes Enborne Junction, near Newbury, with the down " Royal Duchy " in August 1958.
Photo by P. S. Desbrow

THE ROYAL DUCHY
4706

The Mayflower and the Royal Duchy

In the spate of train naming by the Western Region during the years 1955 to 1957, partly as an excuse by that Region for painting set trains in the former Great Western Railway chocolate-and cream colours (instead of the then standard maroon red), two expresses over the West of England main line received titles, though neither of them was a train of great distinction. One was the 8.30 a.m. from Plymouth to Paddington, with the return service at 5.30 p.m., which because of the association of Plymouth with the Pilgrim Fathers was given the name of " Mayflower ". The other was the 1.30 p.m. from Paddington to Penzance, which in January, 1955, became the " Royal Duchy "—a title which, incidentally, required the consent of Her Majesty the Queen. The headboards carried by the engines of the latter express displayed the arms of the Duchy of Cornwall. These names survived for about ten years, but in 1965 there came a complete reorganisation of the W.R. services to and from the West of England. Because of the more intensive use of main-line rolling stock, including shorter terminal turnrounds, retention of names would have involved a good deal of trouble with carriage headboards. In 1965, therefore, these attractive titles disappeared.

▽ The down " Royal Duchy " leaves Exeter St. Davids with 4-6-0 No. 5020 *Trematon Castle* in charge.

▷ The up " Mayflower " approaches Reading behind 4-6-0 No. 6029 *King Edward VIII*, overtaking sister engine No. 6013 *King Henry VIII* on a Bristol line slow.

Photo by C. J. Blay

▷ " Warship " diesel-hydraulic No. D803 *Albion* gives the up " Mayflower " a new look in September 1959, as it passes Dawlish.

Photo by D. Cross

THE MAYFLOWER
038

035

△ The down "Merchant Venturer" near Corsham in May 1951, soon after its inauguration with new crimson-and-cream-liveried B.R. standard stock as a mark of the Festival of Britain; in charge is 4-6-0 No. 7025 *Sudeley Castle.* *Photo by G. J. Jefferson*

◁ Close-up of later W.R. "Merchant Venturer" headboard on 4-6-0 No. 5048 *Earl of Devon* at Paddington in March 1959. *Photo by A. A. Vickers*

▷ Slip coach at the tail of a Bristol-Paddington express leaving Bath in August 1953. *Photo by G. F. Heiron*

▽ Slipping the coach at Reading: note the special double tail-lamp on the last vehicle of the main train. *Photo by R. C. J. Day*

The Merchant Venturer

In 1951 the ranks of titled trains between Paddington and Bristol were augmented, though not by any train of real distinction. This was the 11.15 a.m. out of Paddington, which with the 5.25 p.m. back from Temple Meads became the "Merchant Venturer". From about A.D. 1200 onwards the city of Bristol had become a trading centre of no mean importance, and in 1373 it received a charter, the first of its kind in Great Britain, establishing the city as a self-contained county, and this was followed in 1467 by the founding of the Society of Merchant Venturers to supervise and direct the city's trading activity. So the train title "Merchant Venturer" originated.

In steam days, up to 1939, the 11.15 a.m. from Paddington was a two-hour train to Bristol, with one intermediate stop, at Bath, and an allowance of 102 minutes for the 106.85 miles; it then continued to Weston-super-Mare, arriving at 1.47 p.m. After a turn-around time of nearly three hours, it then left Weston at 4.35 p.m., called at Yatton, had 10 minutes in Temple Meads, and restarted at 5.15 p.m. on a two-hour run to Paddington, slipping coaches en route at both Swindon and Reading. In the restoration period after the 1939–1945 war neither train regained two-hour status between Paddington and Bristol, though the 11.15 a.m. down did just return to mile-a minute running with a time of 106 minutes down to Bath; the up departure from Bristol became 5.25 p.m. and various intermediate stops were introduced. The title "Merchant Venturer" disappeared in the timetable reorganisation of 1965.

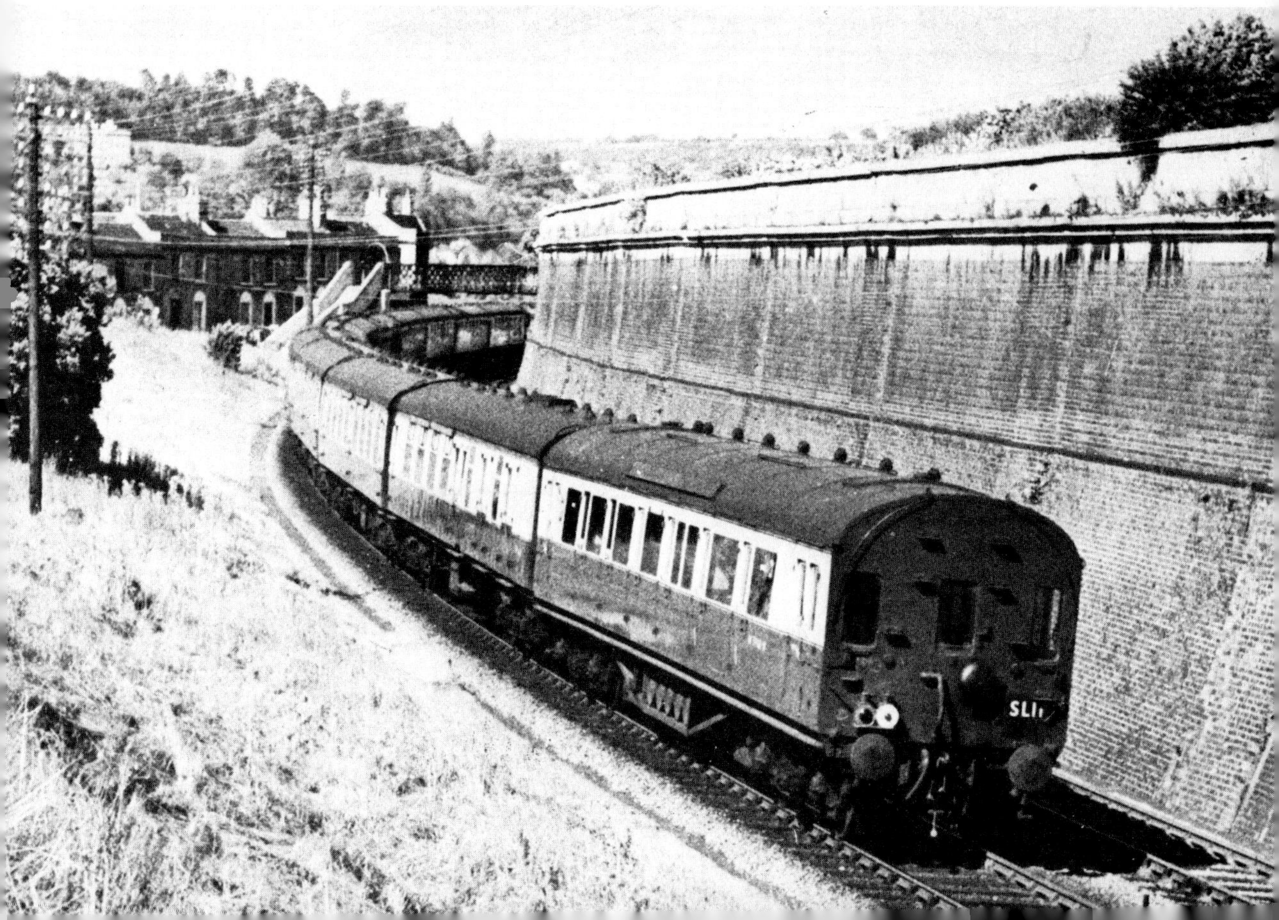

The Pembroke Coast Express and the Red Dragon

For many years, as has been described earlier, the passenger services between Paddington and South Wales had little claim to distinction in the matter of speed. But in 1953 the first sign of change was seen in the inauguration of a new express from London, breaking the gap between the 8.55 and the 11.55 a.m. down by a start at 10.55 a.m. The first stop was Newport, and within a year the new train, christened the " Pembroke Coast Express ", had become the fastest of all South Wales services worked by steam power with its Paddington–Newport timing of 128 minutes only for the 133.4 miles. Calling thereafter at Cardiff and principal stations beyond, the train reached Swansea in $3\frac{3}{4}$ hours from London, and a through portion was worked from there to Pembroke Dock. In the return direction the start at first was from Pembroke Dock at 7.45 a.m., from Swansea at 10.35 a.m. and Cardiff at 11.56 a.m., with a Paddington arrival at 3.10 p.m., a much slower journey than that in the westbound direction, but later the express was moved to the afternoon, and the Swansea–Paddington time was cut to 3 hours 55 minutes.

Another title conferred on a South Wales train was " Red Dragon ", the well-patronised service leaving Paddington at 5.55 p.m. But it was a distinctly lethargic beast, as it was not until ten minutes before midnight that the last of it tail dragged its weary way into Carmarthen. The up journey was rather better, for although the Carmarthen section had to be away by 7.30 a.m., the main train did not leave Swansea until 8.45 a.m., and ran non-stop up from Newport to arrive in Paddington by 1.5 p.m. But what a contrast with 1973 by which year diesel power was hurrying the 8.55 a.m. up from Swansea to London by 12.15 p.m. —an acceleration of exactly one hour, and with the Newport–Paddington non-stop time cut from 165 to 120 minutes! In common with many other Western Region titles, " Red Dragon " vanished in 1965.

△ The Pembroke Dock portion of the "Pembroke Coast Express" is taken over by 4-6-0 No. 7804 *Baydon Manor* from a "Western" diesel after reversal at Carmarthen in August 1963. *Photo by A. A. Vickers*

◁ Following a "Castle" failure, 4-6-0 No. 6847 *Tidmarsh Grange* unusually wears the "Pembroke Coast Express" headboard after working the train from London to Swansea in July 1953. *Photo by J. N. Westwood*

▽ The westbound "Pembroke Coast Express" emerges from Chipping Sodbury tunnel behind 4-6-0 No. 5029 *Nunney Castle* in April 1955. *Photo by G. F. Heiron*

The Pines Express

From 1904 onwards, when the first through coaches were arranged by the London & North Western and London Brighton & South Coast Railways to run between Liverpool, Manchester and Brighton, a keen competition began between a number of railways, and continued for years with numerous new developments, to provide through service between the great cities of Merseyside and the Midlands and the South, South-East and South-West coasts. Thus the Great Western and London & South Western inaugurated a new restaurant car express between Birkenhead and Bournemouth, and the G.W.R., by virtue of its right of access to Manchester either *via* Crewe or *via* Warrington, in 1910 began to run a through section of this train to and from Manchester London Road, by the Crewe route, connecting with the main train at Wellington.

This was too much for the London & North Western, and as a result of negotiations with the Midland, the precursor of the "Pines Express" came into service in October, 1910. It was arranged to use L.N.W.R. metals between Manchester and Birmingham, and between these cities it provided a useful new service, with a time of 1¾ hours from Birmingham to Manchester—the fastest that had been known up to that time. From New Street Station in Birmingham it was worked by the Midland Railway to Bath—and, incidentally, to avoid reversal travelled out of the east end of New Street and *via* Camp Hill to King's Norton—while at Bath the Somerset & Dorset Joint Railway (Midland and London & South Western) took charge for the final stage of the journey.

After suspension during the First World War, the train was reinstated much in its old times and received the title of "Pines Express" in 1927. It became even more exclusively L.M.S.R. in 1930, when this company took over the provision of motive power on the Somerset & Dorset Joint Line, which previously had its own independent locomotives. The only stretch of purely "foreign" territory traversed was 7¾ miles of Southern metals from Broadstone through Poole into Bournemouth.

By 1939 the main restaurant car section of the southbound "Pines Express" was leaving Manchester London Road at 10.10 a.m., and at Crewe was picking up a four-coach set for Birmingham, and through coaches for both Bournemouth and Southampton, which had left Liverpool Lime Street at 9.40 a.m. The combined train was due away from Crewe at 10.49 a.m., and—most unusually for an express—was booked to take the slow road to Stafford, through which it passed on the west side of the station. This was to avoid fouling the path of the up "Merseyside Express", due through Crewe at 10.57 a.m., and the result often was a race from Whitmore down to Stafford, if the "Pines" was behind time. The latter stopped next at Wolverhampton, and then ran across into the Midland Division side at Birmingham New Street, arriving at 12.2 noon. Here the four-coach set from Liverpool was detached, and a Midland Division locomotive took charge of the remainder, usually about six for Bournemouth, one of which was a through coach from Bradford, and the Southampton coach on the rear.

Departure from Birmingham was at 12.13 p.m., and by 1.10 p.m. the express was in Cheltenham, where the Southampton coach was detached; the latter was handed over to the Great Western Railway, to be worked over the one-time Midland & South Western Junction line through Swindon to Andover, and thence over the Southern to Southampton Terminus, arriving at 5.5 p.m. The main train stopped next at Gloucester, and then had 48 minutes for the 41¾ miles to Bath. In the Queen Square station at Bath reversal was necessary.

After Bath came the locomotive tug-of-war, for the tremendous gradients through the Mendips had to be tackled. One result of the L.M.S.R. assumption of locomotive responsibility was the

The ultimate, B.R. standardised look of the " Pines Express ": Class 4 4-6-0 No. 75009 and Class 9 2-10-0 No. 92001 double-head the up train past Masbury Halt, on the Somerset & Dorset line, in September 1962.
Photo by G. A. Richardson

introduction between Bath and Bournemouth of the ubiquitous and capable Class " 5 " 4-6-0s, which greatly eased the power problem. Beginning at Bath Junction, there was first a 2-mile climb at 1 in 50 to the north portal of Combe Down tunnel; again from beyond Radstock there were three miles up to 1 in 50, followed by another 4 miles almost as steeply inclined to the summit at Masbury, and then by a descent to Evercreech Junction which for 7 miles also was largely at 1 in 50. From Templecombe to Blandford the line was single-track, which, though equipped for automatic table-changing, involved slacks through the station loops. In the circumstances, 2 hours 17 minutes for the $71\frac{1}{2}$ miles from Bath to Bournemouth West, with four intermediate stops, was not bad going. The total time for the run of 252 miles from Manchester to Bournemouth, reached at 4.37 p.m., was 6 hours 27 minutes.

Northbound, the " Pines Express " left Bournemouth West at 10.35 a.m., and with six intermediate stops made the better time of 2 hours 5 minutes to Bath. Departure from Bath was at 12.44 p.m., from Gloucester at 1.37 p.m., and from Cheltenham (where the " Pines " picked up from the G.W.R. the through coach which had made its way out of Southampton Terminus at 10.10 a.m.) at 1.51 p.m. From here a fast run was made to Bromsgrove, 31.1 miles in 31 minutes, at just over a mile a minute. The Bromsgrove stop was necessary for taking banking assistance up the formidable Lickey incline, which climbs two miles at 1 in 37¾ up to Blackwell, From King's Norton the direct line was taken into Birmingham, *via* Selly Oak, and this meant that the train passed through New Street in the same direction—from west to east—on both southbound and northbound journeys, and even used the same platform at that station.

To avoid reversal in this direction, the Western Division locomotive thus had to take its train out of New Street from the eastern end, and in consequence the train left Birmingham *via* Aston and Bexscot. In this direction, also, Wolverhampton was avoided by taking the straight line northwards from Willenhall to Bushbury. With the 4-coach Liverpool section added, and now a formation of about 11 bogies, the " Pines Express " ran the 54 miles to Crewe non-stop in 70 minutes, arriving at 4.2 p.m. Here the severance of Liverpool and Manchester sections took place; the Liverpool section reached Lime Street at 5.21 p.m. and the " Pines Express " proper was into Manchester London Road at 4.51 p.m., in a minute over 6¼ hours from Bournemouth.

At summer week-ends, on Mondays, Fridays and Saturdays, the express was divided, and the principal section of the train then followed a very curious route, used by no other regular express train, and avoiding both Wolverhampton and Birmingham. From Bushbury it continued direct to Darlaston and there turned leftwards into Walsall, where the change from Western to Midland Division engine took place. From Walsall the old Midland branch through Sutton Coldfield was used down to Castle Bromwich, on the Derby–Birmingham main line, from which it was a straight run to Saltley and then on through Camp Hill by the train's normal route. The same course was followed in the opposite direction.

The " Pines Express " was withdrawn on the outbreak of the Second World War, but it was restored between Manchester and Bournemouth on October 7th 1946, with a timing of 7 hours southbound and 7¼ hours northbound. It was soon accelerated to 6 hours 56 minutes southbound and 6 hours 51 minutes northbound, but the southbound schedule was later eased to 7 hours 12 minutes. Restaurant cars reappeared, and through coaches to and from Sheffield were added to those between Liverpool and Bournemouth. Departure from Manchester was at 10.20 a.m., and from Bournemouth West at 9.45 a.m.; rather unusually, the latter train finished its journey, not in London Road, but at Manchester Mayfield. The Southern Region had now taken over the responsibility for the locomotive power between Bath and Bournemouth, and used its light Pacifics over this section.

From then up to the time of its disappearance the " Pines Express " suffered further changes of route. The first and most revolutionary change followed the closure of the Somerset & Dorset Joint Line; this resulted in a transfer of the " Pines Express " from the former route through Stafford, Birmingham New Street, Cheltenham and Bath to the former Great Western line *via* Market Drayton, Wellington, Birmingham Snow Hill, Oxford, Reading West, Basingstoke and the Southern line from there, so that the " Pines " entered Bournemouth from the east instead of the west, and incidentally could now serve Southampton. The final change was when in 1963 closure of the line from Nantwich through Market Drayton to Wellington compelled a further diversion *via* Shrewsbury, with a stop there; but the increased speed made possible with diesel power allowed the switch without increase in overall journey time. Thus (apart from the through Southampton coach) it was not until the end of the history of the " Pines Express " that the former competitor, the Great Western Railway, had to take a share in the working of the train, and a very limited share at that, as by now the London Midland Region was in control of the former G.W.R. Birmingham main line as far south as Banbury. In its final form the southbound " Pines Express " left Liverpool at 9.45 a.m. and Manchester at 10 a.m.; it reached Southampton at 3.54 p.m., Bournemouth at 4.44 p.m. and Poole at 5.10 p.m. Northbound, at 9.38 a.m. from Poole, 10.2 a.m. from Bournemouth and 10.43 a.m. from Southampton it was due in Manchester by 5.6 p.m. and Liverpool at 5.11 p.m. But in March, 1967, with the opening of the electrification through Birmingham, the " Pines Express " ceased to run; since then through passengers have been compelled either to travel *via* London, or by L.M.R. electric train from Lancashire to Birmingham New Street, changing there into one of the two diesel-hauled trains that now run daily between Birmingham and Bournemouth, and similarly in the reverse direction.

The Ports-to-Ports Express

In 1897 what until then had been the Manchester Sheffield & Lincolnshire Railway changed its name to Great Central Railway, and greatly enhanced its importance and its range by the new main line opened in 1899 from north of Nottingham to London. The next business was to attract traffic to the new route, and the possibilities were further increased when in 1900 a short spur line was opened from Woodford and Hinton, 34 miles south of Leicester, to Banbury on the Great Western. In course of time various through passenger services were established over this connection between the North-East of England and the West and South.

With one exception, all these through trains continued southwards over the G.W.R. to Oxford and beyond. This exception was the unofficially-named " Ports-to-Ports Express ", for which a more direct route had to be found in order to link Banbury with South Wales. It was planned by making use of a sleepy country branch, single-track throughout, which never previously had seen an express train. This was the line from King's Sutton, just south of Banbury, through the old-world towns of Chipping Norton, Stow-on-the-Wold and Bourton-on-the-Water to Cheltenham, from which town main line running could be resumed through Gloucester to Newport, Cardiff and beyond.

Originally the " Ports-to-Ports Express ", which began it career in May, 1906, was designed to run between Newcastle-on-Tyne and the port of Barry. In later years it was extended westwards to Swansea, though still running between Cardiff and Bridgend by way of Barry instead of by the direct main line. In addition to connecting the ports of Tyneside and Teesside with those of South Wales, in L.N.E.R. days two further ports were linked with the service by the running of a through coach to and from Hull and Goole, detached and attached at Sheffield.

In 1939 the express was leaving Newcastle at 9.30 in the morning and with stops at Durham, Darlington and Northallerton reached York at 11.32 a.m. On the way it suffered the indignity of being put on to the slow loop south of Eryholme to let the " Silver Jubilee " streamliner get by. The next stage, from York at 11.42 a.m., was a non-stop run to Sheffield, by way of the Swinton & Knottingley Joint Line through Pontefract, with an arrival in Sheffield at 12.51 p.m. Here reversal was necessary, and with the through coach from Hull—which had left there at 10.35 a.m. and had travelled to Sheffield *via* Doncaster—at the head end, the train left for the south at 1 p.m. A fast run was made over Great Central metals to Banbury, with calls at Nottingham, Loughborough, Leicester and Rugby, and the G.W.R. station was reached at 3.30 p.m.

To this point the locomotive power had been similar to that of the " Aberdeen–Penzance " service, but something much lighter was needed for the Banbury–Cheltenham line, and for years, until the advent of the 4–6–0 " Manors ", the G.W.R. used Moguls over this section, through between Banbury and Cardiff. After the fast L.N.E.R. running, the allowance of 82 minutes for the 44¾ miles from Banbury to Cheltenham

The " Ports-to-Ports Express " on Great Central tracks early in this century: a train of G.W.R. clerestory stock, apart from the leading G.C. coach, it is headed by G.C. 4-4-0 No. 1015.

South came somewhat as an anticlimax, even if the lethargy, in the circumstances, was unavoidable. Stopping at Gloucester and at Chepstow, the " Ports-to-Ports Express " skirted the Severn estuary to reach Newport at 6.30 and Cardiff at 6.51 p.m.

Up to 1922, the Great Western Railway relinquished their charge of the train at Cardiff and handed over to the Barry Railway for the short run between Cardiff and Barry, but from the grouping this line, with its extension through Aberthaw to Bridgend, became part of the G.W.R. It was considerably more circuitous, of course, than the direct main line from Cardiff to Bridgend, and the 54 miles from Cardiff to Swansea, with stops at Barry Docks, Barry, Bridgend, Pyle, Port Talbot and Neath, took just over $1\frac{3}{4}$ hours. Swansea was reached at 8.45 p.m., after a 397-mile journey taking $11\frac{1}{4}$ hours.

In the northbound direction, the G.W.R. in later years cut out the journey by the Barry loop, and leaving Swansea at 8.15 a.m., ran the "Ports-to-Ports Express" direct to Cardiff, with stops at Neath, Briton Ferry, Port Talbot, Bridgend and Llantrisant. Cardiff was left at 9.40 a.m. and Newport at 10 a.m., and with the same stops on Great Western territory beyond Newport as in the reverse direction, the express found its way into Banbury at 12.40 p.m. Four minutes later the L.N.E.R. were away on the journey to Sheffield, and with halts at Rugby, Leicester and Nottingham this stretch of $107\frac{1}{4}$ miles was completed in 2 hours 19 minutes. The Hull coach, detached at Sheffield, found its way into that port at 4.45 p.m.; the main train, reversing in Sheffield, got to York by 4.19 p.m. A stop of 11 minutes sufficed here, and again with the same stops as coming south the end of the journey, at Newcastle, was attained by 6.15 p.m. This was a considerably faster effort than that of the south-bound train, and cut the through journey to 10 hours precisely.

For most of the year a 6-coach corridor set, including restaurant car, and the through composite corridor coach to and from Hull, provided comfortably adequate accommodation, though the formation was added to as required during the summer. London & North-Eastern and Great Western coaches were used on alternate days. The train was withdrawn on the outbreak of war. The only through passenger trains in wartime continuing to use the Woodford–Banbury link between the L.N.E.R. and the G.W.R. were the York–Swindon service, and the through train between Newcastle and Ashford, later diverted to Southampton.

The "Ports-to-Ports Express" reappeared in October, 1946, but modified at the G.W.R. end by being run between Banbury and Newport *via* Oxford, Swindon and the Severn Tunnel, a considerably longer route than the previous one *via* Cheltenham. Except on summer Saturdays, at the northern end of the route the terminal point was York and not Newcastle. Leaving York at 12.20 p.m., the "Ports-to-Ports Express" was in Swansea by 9.8 p.m., and coming north, with a departure from Swansea at 8.15 a.m., York was reached at 5.12 p.m.

In the winter of 1952–1953 the working of the train was cut short at Banbury, and to Fridays and Saturdays only; thus it ceased to touch any ports at all. But this was largely because of the establishment of a new and far more direct through service between Cardiff and Newcastle by way of Gloucester and the L.M.R. line through Birmingham and Derby to York; this cut the Cardiff-Newcastle time to 8 hours 32 minutes, and that in the reverse direction to $8\frac{1}{4}$ hours, both faster than before. By 1973 the through service had become far faster still; the 10.4 a.m. restaurant car express from Newcastle made its way into Cardiff by

4.11 p.m., in no more than 6 hours 7 minutes, while in the opposite direction the 11.45 a.m. from Cardiff arrived in Newcastle by 6 p.m., taking 6¼ hours for the journey. Such is the vast cross-country train service improvement that has taken place with the bringing up to high speed standards of the Sheffield–Derby–Birmingham–West of England main line. Reversion to the original route would be impossible, as between Nottingham and Cheltenham it no longer exists.

The South Wales Pullman

The chapter on the " Birmingham Pullman " has described how in 1929 the Great Western Railway made an experiment in Pullman travel, with an all-Pullman car express between Paddington and Torquay, and with the inclusion of Pullmans in its Transatlantic boat trains between Plymouth and London. But the public response was not encouraging, and a year later the cars were withdrawn. Not until the summer of 1955, after the G.W.R. had become swallowed up in the nationalised British Railways, did Pullman cars reappear on Western metals. And not, this time, as an attraction for holidaymakers, but in recognition of the fact that a business *clientèle* favours this kind of comfort and service. So it was the growing industrial and commercial importance of South Wales that suggested the South Wales main line as a suitable *venue* for a new Pullman venture, this time destined not merely to be permanent, but eventually to justify a Pullman service three times daily in each direction. The first " South Wales Pullman " was an eight-coach train of standard cars, in the Pullman chocolate-and-cream livery, steam-hauled in each direction by a " Castle " class 4–6–0. It left Paddington at 9.55 a.m., ran non-stop to Newport and with halts after that at Cardiff and Port Talbot reached Swansea at 2.0 p.m. The return journey was begun at 4.35 p.m., and with the same stops Paddington was reached at 8.45 p.m.

Five years later the Western Region invested in its three eight-car diesel " Blue Pullman " sets, and in 1961 one of these replaced the locomotive-hauled " South Wales Pullman ". For some time the latter had been running an hour earlier in the down direction than when first introduced, leaving London at 8.50 a.m., though the up working had been but little altered. But with the introduction of the new train set in September, 1961, as with the other W.R. " Blue Pullmans " working of the " South Wales Pullman " was completely reversed. The new train started out of Swansea bright and early at 6.40 a.m., added Bridgend to the Neath and Port Talbot stops, and after the customary halts at Cardiff and Newport ran the 133.4 miles from the latter town to Paddington in 127 minutes, arriving at 10.15 a.m. The down journey was begun at 4.55 p.m., and with a 127-minute timing to Newport and the same stops as coming up, Swansea was reached at 8.40 p.m. The 3 hours 35 minutes of the up journey was easily the fastest ever tabled between Swansea and London, and 35 minutes quicker than that of the steam-hauled train.

In 1964 it was decided that just as with the other two " Blue Pullmans " the " South Wales Pullman " should no longer stand idle all day at Paddington, and that there was plenty of time available to make a midday run as far as Cardiff and back. So at 11.0 a.m. it started out on a non-stop timing of 122 minutes to Newport, and reached reached Cardiff at 1.19 p.m.; returning at 2.30 p.m., it was into London by 4.50 p.m., but this, of course, necessitated a later start of the final run, which was put back to 5.40 p.m., Swansea now being reached at 9.10 p.m. This pattern was then substantially accelerated. Soon the Swansea start became 15 minutes later, at 6.55 a.m., and with a 2-hour run over the 133.4 miles from Newport the Pullman achieved a time of no more than 3 hours 20 minutes from Swansea to London; in the reverse direction the 5.40 p.m. down took 3½ hours. The 11.0 a.m. down Cardiff Pullman

▷ In its final B.R. blue-and-grey dress, a " Blue Pullman " dmu hurries through Acton on the up " South Wales Pullman " service in August 1971. *Photo by J. H. Cooper-Smith*

▽ The up " South Wales Pullman " in July 1961 : 4-6-0 No. 4099 *Kilgerran Castle* storms past Wapley Sidings. *Photo by G. F. Heiron*

and the 2.30 p.m. up from then on were allowed 2¼ hours.

Even more important, from the summer of 1967 a third "Blue Pullman" began to serve South Wales, and, moreover, was booked to make the run of 133.4 miles from Paddington to Newport in 113 minutes, at an average of 70.8 m.p.h. It took its place at 9.0 a.m. in the sequence of even-hour departures from Paddington, and with stops at Newport, Cardiff, Bridgend and Neath was into Swansea by 12.20 p.m. It then provided an evening service from South Wales to London, at 4.20 p.m. from Swansea, arriving in Paddington by 7.45 p.m. The set of " Blue Pullmans " making the morning up and evening down runs, with the midday trip to Cardiff and back, covered no less than 672 miles each day.

But none of the Western Region midday Pullman experiments survived for long; the business fraternity wanted the morning and evening workings, but patronage of the midday Pullman trains was not sufficient to justify continuance. South Wales continued to enjoy its morning and evening Pullmans in each direction until April, 1973. however. The morning up Pullman was back to its former 6.40 a.m. starting time from Swansea, and after calls at Neath, Port Talbot and Bridgend left Cardiff at 7.40 a.m. and Newport at 7.55 a.m., with a non-stop timing of 115 minutes for the 133.4 miles to Paddington. So with a Paddington arrival at 9.50 a.m., the Swansea–London time had come down to 3 hours, 10 minutes, for an overall average of almost exactly 60 m.p.h. The afternoon up " South Wales Pullman " was starting at 3.55 p.m. from Swansea, and was allowed 5 minutes more to Newport, but the same time thence to Paddington, with an arrival at 7.10 p.m.

In the down direction the morning " South Wales Pullman " fitted into the pattern of departures on the hour for South Wales by leaving Paddington at 9.0 a.m., and with its Newport arrival at 10.50 a.m. had to cover the 133.4 miles at an average of 72.8 m.p.h. Cardiff was reached at 11.7 a.m., and with stops as in the up direction at Bridgend, Port Talbot and Neath the Swansea arrival was at 12.10 p.m., also in 3 hours 10 minutes from London. The evening down Pullman was starting at 5.33 p.m., 3 minutes behind the " Golden Hind ", taking 111 minutes to Newport and 2 hours 8 minutes to Cardiff, and was making Swansea by 8.45 p.m.

But in May, 1973, as we have seen already, the decision was reached to abandon all the Western Region Pullman workings, and in the case of the South Wales services to substitute trains of ordinary first and second class stock in much the same times. A new 9.0 a.m. down took 5 minutes longer to Swansea (3¼ hours), though evening travellers had to be content with the 5.0 p.m. down, which did not reach Swansea until 8.26 p.m., a longer journey by 14 minutes. Coming up in the morning, the 6.40 a.m. from Swansea was into Paddington by 9.55 a.m., which was only 5 minutes later, while the 3.53 p.m. up, arriving at 7.15 p.m., added only 7 minutes to the journey time.

It remains to add that when the 125 m.p.h. HST diesel trains take over the South Wales express service in 1976 the fastest London-Cardiff journey time will be 1 hour 46 minutes, the quickest London-Swansea only 2 hours 45 minutes.

The Torbay Express

Little special interest attached to the "Torbay Express" of the G.W.R., other than that of being a fast and popular train. Before the First World War it left Paddington at 11.50 a.m., and followed the then prevailing G.W.R. fashion of slipping coaches by having a slip portion on the tail as far as Taunton, for Ilfracombe, in the course of its 3-hour non-stop run to Exeter. In the summer this Ilfracombe section achieved distinction by being the only slip portion in history to include a restaurant car in its four-coach formation. Just before the outbreak of war, the starting time was changed to 12 noon, and in the post-war recovery this became the permanent departure, though the Taunton "slip" did not reappear.

Before the outbreak of the Second World War, the "Torbay", leaving Paddington at 12 noon, was due into St. David's station at Exeter at 2.49 p.m., having covered the 173.5 miles in 169 minutes, at 61.6 m.p.h. A stop of 6 minutes was scheduled here, and the 26.1 miles on to Torquay required 35 minutes, making exactly $3\frac{1}{2}$ hours from London. From Torquay the London engine, almost invariably a "King" 4-6-0, continued with the train, calling at Paignton, taking the train-staff for the single line at Goodrington Sands, calling at Churston, and descending the steep incline to Kingswear, to come to rest on the banks of the Dart opposite Dartmouth at 4.5 p.m. The Goodrington–Kingswear stretch of 6 miles was probably the only piece of single track on the G.W.R. used regularly by a "King". On Saturdays in summer the traffic for Torbay was sufficient to justify a non-stop run over 199.6 miles from Paddington to Torquay, and the "Torbay Express" was allowed 3 hours 28 minutes to do it. Times beyond Torquay, however, were unchanged.

How the "Torbay Express" roofboards were displayed on Hawksworth coaching stock—a September 1953 shot at Reading, as 4-6-0 No. 5028 *Llantilio Castle* takes the Berks & Hants line. *Photo by M. W. Earley*

In the reverse direction, the "King", after a level mile out of Kingswear, had first to tackle the nasty climb to Churston, including 2 miles at 1 in 66 and 1 in 75. The start from Torquay is even worse; it begins at 1 in 55 for $\frac{3}{4}$-mile to Torre, and continues for another $\frac{3}{4}$-mile at 1 in 73, so that banking assistance was often needed. Leaving Torquay at 12 noon, the "Torbay" was due in Exeter 35 minutes later, and after 6 minutes there, made the run of 173.5 miles to Paddington in 174 minutes, at an average of almost exactly a mile-a-minute, arriving at 3.35 p.m. On summer Saturdays a non-stop relief was run from Torquay at 11.50 a.m., taking $3\frac{3}{4}$ hours, and the main train was allowed an extra quarter of an hour.

The Second World War at first saw the down "Torbay Express" married to the "Cornish Riviera Limited", but the load of the combined train soon became too great for single engine haulage, and the "Torbay" was split off and started separately at 10.40 a.m. With additional stops at Taunton, Dawlish, Teignmouth and Torre, it was due in Torquay at 3.18 p.m. and Kingswear at 3.50 p.m.—only 15 minutes before its peacetime arrival, when the start was 80 minutes later. Going up, the "Torbay" left Kingswear at 11.25 a.m., as before the war, and Torquay 5 minutes earlier, at 11.55 a.m.; at Newton Abbot it was linked up with a through portion which had started from Penzance at 8 a.m., and the combined train, calling at Exeter, Taunton and Reading, was due in Paddington at 4.50 p.m. In the up direction, therefore, war added $1\frac{1}{4}$ hours to the Torquay–London journey, but from October 1st, 1945, the train was accelerated to arrive at 4.35 p.m.

In the summer of 1946 the old 12 noon departure from Paddington was restored, and with a non-stop schedule of 183 minutes to Exeter, the down "Torbay" was accelerated to reach Torquay in $3\frac{3}{4}$ hours. The up "Torbay" came down to a

Resplendent in chocolate and cream coaching stock livery, the "Torbay Express" in August 1956: with final W.R.-style headboard up, 4-6-0 No. 5082 *Swordfish* hurries through Kingskerswell, on the Torquay branch, with the down train. *Photo by P. F. Bowles*

run of 3 hours 50 minutes from Torquay to Paddington.

The " Torbay Express " maintained its separate existence until the Western Region timetable reorganisation of 1961, when it was decided that all West of England expresses, leaving Paddington at 30 minutes past the even hours, should be made up of portions for both Plymouth and Torbay, including the " Cornish Riviera Express ". The " Torbay Express " thus became the 12.30 p.m. departure from Paddington, but with stops at Reading, Westbury, Taunton and Newton Abbot added to its previous stop at Exeter only. Before this change the time from Paddington had come down to 3 hours 25 minutes, but this was now lengthened to 3 hours 52 minutes; and the up " Torbay " had its 3 hours 35 minutes timing from Torquay increased to 4 hours 1 minute.

In 1965 the 12.30 p.m. from Paddington and the 10.55 a.m. up from Paignton lost their name, but then from mid-May to mid-September the Torbay portion was split off from the " Cornish Riviera Express " to form a separate train which carried the title " Torbay Express ". This left Paddington at 10.50 a.m., and ran non-stop over the 142.7 miles to Taunton in 124 minutes; after a stop at Exeter from 1.31 to 1.35 p.m., passengers for Dawlish and Teignmouth had the privilege of a fast through service from London before the " Torbay Express " stopped at Newton Abbot and was into Torquay by 2.22 p.m. and Paignton by 2.30 p.m. On Saturdays the train did not stop at Taunton, but continued from Paignton to Kingswear, as in pre-war days. Coming up, the " Torbay Express " got away from Paignton at 11.50 a.m., and from Torquay at 11.58 a.m., with the same stops as on the down run but an easier timing it reached Paddington at 3.35 p.m.

In 1973 no train carried the title " Torbay Express ", as every departure from Paddington at 30 minutes past the even hours, from 8.30 a.m. to 4.40 p.m., was for Torbay. The quickest of these, and the nearest approach to the former " Torbay Express ", was the 12.30 p.m. down, which with stops at Reading, Westbury, Taunton, Exeter and Newton Abbot reached Torquay at 3.56 p.m., in 3 hours 26 minutes from London. Travel by the down " Golden Hind " cut the time to 3 hours 13 minutes, but involved a change of train at Newton Abbot.

The Zulu

" Zulu " was another of the rare British train nicknames to have originated from overseas. In 1879 the Zulu War was so much in the public mind that the name " Zulu " became attached to a new G.W.R. express from Paddington at 3 p.m. to Plymouth, to which reference has been made already in the " Cornish Riviera Express " article.

However, it is with an express introduced in the following year, and travelling in an entirely different direction, that the name " Zulu " is usually associated. Perhaps " Northern Zulu " might be the more appropriate title, as this was a new 4.45 p.m. express from Paddington to Birmingham and Birkenhead. And whereas the original " Zulu " had been put on to compete with the London & South Western Railway to Exeter and beyond, the " Northern Zulu " was attacking the London & North Western Railway to Birmingham and beyond. The new express, calling at Oxford and Leamington, took 2 hours 42 minutes to cover the 129.4 miles to Birmingham, which was not much of a threat to the L.N.W.R. with its route of 112.9 miles only; but to Shrewsbury, Chester and Birkenhead it was another matter. Shrewsbury was reached in 3 hours 50 minutes, Chester in 4 hours 50 minutes and Birkenhead in 5 hours 10 minutes, these two last over an hour less than the shortest previous times. The new up service was not so fast; leaving Birkenhead at 11.45 a.m. it was not into Paddington until 5.25 p.m.

TORBAY EXPRESS
146

25
40

△ The down broad-gauge "Zulu" passes Ealing in 1890, headed by 8 ft. driving-wheel 4-2-2 *Great Western*.

◁ The double-headed "Torbay Express" emerges from Parsons Tunnel, Teignmouth, in October 1955 behind 4-6-0s Nos. 4099 *Kilgerran Castle* and 5024 *Carew Castle*.
Photo by D. S. Fish

◁ Successor to the "Zulu": 4-6-0 No. 6011 *King James I* strides away from Leamington Spa with the 3.0 p.m. Birmingham-Paddington in March 1957. *Photo by R. J. Blenkinsop*

Originally the " Zulu ", after leaving Wolverhampton, stopped at Wellington, Gobowen and Wrexham in addition to Shrewsbury, but not, strangely enough, at Chester; this city was served by a through coach detached at Wrexham, whereas the main train by-passed Chester General by taking the direct spur line to the north. Soon, however, at the cost of omitting the Wellington, Gobowen and Wrexham stops, sufficient time was gained to permit of a stop and reversal at Chester General, but this was a temporary phase only, for in 1888, though the Wellington stop was restored, no passenger stop was scheduled between Shrewsbury and Birkenhead, a momentary stop at Chester Cutting Box being made to detach a through Chester coach. From Shrewsbury to Chester Cutting the booked time called for a start-to-stop speed of 50.6 m.p.h., which over this sharply-graded course required some hard locomotive work. To operate this express three of the " Sir Daniel " class 2–2–2s, including *Sir Daniel* himself, were stationed at Birkenhead, and one of them made the trip to and from Wolverhampton daily.

By the first decade of the century the " Zulu " was still the fastest train on the Northern main line of the Great Western. In the down direction its starting time from Paddington had been altered to 4.55 p.m., and the first stop was at Oxford from 6.10 to 6.12 p.m. Banbury and Leamington were both served by slip coaches, and Birmingham was reached at 7.30 p.m. After a stop at Wolverhampton a third slip coach came off the train, this time at Wellington; arrival at Shrewsbury was at 8.33 p.m., and thenceforward stops at Gobowen, Ruabon (conditional) and Wrexham preceded a Chester arrival at 9.42 p.m. The " Zulu " was then considerate enough to stop at any station between Chester and Birkenhead on request to set down passengers, and arrival in Woodside station was at 10.2 p.m., in 5 hours 7 minutes from London, only 3 minutes faster than when the train was first introduced in 1880.

Coming up, the start from Birkenhead Woodside was now at 11.47 a.m., with the same willingness to pick up passengers at any station between there and Chester for Wolverhampton or beyond. In this direction there was now a regular stop at Ruabon, but none at Gobowen; Shrewsbury was left at 1.33 p.m., Wolverhampton at 2.18 p.m. and Birmingham at 2.44 p.m., after this Leamington was the only halt, and the 106 miles to Paddington were then run non-stop in 125 minutes, for an arrival at 5.20 p.m. Two slip portions were detached, at Oxford and Reading. For some unexplained reason, all the point-to-point times in the up direction were slower than in the down, the entire journey taking 5 hours 33 minutes.

So matters continued until 1910, when there came the complete reorganisation of the service with the opening of the short route *via* Bicester. After this there was little recognisable resemblance between the new trains and the old.

Slipping on the West Midlands main line—a 1928 scene at Wellington (Salop), as a slip coach off the 2.10 p.m. from Paddington enters the station.

'Drama classrooms can offer students critical opportunities to re-think and re-enact themselves as social beings and citizens. Dramatherapy, integrated into mainstream classes, offers long-term exploration of values and identities rather than short-term cultivation of marketable skills. Jeanne Roberts helps us think our way out of the overly-managed classroom and into a space of potential transformation. This splendid adventure in creative, student-centered, drama-based classroom education will appeal to teachers at all levels of education who long for more active and enjoyable ways to engage students and open up their worlds'.

Dr Kathy E. Ferguson,
University of Hawai'i, Mānoa

'This is a book for all those educators, policy makers, and students of education who are interested in educating for children's self-actualisation and critical agency. It powerfully highlights the role of dramatherapeutically informed drama for promoting the embodied, psychosocial, and relational identity-work which is fundamental to enabling children in this. Rooted in Roberts' empirical research and over thirty years' practice experience, the book offers searing critique of neoliberalised narrowing of learning, and evidences new possibilities enacted in current dramatherapeutically informed classrooms. The book makes a passionate, rigorously articulated case for the importance of relationality and embodiment in learning and the development of a dramatherapeutic sensibility in drama-teaching practice'.

Dr Shona Hunter, *Leeds Beckett University,*
Author of Power, Politics and the Emotions

Ethics, Identity, and the Dramatherapy-informed Classroom

Using the drama classroom to shape an active, student-centred space and foster a new perspective for understanding the dramatherapeutic change-process, this book explores the processes that underpin the ways young people negotiate and perform their identities as ethical people.

Arguing for the retention of process-based exploratory drama on the curriculum, chapters critique the impact of neoliberalism and managerialism on the development of young people's ethics and values. Using concepts such as aesthetic distance, encoding, the role of audience and witness, and the contrast between individual, multi, and group roles, to enable students to develop as thinking, reflecting people, the book argues that dramatherapy should not be limited to clinical settings, disconnected from classrooms and the pedagogical contributions that it can make. By absorbing dramatherapy into the broader field of education, an expanded understanding of the concept of the managed classroom space can be gained, based on an understanding of the multiple embodied psychosocial relational processes at play in the drama classroom.

This innately multidisciplinary book will be of use to scholars, researchers, and postgraduate students studying drama education, dramatherapy, and curriculum studies more broadly. Drama teachers and educators will also find this volume of use.

Jeanne Roberts worked as head of drama in secondary schools for over 30 years in the UK and the Crown Dependencies. She received her doctorate from Leeds Beckett University, UK, and is a full member of the British Association of Dramatherapists (BADth).

Routledge Research in Creative Arts and Expressive Therapies

This series provides a forum to discuss the latest research, debates and practice in creative arts and expressive therapies; including arts therapy, dance therapy, dramatherapy and music therapy.

Intercultural Music Therapy Consultation Research
Shared Humanity in Collaborative Theory and Practice
Lisa Margetts

Reflections on Authentic Movement
Theory, Practice and Arts-Led Research
Eila Goldhahn

Space, Place and Dramatherapy
International Perspectives
Edited by Eliza Sweeney

Posthuman Possibilities of Dance Movement Psychotherapy
Moving through Eco-feminist and New Materialist Entanglements of Differently Enabled Bodies in Research
Caroline Frizell

Ethics, Identity, and the Dramatherapy-informed Classroom
Processes of Identity Negotiation and Performance
Jeanne Roberts

Ethics, Identity, and the Dramatherapy-informed Classroom

Processes of Identity Negotiation and Performance

Jeanne Roberts

Routledge
Taylor & Francis Group
LONDON AND NEW YORK

First published 2025
by Routledge
4 Park Square, Milton Park, Abingdon, Oxon OX14 4RN

and by Routledge
605 Third Avenue, New York, NY 10158

Routledge is an imprint of the Taylor & Francis Group, an informa business

British Library Cataloguing-in-Publication Data
A catalogue record for this book is available from the British Library

ISBN: 978-1-032-72985-5 (hbk)
ISBN: 978-1-032-73510-8 (pbk)
ISBN: 978-1-003-46453-2 (ebk)

DOI: 10.4324/9781003464532

Typeset in Galliard
by Newgen Publishing UK

And to my Dad who continues to live on inside of me, and who I know is so proud.

Contents

Foreword

Clive Holmwood

My relationship to drama education and dramatherapy goes back many years to my own doctoral research, and before, and subsequent publication (Holmwood, 2016). However, Roberts, as she accurately depicts, has taken this thinking to a new, stimulating, and nuanced level and has created a book which will be of great interest to *both* professions, and more importantly to the very soul of the work with young people, using drama, the art form that lies between these two professions. It is with incredible pride and pleasure that I have been asked to write the foreword to this new, exciting, relevant, scholarly, and much needed book that attempts to challenge current binary thinking.

My own work considered the difference between drama education and dramatherapy. Roberts' work takes this a step further and suggests the idea of a dramatherapeutically *informed* drama classroom, allowing ideas from both professions to converge to the benefit of all. She does not suggest a quasi-dramatherapy session in the classroom environment, or teaching drama within a dramatherapy setting but suggests that a carefully considered amalgamation of educational drama with informed dramatherapy theory can aid the thinking and relational process between student and teacher in the classroom.

Roberts begins by setting a contemporary context for drama in education. She does not avoid some of the difficult and more challenging philosophy around the predominant neoliberal ideation of education in general, and arts and drama in particular, stating that: 'Neoliberalism is an expression of the advanced global capitalism that frames the modern world' (Chapter 1). Even though in UK classrooms drama as a subject lies outside of the main national curriculum, it does not escape from these neoliberal ideologies. Moving drama away from technical and bureaucratic 'easily measurable so-called marketable skills and towards the exploration of values and identities' (Chapter 1) is one of the primary considerations.

What lies at the centre of this book is the idea of 'relationality', and the idea, often overlooked in the busy classroom environment, that the relationship not only between pupils, but centrally, the relationship between teacher and student is important and worthy of consideration; the focus being around the importance of 'embodied psychosocial relational processes' (Chapter 1). Relationality is seen through the prism of the work between student and teacher and an ability to further focus on the nuanced identities, roles, and experiences of the students when using drama. What the drama shows and what they gain through the drama is seen in safe and distanced ways that are not in their own right therapy but are tried and tested dramatherapy practices, used dramatherapeutically in the classroom.

Through beautifully described and theoretically sound spotlighted case studies, we are taken on a journey. We witness the challenges of being in a secondary school, one not even designed with drama in mind. We are witness to the wonderful and relational work carried out by Roberts and her students using this blended dramatherapeutic process. I am also struck by the importance of the need for teacher self-reflection. As Roberts points out, teachers do not sit outside of the relational dynamic. Their own ability to self-reflect on these powerful underlying forces is key here, with teachers needing to be open to the internal and external pressures both within the room but also within the wider neoliberal expectations of the education system. Roberts suggests that this is a difficult course to navigate. Offering drama teachers supervision might be one interesting insight to come from this work.

There is, I imagine, one major criticism that some might aim at this work. Roberts is in a privileged position, having been dual trained as both drama teacher and dramatherapist. The vast majority of drama teachers will not have had this background. Therefore, how can they be expected to have this dramatherapeutically engaged lens? In Chapter 8, Roberts makes some useful suggestions, including offering initial training to drama teachers on some of the fundamental theoretical approaches that dramatherapists use in order to help them better understand and use relational practice and attachment-based ideas in the drama classroom.

Dramatherapy has its historical roots, in the UK at least, in drama education and special needs education: the pioneering work of Slade (1954) and Jennings (1984) for example. It then moved in more of a clinical direction (and to an extent, rightly so) in the 1980s. However, the separation of the two also had disadvantages; in more siloed approaches, with drama teachers and dramatherapists seeing each other with some suspicion and not sharing practice. Nevertheless, there is now a move towards less binary approaches, with closer relationships between these two professions. Roberts' work fits into this new more liminal and enlightened philosophy between the two professions, as for example does the work of Ma and Subbiondo (2022), who advocate for an Integral Drama Based Pedagogy in the training of drama teachers using the more embodied approach of integral education, based on Eastern philosophy. Roberts' teaching processes appear very similar as 'the focus of this book is an exploration of the embodied psychosocial relational processes that facilitate the shifts in discourses, and shifts in alignment to discourses, that inform, consciously or unconsciously, student identity' (Chapter 1) when in the drama classroom. Thus, Roberts suggests 'that an approach other than an "outcome-measured" approach can have outcomes that are of value' (Chapter 8), and this directly challenges the current homogenised neoliberal approach to education that is prevalent in much of the West.

If nothing else, I hope that this book will further develop the relationship between drama educators and dramatherapists who share both a common heritage and a common art form. I would also like to think that it might impact current and future educational policy around drama as it is taught within Western-based educational systems and that educational policy makers and school managers will see that drama as a subject cannot just be seen as a form of neoliberal managerialism but as an important part of a young person's abilities to creatively problem solve, work on their own and with others, and to understand their place in a complex inter-relational world, where they can develop confidence, achieve, and ultimately *be* themselves and not the product of a system.

Clive Holmwood is a qualified dramatherapist of almost 30 years' experience and is Associate Professor, lecturer, and researcher in the Discipline of Therapeutic Arts, School of Arts, University of Derby, UK. He has a particular interest in drama, drama education, and dramatherapy.

References

Holmwood, C. (2016). *Drama education and dramatherapy: Exploring the space between disciplines*. London: Routledge.
Jennings, S. (1984). *Remedial drama*. London: A & C Black Publishing Limited.
Ma, L., & Subbiondo, J. (2022). Integral drama based pedagogy as a practice of integral education: Facilitating the journey of personal transformation. *Beijing International Review of Education, 3*, 499–515. doi:10.1163/25902539-03040001
Slade, P. (1954). *Child drama*. London: University of London Press.

Acknowledgements

I would like to take this opportunity to extend a heartfelt thank you to my supervisors Tom and Shona for their guidance, to my 'critical-friend' Eleanor for her support, to Clive for his encouragement, to Gary for his endless tolerance of this project, to my Mum for asking me every day how it was going, and to Rebekah for making everything worthwhile.

And to my Dad who continues to live on inside of me, and who I know is so proud.

Acronyms and Abbreviations

GCSE	General Certificate of Secondary Education
KS3	Key Stage Three
KS4	Key Stage Four
OECD	Organisation for Economic Co-operation and Development
OFSTED	Office for Standards in Education
PISA	Programme for International Student Assessment
SISRA	Service for Improved Schools' Results Analysis

Note:

Dramatherapy is the British spelling and is used throughout when referring to dramatherapy.

Drama therapy is the American spelling and is used when quoting from American texts which give the spelling as drama therapy.

1 Introduction

By law, the state schools of the Crown Dependencies have an obligation to provide for their young people an education that enables them to leave school as responsible and capable citizens, who are fit for taking an active role in and of contributing economically to their communities whilst maintaining positive mental health and well-being (Isle of Man Government, 2006; States of Guernsey, 2020; States of Jersey, 2023b). Historically, drama has been a subject ideally placed to help schools achieve this goal. For example, in the past, drama was often about allowing students to explore their individual and group relationships to social, ethical, and moral conundrums (Heathcote & Herbert, 1985). Furthermore, as a formalisation of child-play, drama has often facilitated a high level of fun and enjoyment in the classroom. However, within current education policy, which is framed through discourses and technologies of neo-liberal governance (Ball, 2003, 2016; Burman, 2012; Hess, 2015), the moral exploration and the play aspects of the drama curriculum have been side-lined, and what was once valued for its intrinsic worth has become commodified (Beck & Beck-Gernsheim, 2002; Curran & Hill, 2019). In line with that commodification, what is now considered educational success tends to be what can be assessed by pre-determined and easily measurable but superficial outcome indicators (Moos, 2017; Shore & Wright, 1999). This causes staff, who are increasingly subject to excessive scrutiny, to experience a fundamental shift in the nature of their relationship to the institution, to teaching, and to students (Davies & Bansel, 2007). For example, what develops is an overconcern with second-order activities to do with managing performance indicators, at the expense of the first-order activity of helping children learn about their world and their place within it (Ball, 2016; Stronach & Clarke, 2011).

The result has been that in the current education policy-climate, the exploratory and play aspects of drama have been marginalised and replaced by a focus on the teaching of skills as an end in itself. On the other hand, the exploratory and developmental use of drama remains strong in the theorising and practice of dramatherapy. Dramatherapy shares joint ancestry with educational drama; however, its potential as a tool to further personal development is rarely if ever made available to students in mainstream drama classes. In the context of the

DOI: 10.4324/9781003464532-1

above, this book considers what the benefits might be of a drama curriculum that returns the developmental and exploratory aspects of drama to the foreground. I observe what happens when drama skills are taught because they facilitate deeper exploration of the material but where it is the deeper exploration of the material that is the primary focus. I investigate what happens when the crafting of material for performance remains an important aspect of the drama experience but where that crafting is held in balance with exploration and play. I ask what happens when the dramatherapeutic focus on development is re-introduced to the classroom to create dramatherapeutically informed classroom drama. In short, I consider what happens when classroom drama is facilitated by a practitioner who understands the value of exploratory play and developmental story-making (Lahad, 1992); who understands the drama change-processes (Jones, 1996c); and who is able to use these understandings to support students' personal and collective critical, ethical, and identity-work. In other words, this book considers the kinds of exploratory and identity-work done through embodied, psychosocial, and relational mechanisms for which dramatherapeutically informed classroom drama is a vector. By identity-work, I mean 'the ongoing processes through which people come to understand "who I am" and their place in the world' (Allen & Mendick, 2013, p. 80) (see Chapter 3).

Bringing together my enjoyment of being with young people and my love of drama, I came to drama-teaching in the late 1980s armed with an honour's degree in drama and theatre arts and a postgraduate certificate in education that qualified me to teach drama and what was in those days called Special Educational Needs. However, I quickly became dissatisfied with the drama journey I was facilitating in the classroom and undertook qualifying training in dramatherapy, hoping that this would help me deepen the dramatic experience I was able to offer my students. The school in which I currently teach is the fifth school I have worked in, and the one to which I am most deeply attached, having been a member of staff there for nearly 30 years. At this school, I have always used my dramatherapy training to support my drama-teaching practice. As a member of staff at this school, I have worked under five head-teachers, alongside scores of colleagues and with thousands of children. I am privileged to work in a context where I see the children I teach become the adults I work with, and who, ultimately, will offer me care, make policy decisions for the community, and maintain the social infrastructure as I move into the later stages of life. I wonder what kinds of adults these people will be, what ethics and values they will hold, and what contribution, as their small, East-Asian, female drama teacher, I will have made.

As a classroom practitioner who is a teacher, a dramatherapist, and a social being, I stand between competing paradigms, and those paradigms cannot be defined or explained as being simply the disciplinary differences between teaching classroom drama on one hand and practicing dramatherapy on the other. The tension is more nuanced than that and is to do with the interplay of my social beingness with the effects-in-practice of policy that is informed by the current 'global order' of neoliberalism on one hand (Burman, 2008, 2012) and the desire for a more humancentric or developmental orientation on the other (Uljens & Ylimaki, 2017). The neoliberal version of education tends to commodify people and experiences. Outcomes need to be pre-determinable and easily measured and are therefore simplified and superficial (Morales & Abegglen, 2020). In practice, this is epitomised by: the imposition on state schools in some jurisdictions of the England and Wales initiative known as 'Attainment 8' or of regimes that are 'Attainment 8' adjacent (States of Guernsey, 2023; States of Jersey, 2023a), where 'Attainment 8' is a way of measuring the quality of a school based on the academic outcomes of a select range of subjects; by increasing managerialism; and with a preoccupation with pre-determinable outcome-measures. My preferred educational model stands in stark contrast to the above. It is developmental: a model where in a process of 'self-actualisation' (Culler, 2011 quoted in Priestly, 2017, p. 45) within the arts and drama, space is made for the kinds of learning where students are allowed to rearticulate themselves through their responses to the material. Because self-actualisation happens personally for each student, outcomes cannot be pre-determined and the teacher must respond to the evolving classroom context and make in-situ choices that cannot be planned for in advance. The choices that I make as I hold and navigate the tensions between these competing paradigms are instrumental in determining my classroom environment. In turn, the classroom environment influences the kinds of learning the students can experience.

A teacher's embodied presence in the classroom constitutes part of the relational environment and cannot be disregarded. The meanings attached to that embodied presence are multifaceted and relationally negotiated and held. Two aspects of my embodied presence are my various identities as a teacher and my various identities as a dramatherapist. As a teacher, I hope to develop my students' knowledge of the theatre and to diversify their experience of an increasing range of drama skills and conventions. As a teacher, I also have a responsibility for my students' overall well-being, and it is at this point that, in resistance to the splitting and fragmentation which is fundamental to the articulation of identity in neoliberally informed contexts (Baker & Kelan, 2019; Hunter, 2015), the dramatherapist and the teacher in me start to coincide. However, my dramatherapy sensibilities take me further than a simple concern for the pastoral oversight of the students in my classes. I believe that there is potential, which is neither widely understood nor widely comprehended within the mainstream drama-teaching classroom, for a different kind of developmental work; the kind of moral and ethical work – identity-work – that inspired the work of practitioners such as Heathcote (Edmiston & Towler-Evans, 2022) and Jennings (Jennings, 1987), in the 'early days' of both drama-teaching and dramatherapy. In those early days, much drama-teaching in the classroom tended to the experiential rather than towards skills training (Baldwin, 2007), and the profession of dramatherapy had not yet distanced itself from its educational roots in its struggle to redefine itself as a clinical profession (Holmwood, 2016). It was from those early days that I took my own formative experiences of classroom drama and dramatherapy, and from where my own inspirations and ambitions derive.

My professional identities work relationally with other aspects of my identity. As is characteristic in neoliberalised frameworks, the impact of some aspects of identity, such as gender and age, are in danger of being split off and their political impact minimised (Baker & Kelan, 2019). However, the relational impact of my ethnicity is hard for me to ignore because the students often respond to it in overtly negative ways. I am both Japanese and white-English. In resistance to neoliberal logics which facilitate inclusion by assigning people to recognised and measurable subgroups such as 'ethnic minority', which would force me to hold these two identities apart (Baker & Kelan, 2019; Hunter, 2015), I insist on drawing threads of these parts of myself together and enacting both these identities in everyday life. In the same way I am both drama teacher and dramatherapist. There are significant differences in the knowledges and practices of these two separate professions. However, there are also significant overlaps between them, and there are contexts where holding on to the split that holds the two professions apart is unnecessary and artificial and in which a judicious drawing together again of some of the coinciding aspects of both professions would be beneficial. One of those contexts is the mainstream drama classroom.

The drama that forms the basis of this book was conducted in a state-funded mainstream school located somewhere in the British Isles, in one of the three Crown Dependencies. As a Crown Dependency, the community where the school is located enjoys semi-independence from UK policy. At the same time, the community is subject to the gravitational weight of policy that is implemented in England and Wales. The community is also subject to the same global ideological and market trends as are felt in the UK and beyond. Straddling the three loci of local, national, and global pressures, and feeling the impact locally of national and global demands and influences, these communities are ideal contexts from which to explore the effects of those competing influences and pressures on, for example, educational policy and outcome. Furthermore, if the community that hosted the work on which this book is based provides a microcosm of national and global processes, then within that, the world of the drama classroom provides a further microcosm that contains and reflects a version of those same pressures.

In the following sections of this chapter, I explore the performative and relational basis of identity and build on the premise introduced above that exploratory drama facilitates individual and group exploration of social, ethical, and moral conundrums, and that this constitutes identity-work, but that this kind of drama has been side-lined within current educational policy. I explore the idea that neoliberal discourses and technologies of governance change the performative expectations of individuals and groups and therefore the basis of relationality. Throughout the book, the identities of the school and of the young people with whom I worked have been anonymised.

Identities Are Performatively and Relationally Constituted

From an embodied psychosocial relational perspective, which is the perspective adopted in this book (see Chapter 3), identities develop over time in embodied psychosocial relationship with others, including primary carers. We learn who we are by experiencing ourselves being witnessed by others (Bowlby, 1988; Klein, 1932; Lacan, 2004; Mitchell, 2014; Shelton, 2019). This 'being witnessed' creates a 'relational encounter' (Mayor & Frydman, 2021, p.73). In an ongoing process, relational encounters determine the ways we present ourselves to the world by defining our beliefs about ourselves, about who we are, and about what we mean to those around us. Our identities are repeatedly contextually re-negotiated, and re-performed, including through social and discourse contexts (Craib, 1992; Elliott & Lemert, 2009). We internalise the feedback we experience in the world and act into and out of roles made available by psychosocial relational contexts, in a relational and embodied performative process. For some people, some of the time, those roles offer privilege. For others, often, those roles are less emancipating. In all cases, those roles are collectively and contextually emergent. This perspective implies that identity is not an individual concern and offers an alternative to essentialist anti-relational models of identity.

Identities Are Influenced by Prevailing Neoliberal Discourses

Neoliberalism is an expression of the advanced global capitalism that frames the modern world (Ball, 2003, 2016; Burman, 2012; Hess, 2015). Discourses associated with neoliberalism are pervasive to the extent that they change the performative expectations of groups and individuals, which in turn changes the nature of the performativity and relationality that underpins identity (Hess, 2015). For example, neoliberal discourses appropriate and commodify natural identity-forming processes (Burman, 2008; Gandesha, 2020; Teo, 2018) in that they lead to increasing internalised concern with outcomes and impression management (Ball, 2003). In effect, as explained further in Chapter 2, as the model of advanced capitalism is applied to multiplying aspects of our lives, our discursive contexts become steeped in neoliberal assumptions and technologies, including: managerialism; self-marketing; the commodification and dehumanising of relationships; the re-alignment of our public persona to fall in line with or accommodate workplace policy rhetoric (Ball, 2003); the internalisation of that rhetoric, or the alternatives of resistance and splitting (Baker & Kelan, 2019); the polarising of identity into increasingly fragmented reference groups (Hunter, 2015); increased concern with secondary tasks to do with being seen to fulfil externally imposed and superficial outcome-measures at the expense of fulfilling the primary tasks that the outcome-measures were intended to ensure (Stronach & Clarke, 2011); and the impact of globalisation, including the impact of social media and its 'memes' (Hess, 2015, p. 326). Owing more to the binary of Taylorism and associated technologies of audit (see Chapter 2) than to Human Relations (Fournier, 2017), the combined result of the internalising of and being steeped in a neoliberal world-view is that neoliberalism impacts the relational processes by which people's identities are formed (Archer, 2008; Ball, 2003, 2008, 2012, 2013, 2016; Butler, 2000, 2006, 2011, 2015; Elliott & Lemert, 2009; Elliott & Urry, 2010).

With That in Mind

Using an embodied psychosocial relational conceptualisation of identity, this book explores the processes that underpin the development of students' 'identity-work' as they engage with classroom drama in a context where I endeavour to hold in balance the embodied-performative and the developmental aspects of the work. By embodied psychosocial relational identity, I mean a conceptualisation whereby it is understood that identity arises through embodied, emotionally, socially, economically, culturally, and politically contextualised negotiated dialogue and witnessing (Barad, 2007; Haraway, 1997). It implies a concern with the ways individuals negotiate identity positions within groups, in relationship to others.

The book considers the relational and performative drama-processes involved when school-aged students engage in identity-work in the context of dramatherapeutically informed classroom drama (see Chapters 5, 6, and 7). It explores the processes involved when students take the opportunity, in relational negotiation with their peers, to subtly re-position their identities relative to dominant neoliberal discourses and market 'memes'. By memes, I mean free-floating metaphors that have become disconnected from their paradigmatic roots. They influence people, but the disconnect limits people's ability to critically reflect on them (Hess, 2015). This book considers what processes occur when, in the classroom rehearsal space, students encounter situations of 'discrepant communication' (Sajnani, 2012, p.17), i.e., when they encounter differences between the discourses that underpin their world-views and those encountered in the group-created fiction (Yacobi, 1987). Those moments help them to discover alternative aspects of self and new relational possibilities. It considers the classroom environment and inter/intra student dynamics, and how the classroom environment relates to the wider socio-political and economic context, as dominated by the performative demands of neoliberalism. It considers ways in which competing demands made on my own identity-performance at work influence the choices I make in the classroom, and the effects that those choices have on student identity-work. Identity-work is inevitably undertaken in an embodied (Haraway & Wolfe, 2016) psychosocial relational context (Hunter, 2008, 2015) where relationality is the vector through which cultural-social (Archer, 2008) and political-economic factors (Allen & Mendick, 2013; Lanskey, 2015) come together to frame the negotiated parameters of what is possible.

However, by suggesting a drawing together in the drama classroom of some of the coinciding aspects of both professions, I am not advocating a simple turning back of the educational and dramatherapeutic clock. That would be impossible anyway because everything, including teaching practice, is articulated in response to context, which is now changed. For example, in the early days of Heathcotian educational drama, neoliberalism had not yet influenced educational policy to its current extent, and the world of dramatherapy had not yet benefitted from some of the more recent research and thinking which has taken the initial work of, for example, Jones's theorising on the dramatherapeutic core processes (Jones, 1991, 1996a, 1996b, 1996c, 2008), and Lahad's exploration of storying (Lahad, 1992, 2017; Lahad & Dent Brown, 2012; Lahad, Shacham, & Ayalon, 2013; Lahad, Shacham, & Niv, 2000), and developed and deepened it, and begun to lay bare our understandings of the processes by which drama effects change in people (for example, Mayor & Frydman, 2021; Pendzik, 2013). It is apparent that the way is forward, and that just as I can jointly enact rather than polarise my own identities as, for example, both Japanese and white-English, and as both drama teacher and dramatherapist, so too can the positive aspects of the past and the present-future be jointly enacted. In this way, the developmental aspects of education and dramatherapy that are currently out of fashion in the classroom but which were embedded in the genesis of both professions could be woven into a strand of dramatherapeutically informed drama education by judiciously combining them with current classroom drama and dramatherapy practice. The result-in-practice of an in-classroom weaving together of those skills and knowledges would be a classroom environment that allows students to develop skills that would equip them to navigate and resist the more dehumanising aspects of the neoliberal context.

My overall orientation is embodied, psychosocial, and relational. As both drama practitioner and teacher, I spend my professional life immersed in the students' group-negotiated, physically embodied imaginative worlds and their multiple contextualised meanings. Informed by a dramatherapy sensibility, I am interested not only in the content of the students' drama and the skills and drama conventions students use to realise their ideas but also in the ways they relate to their drama and to each other in the context of their drama, and how those relational positionings are reflective of their contextualised identities and the discourses that organise them, including ethical positionings (Jones, 2008; Lahad, 2017; Lahad et al., 2013; Landy, 1993). Although I work to remain aware of the content of the discourses that impact and organise the identity-performances and relational positionings of the students, the focus of this book is not an exploration of the content of student discourses per se. The contents of the discourses are relevant in so far as they help to shed light on the currently prevailing 'memes' with which students might identify and that influence the positionings of the students as they engage in the drama-process. However, the focus of this book is an exploration of the embodied psychosocial relational processes that facilitate the shifts in discourses, and shifts in alignment to discourses, that inform, consciously or unconsciously, student identity-performances, and that, potentially, facilitate shifts in the nuance and inflection of student identity-performance. I am interested in how student identities are both performed through and performative of the relationally negotiated aesthetic aspects of their embodied drama work (Pendzik, 2013). Therefore, in the classroom, I value collaboration, negotiation, personhood, and choice (for example, Bondy, Ross, Gallingane, & Hambacher, 2007; Cheon, Reeve, & Vansteenkiste, 2020; Mihalas, Morse, Allsopp, & McHatton, 2009; Patall et al., 2018; Reeve & Jang, 2006; Sierens, Vansteenkiste, Goossens, Soenens, & Dochy, 2009; Teven & Hanson, 2004; Tsai, Kunter, LÜDtke, Trautwein, & Ryan, 2008; Vansteenkiste et al., 2012; Vansteenkiste, Simons, Lens, Sheldon, & Deci, 2004). Furthermore, it is my understanding that the kinds of development I am looking for in the classroom cannot be pre-determined and take time to evolve (Assor, Kaplan, & Roth, 2002). I work on the basis that there is emancipatory potential in the work I do (Freire, 2013) and that boundaries, including frameworks and ritual, provide security (Cothran, Kulinna, & Garrahy, 2003) and therefore I provide them for the students. I work responsibly and ethically within the school administrative and curriculum structures and policy framework.

Within current research, despite the shared beginnings and overlapping interests of dramatherapy and drama-teaching, there is scant research into what a true synthesis of the dramatherapeutic and the educational might look like, or what such a synthesis might be able to achieve, in the mainstream drama classroom. There is interest in using dramatherapy in schools but not usually in a mainstream context. There is interest in using a developmental model of drama-teaching in schools but usually not through the mainstream curriculum, and in addition, much of the research done in the context of education focuses on the extent of the efficacy of drama to effect change rather than on the processes by which that change is effected. This represents a gap in practice and research that this book addresses. Furthermore, it is my belief that it is not what students know and what skills they leave school with that will determine the ethical trajectory of their decision-making, including policy decision-making. Rather, that trajectory will be determined by the values and ethics to which the students hold allegiance. Although in the published statutory guidelines 2014 for schools in England the word democracy is entirely absent (GOV.UK, 2014), and likewise, the word democracy is missing from the headline aims of educational policies of the Crown Dependencies, as given at the opening of this chapter, the written aims of the curriculums of the Crown Dependencies do include an intention to prepare students to take an active part in the island's community as productive and fulfilled individuals. In line with this, the model of drama I offer in the classroom tends to the exploratory and the developmental and allows for identity-work and values exploration (Adams, 2013). This book highlights the importance of maintaining developmental drama rather than pseudo-vocational drama on the school curriculum despite pressure not to do so. It advocates for the need to move the focus of school drama away from easily measurable so-called marketable skills and towards the exploration of values and identities. It foregrounds the desirability of an approach to drama education that provides an alternative to the drama-as-commodity, performative, and mainly audience-oriented curriculum that is current practice. It notes the benefits inherent in a move away from curriculum design that uses as its Key Stage 3 (KS3) curriculum model the General Certificate of Secondary Education (GCSE) curriculum, where the over-riding justification for the KS3 curriculum is how well it fits students for work at Key Stage 4 (KS4). Finally, it discusses the potential benefits of a move away from a model where linear progression against pre-determined skills-outcomes is the primary goal.

This book explores a kind of drama that facilitates ethical exploration and identity-work and which equips students with greater role flexibility and is therefore fully relevant to all students. In addition, it explores the embodied psychosocial relational processes that underpin the efficacy of drama as a container and facilitator of that kind of identity-work. This work validates practitioners like myself who recognise the extended value of enabling students to engage in the relational crucible of role, performance, and story that is drama. Moreover, this work offers encouragement to persist with the ongoing struggle to straddle competing paradigms and to maintain a space of witnessing in the face of increasing pressure to focus on audience-oriented 'performative' work. It represents a call for schools to move away from a model of drama that has as its focus the teaching of pseudo-vocational knowledge and skills and to re-introduce and re-validate the developmental. This book is relevant to educational policy makers, curriculum developers, school leaders, teacher-trainers, drama teachers, dramatherapists, and anyone interested in understanding what the processes are that lead to educational, ethical, and developmental change.

Chapter Overview for the Rest of the Book

Chapter 2 locates the school and community where I worked in its local and global context, and in doing so, offers the reader the opportunity to consider the local and global context of their own situation. I define the terms neoliberalism and performativity as they have been conceptualised in this book and consider the influences of the school's built environment when the architecture itself de-values congregational spaces and prioritises 'flow'. The contested relationship that my community has with neoliberalism is explored, and I observe that my own resistance to encroaching managerialism takes the form of maintaining a concern with relationship, emancipation, dialogue, multiplicity, and democracy. The context of the book is a synthesis of marginality.

In Chapter 3, I explore what a fluid identity looks like in the context of neoliberalism and explain the concept of embodied psychosocial relational identity, which draws together the threads and influences of various theories of identity. Each influencing theory acknowledges that there is a balance or tension between internal and external influencing factors, and this results in identity being understood as an embodied (Strathern & Stewart, 2008), performative (Butler, 2015), relational (Haraway & Wolfe, 2016), contextual

(Hekman, 2014), multiplicity (Hunter, 2015). The chapter includes reference to the ways that identity arises relationally and the relevance of roles. It investigates the performative and embodied natures of identity and the relationship between performance on the one hand and critiques of neoliberal performativity on the other. It acknowledges that our lives are storied and can therefore be re-storied and explores our ability to make values-based ethical choices in places of moral uncertainty. The chapter explores the way that drama is made up of roles, performances, and stories and makes the argument that drama is a container for ethical negotiations. It links the component parts of drama which are role, performance, and story, to an embodied psychosocial relational understanding of identity. It also introduces the idea that identity is enacted relative to normative social discourses and explores some of the more powerful constituting discourses. I look at how enlightenment thinking still strongly influences the ways that gender is perceived today and at the ongoing legacy of psychodynamic theory, including attachment theory. There is consideration of the ways that the introduction of the concept of intersectionality effects how we think about marginalisation, and exploration of what is meant by psychosocial relationality, performativity, and embodiment, and how these concepts change how we think about identity.

In Chapter 4, I look at how it is possible to bridge the theory/practice divide to see not only what is going on inside the classroom but how it is going on and offer a brief background to the research element of this book. I take the perspective of exploring contestation and address the question of how we make meaning. I look at the pedagogic landscape and note the mismatch between policy and practice that needs resolving in the classroom. I note the fact/fiction boundary that must be straddled in the drama classroom, where all meanings are contestable as students negotiate the meaning of their work as they go. I suggest that practitioner enquiry is a methodology that is flexible enough to make a coherence of this level of contestation, and that it is appropriate for use in schools because it follows the cyclical and iterative 'plan, do, review' format that is often used in teaching. I take a look at the data strands that were used in the development of the thinking that underpins the writing of this book and give a description of the work that the young people and I did together. I note that sitting at the centre of all the drama that the young people did was a negotiated ethical exploration. This chapter is of relevance to everyone who works with groups of people whether in a classroom or in another group-oriented context, and who is trying to make sense of what they are seeing and experiencing.

Chapter 5 explores seven key group-drama-processes and foregrounds the embodiment, the psychosocial, and the relational aspects of identity negotiation. I introduce the four-part structure as a framework that can be used to make those processes visible. Chapter 6 considers the individual student journey through the development of and engagement with functional-, fictional-, and relational-roles. This chapter looks in depth at the embodied psychosocial relational processes that effect change for two young people: Peter First and Kelly

Burk (pseudonyms). In Chapter 7, I consider the role the teacher's choices make as part of the identity-work being negotiated in the classroom. I identify four teacher use-of-self dimensions and four drama-processes that have an impact on the identity-work of the young people and consider those processes in the context of current policy and managerial practice.

Chapter 8 concludes. This chapter summarises what the change-processes are and looks at how the practices and contexts that facilitate those change-processes can be created and maintained. I point out that student participation in drama and student identity expression hinges on the dynamic of their embodiment and their psychosocial relationships, which are inflected by the classroom environment, contained by the drama, and mediated by the drama-processes. In other words, identity-work is done in the relational spaces that are created by the drama. This chapter also looks to the future and considers where resistance to the outcome-measures culture is happening and what that looks like.

Conclusion

As a class and as individuals, the student participants who created the drama work that fed into the thinking that underpins this book created a significant corpus of rich, interesting, and unique work. There would never be enough space in a book such as this to refer to all of it; therefore, I have tried to select illustrative material that best supported my crafted narrative. However, none of the students' work was of no consequence, and it all deserves acknowledgement. What I hope this book will offer is an insight into the processes by which working in and through the crucible of role, performance, and story, that is the drama medium, facilitates student identity-work. This book will be of interest to drama teachers who have found their developmental practice marginalised by education policy changes, and to dramatherapists who are interested in continuing to work in and through a non-clinical model of dramatherapy. It also has wider pedagogical implications and will be of interest to educationalists and teachers from a range of backgrounds and roles, including teacher-trainers. I also hope that in the current political context, this book will support the idea that there might be other, better, ways of providing a balanced, effective, and nurturing education not only to the children of the Crown Dependencies but to all children who live in a community where a managerialist culture is taking hold than the current policy of pursuing, exclusively, micro-managed outcomes.

References

Adams, J. (2013). The Artful Dodger: Creative resistance to neoliberalism in education. *Education, Review of Education, Pedagogy, and Cultural Studies, 35*(4), 242–255. doi:10.1080/10714413.2013.819726

Allen, K., & Mendick, H. (2013). Young people's uses of celebrity: Class, gender and 'improper' celebrity. *Discourse: Studies in the Cultural Politics of Education, 34*(1), 77–93. doi:10.1080/01596306.2012.698865
Archer, L. (2008). The new neoliberal subjects? Young/er academics' constructions of professional identity. *Journal of Education Policy, 22*(3), 265. doi:10.1080/02680930701754047
Assor, A., Kaplan, H., & Roth, G. (2002). Choice is good, but relevance is excellent: Autonomy-enhancing and suppressing teacher behaviours predicting students' engagement in schoolwork. *British Journal of Educational Psychology, 72*(2), 261. doi:10.1348/000709902158883
Baker, D. T., & Kelan, E. K. (2019). Splitting and blaming: The psychic life of neoliberal executive women. *Human Relations, 72*, 96–97. doi:10.1177/0018726718772010
Baldwin, P. (2007). *With drama in mind: Real learning in imagined worlds*. Great Britain: Network Continuum.
Ball, S. (2003). The teacher's soul and the terrors of performativity. *Journal of Education Policy, 18*(2), 215–228. doi:10.1080/0268093022000043065
Ball, S. (2008). Performativity, privatisation, professionals and the state. In B. Cunningham (Ed.), *Exploring professionalism* (pp. 50). London: The Institute of Education, University of London.
Ball, S. (2012). *Foucault, power, and education*. New York: Routledge Ltd.
Ball, S. (2013). *The education debate* (2nd ed.). Bristol, UK: The Policy Press.
Ball, S. (2016). Neoliberal education? Confronting the slouching beast. *Policy Futures in Education, 14*(8), 1046–1059. doi:10.1177/1478210316664259
Barad, K. M. (2007). *Meeting the universe halfway: Quantum physics and the entanglement of matter and meaning*. Durham: Duke University Press.
Beck, U., & Beck-Gernsheim, E. (2002). *Individualization: Institutionalized individualism and its social and political consequences* (Kindle ed.). London, Thousand Oaks, New Delhi: SAGE Publications.
Bondy, E., Ross, D. D., Gallingane, C., & Hambacher, E. (2007). Creating environments of success and resilience: Culturally responsive classroom management and more. *Urban Education, 42*(4), 326. doi:10.1177/0042085907303406
Bowlby, J. (1988). *A secure base: Clinical applications of attachment theory*. London: Routledge.
Burman, E. (2008). *Developments: Child, image, nation*. London and New York: Routledge.
Burman, E. (2012). Deconstructing neoliberal childhood: Towards a feminist antipsychological approach. *Childhood, 19*(4), 423–438. doi:10.1177/0907568211430767
Butler, J. (2000). *Antigone's claim: Kinship between life and death*. New York: Columbia University Press.
Butler, J. (2006). *Gender trouble* (1st ed.). New York and London: Routledge.
Butler, J. (2011). *Bodies that matter: On the discursive limits of sex*. Oxon and New York: Routledge Ltd.
Butler, J. (2015). *Notes towards a performative theory of assembly* (Kindle ed.). Cambridge: Harvard University Press.
Cheon, S. H., Reeve, J., & Vansteenkiste, M. (2020). When teachers learn how to provide classroom structure in an autonomy-supportive way: Benefits to teachers and their students. *Science Direct, 90*. doi:10.1016/j.tate.2019.103004

Cothran, D. J., Kulinna, P. H., & Garrahy, D. A. (2003). 'This is kind of giving a secret away…': Students' perspectives on effective class management. *Teaching and Teacher Education, 19*(4), 435. doi:10.1016/S0742-051X(03)00027-1

Craib, I. (1992). *Modern social theory from Parsons to Habermas* (2nd ed.). London and New York: Routledge Taylor and Francis Group.

Curran, T., & Hill, A. P. (2019). Perfectionism is increasing over time: A meta-analysis of birth cohort differences from 1989 to 2016. *Psychological Bulletin, 145*(4), 410–429. doi:10.1037/bul0000138

Davies, B., & Bansel, P. (2007). Neoliberalism and education. *International Journal of Qualitative Studies in Education (QSE), 20*(3), 247–259. doi:10.1080/09518390701281751

Edmiston, B., & Towler-Evans, I. (2022). *Humanizing education with dramatic inquiry: In dialogue with Dorothy Heathcote's transformative pedagogy.* New York and London: Routledge.

Elliott, A., & Lemert, C. (2009). *The new individualism: The emotional costs of globalization* (Revised ed.). New York and Oxon: Routledge.

Elliott, A., & Urry, J. (2010). *Mobile lives.* London and New York: Routledge.

Fournier, V. (2017). *Working in organisations* (2nd ed.). Milton Keynes: The Open University Business School.

Freire, P. (2013). *Education for critical consciousness.* London: Bloomsbury.

Gandesha, S. (2020). The neoliberal personality. *Logos: A Journal of Modern Society and Culture, Spring 2020.*Retrieved from https://logosjournal.com/article/the-neoliberal-personality/]

GOV.UK. (2014). National curriculum in England: Framework for key stages 1 to 4. Retrieved from www.gov.uk/government/publications/national-curriculum-in-england-framework-for-key-stages-1-to-4/the-national-curriculum-in-england-framework-for-key-stages-1-to-4

Haraway, D. (1997). *Modest_Witness@Second_Millennium. FemaleMan_Meets_OncoMouse: Feminism and technoscience.* New York and London: Routledge.

Haraway, D., & Wolfe, C. (2016). *Manifestly Haraway.* Minneapolis, MN: University of Minnesota Press.

Heathcote, D., & Herbert, P. (1985). A drama of learning: Mantle of the expert. *Theory Into Practice, 24*(3), 173–180. doi:10.1080/00405848509543169

Hekman, S. J. (2014). *The feminine subject.* Cambridge, UK: Polity.

Hess, K. (2015). Metaphors matter: Ethics and the memes of the market. *Georgetown Journal of Law and Public Policy, 13,* 321–336.

Holmwood, C. (2016). *Drama education and dramatherapy: Exploring the space between disciplines.* London: Routledge.

Hunter, S. (2008). Living documents: A feminist psychosocial approach to the relational politics of policy documentation. *Critical Social Policy, 28*(4), 506–528. doi:10.1177/0261018308095300

Hunter, S. (2015). *Power, politics and the emotions: Impossible governance?* London, UK: Taylor & Francis Group.

Isle of Man Government. (2006). The Manx curriculum. Retrieved from www.gov.im/media/186468/curriculumlearnachieveapr06_1_.pdf

Jennings, S. (Ed.) (1987). *Dramatherapy theory and practice for teachers and clinicians.* Kent: Routledge.

Jones, P. (1991). Dramatherapy: Five core processes. *Dramatherapy, 14*(1), 8–15. doi:10.1080/02630672.1991.9689804

Jones, P. (1996a). The active witness: The acquisition of meaning in dramatherapy. In H. Payne (Ed.), *Handbook of inquiry in the arts therapies: One river many currents* (pp. 41–55). London: Jessica Kingsley.
Jones, P. (1996b). *Drama as therapy volume 1: Theory, practice and research* (2nd ed.). London and New York: Routledge.
Jones, P. (1996c). *Drama as therapy: Theatre as living.* London and New York: Routledge.
Jones, P. (2008). Audience and witnessing: Research into dramatherapy using vignettes and aMSN messenger. *Research in Drama Education: The Journal of Applied Theatre and Performance, 13*(1), 39–53. doi:10.1080/13569780701825252
Klein, M. (1932). *The psycho-analysis of children* (A. Strachey, Trans.). London: Random House Vintage.
Lacan, J. (2004). *The four fundamental concepts of psycho-analysis* (A. Sheridan, Trans. J.-A. Miller Ed. Karnac Books Ltd. ed.). London and New York: Routledge.
Lahad, M. (1992). Story-making in assessment method for coping with stress: Six piece story making and BASIC-Ph. In S. Jennings (Ed.), *Dramatherapy theory and practice 2* (pp. 150–163). London: Routledge.
Lahad, M. (2017). From victim to victor: The development of the BASIC PH model of coping and resiliency. *Traumatology, 23*(1), 27–34. doi:10.1037/trm0000105
Lahad, M., & Dent Brown, K. (2012). Six-piece story-making revisited: The seven levels of assessment and the clinical assessment. In D. Johnson, S. Pendzik, & S. Snow (Eds.), *Assessment in drama therapy* (1st ed., Vol. January 2012, pp. 121–147). Springfield Illinois: Charles C Thomas.
Lahad, M., Shacham, M., & Ayalon, O. (Eds.). (2013). *The 'BASIC PH' model of coping and resiliency: Theory, research and cross-cultural application.* London and Philadelphia: Jessica Kingsley.
Lahad, M., Shacham, Y., & Niv, S. (2000). Coping and community resources in children facing disaster. In A. Y. Shalev, R. Yehuda, & A. C. McFarlane (Eds.), *International handbook of human response to trauma* (pp. 389–395). Boston, MA: Springer US.
Landy, R. (1993). *Persona and performance: The meaning of role in drama, therapy, and everyday life.* New York, London: Guildford Press.
Lanskey, C. (2015). Up or down and out? A systemic analysis of young people's educational pathways in the youth justice system in England and Wales. *International Journal of Inclusive Education, 19*(6), 568–582. doi:10.1080/13603116.2014.961675
Mayor, C., & Frydman, J. S. (2021). Understanding school-based drama therapy through the core processes: An analysis of intervention vignettes. *The Arts in Psychotherapy, 73.* doi:10.1016/j.aip.2021.101766
Mihalas, S., Morse, W. C., Allsopp, D. H., & McHatton, P. (2009). Cultivating caring relationships between teachers and secondary students with emotional and behavioral disorders: Implications for research and practice. *Remedial and Special Education, 30*(2), 108–125. doi:10.1177/0741932508315950
Mitchell, S. A. (2014). *Relationality: From attachment to intersubjectivity* (Kindle ed. Vol. 20). New York and London: Psychology Press.
Moos, L. (2017). Neo-liberal governance leads education and educational leadership astray. In M. Uljens & R. M. Ylimaki (Eds.), *Bridging educational leadership, curriculum theory and didaktik, educational governance research 5* (Kindle ed., Vol. 5, pp. 4425–5252). Switzerland: Springer Open.
Morales, J. B., & Abegglen, S. (Eds.). (2020). *Understanding education and economics: Key debates and critical perspectives.* London and New York: Routledge.

Patall, E. A., Steingut, R. R., Vasquez, A. C., Trimble, S. S., Pituch, K. A., & Freeman, J. L. (2018). Daily autonomy supporting or thwarting and students' motivation and engagement in the high school science classroom. *Journal of Educational Psychology, 110*(2), 269–288. doi:10.1037/edu0000214

Pendzik, S. (2013). The 6-key model and the assessment of the aesthetic dimension in dramatherapy. *Dramatherapy, 35*(2), 90–98. doi:10.1080/02630672.2013.822524

Priestly, M. (2017). '...two decades of neoliberal policy have generated a cupboard-full of troubles' (Ryan, 2012, p.23). *The STeP Journal: Student Teacher Perspectives 4*(3), 42–49.

Reeve, J., & Jang, H. (2006). What teachers say and do to support students' autonomy during a learning activity. *Journal of Educational Psychology, 98*(1), 209–218. doi:10.1037/0022-0663.98.1.209

Sajnani, N. (2012). The implicated witness: Towards a relational aesthetic in dramatherapy. *Dramatherapy, 34*(March 2012), 6–21. doi:10.1080/02630672.2012.657944

Shelton, L. G. (2019). *The Bronfenbrenner primer: A guide to develecology.* London: Routledge.

Shore, C., & Wright, S. (1999). Audit culture and anthropology: Neo liberalism in British higher education. *The Journal of the Royal Anthropological Institute, 5*, 557–575. doi:10.2307/2661148

Sierens, E., Vansteenkiste, M., Goossens, L., Soenens, B., & Dochy, F. (2009). The synergistic relationship of perceived autonomy support and structure in the prediction of self-regulated learning. *British Journal of Educational Psychology, 79*, 57–68. doi:10.1348/000709908X304398

States of Guernsey. (2020). Education Law Consultation Launched. Retrieved from www.gov.gg/article/176285/Education-Law-Consultation-Launched

States of Guernsey. (2023). Attainment 8. Retrieved from www.gov.gg/attainment8

States of Jersey. (2023a). GCSE and equivalent results in Jersey. Retrieved from www.gov.je/SiteCollectionDocuments/Education/R%20GCSEReport2018-2019%2020200714%20EI.pdf

States of Jersey. (2023b). The Jersey Curriculum. Retrieved from www.gov.je/SiteCollectionDocuments/Education/ID%20Jersey%20Curriculum%20Foreword%2020160531%20PH.pdf

Strathern, A., & Stewart, P. (2008). Embodiment theory in performance and performativity. *Journal of Ritual Studies, 22*(1), 67–71.

Stronach, I., & Clarke, J. (2011). Eight contentions for an educational future: Timely rules for unruly times. *Qualitative Inquiry, 17*(10), 986–996. doi:10.1177/1077800411425155

Teo, T. (2018). Homo neoliberalus: From personality to forms of subjectivity. *Theory and Psychology, 28.* doi:10.1177/0959354318794899

Teven, J. J., & Hanson, T. L. (2004). The impact of teacher immediacy and perceived caring on teacher competence and trustworthiness. *Communication Quarterly, 52*(1), 39–53. doi:10.1080/01463370409370177

Tsai, Y.-M., Kunter, M., LÜDtke, O., Trautwein, U., & Ryan, R. M. (2008). What makes lessons interesting? The role of situational and individual factors in three school subjects. *Journal of Educational Psychology, 100*(2), 460–472. doi:10.1037/0022-0663.100.2.460

Uljens, M., & Ylimaki, R. M. (Eds.). (2017). *Bridging educational leadership, curriculum theory and didaktik: Non-affirmative theory of education* (1 ed. Vol. 5). Cham: Springer International Publishing.

Vansteenkiste, M., Sierens, E., Goossens, L., Soenens, B., Dochy, F., Mouratidis, A., ... Beyers, W. (2012). Identifying configurations of perceived teacher autonomy support and structure: Associations with self-regulated learning, motivation and problem behavior. *Learning and Instruction, 22*(6), 431–439. doi:10.1016/j.learninstruc.2012.04.002

Vansteenkiste, M., Simons, J., Lens, W., Sheldon, K. M., & Deci, E. L. (2004). Motivating learning, performance, and persistence: The synergistic effects of intrinsic goal contents and autonomy-supportive contexts. *Journal of Personality and Social Psychology, 87*(2), 246–260. doi:10.1037/0022-3514.87.2.246

Yacobi, T. (1987). Narrative structure and fictional mediation. *Poetics Today, 8*(2), 335–372. doi:10.2307/1773041

2 Resisting the Neoliberal Binary

The aim of this chapter is to locate the project in its global and local context in terms of the situatedness of the jurisdiction in which I work, with reference to the implementation of increasingly neoliberal modes of governance. In doing so, I invite you to consider the local and global context of your own situation. In the first section of the chapter, I explore the key terms neoliberal and performativity, consider the impacts on and impacts of the school build, explore the relationships that education policy in the Crown Dependencies has with UK educational policy, and address the relationship between the local educational context and tensions arising from the implementing of and resistance to neoliberal policy. Although there are many ways of thinking about neoliberalism, I suggest that one effect of neoliberal policy is that it changes the nature of our relationships with the institution, with teaching, with ourselves, and with students (Davies & Bansel, 2007). For example, in the drama-teaching context, neoliberal policy de-values the relational and developmental aspects of curriculum-drama by imposing superficial target-based assessments (Shore & Wright, 1999). I suggest that in the jurisdiction in which I work, in education, the restructuring technologies associated with neoliberalist modes of governance (Harvey, 2007) have been as much resisted as embraced, and that this has provided an opportunity to reaffirm drama as a developmental, exploratory, creative, and embodied subject. In the second section of the chapter, I explain why a dramatherapeutic approach to the teaching of drama has the potential to equip students to resist neoliberal *value*-thinking and facilitate ethical and *values* exploration, to help students develop enhanced role flexibility, and to equip students to navigate the performativity demanded by neoliberal structures (Edmiston & Towler-Evans, 2022). I further suggest that a dramatherapeutically informed drama curriculum has the potential to focus student experience on meaning-making, ethical exploration, and the development of values and identity. I explain what is meant by 'drama' and 'theatre' and say how they are related but not interchangeable terms and demonstrate that, throughout its history, theatre has facilitated the didactic *and* the developmental. I conclude by suggesting

DOI: 10.4324/9781003464532-2

that students would benefit from more frequent opportunities to engage in values-exploration, to develop their own sets of ethics in critical relationship to prevailing discourses, and to develop greater role flexibility that will help them to cope with the demands of increasing performativity in systems where a concern with values has been replaced by a concern with commodified value.

The Natures of Neoliberalism and Performativity: Neoliberalism

Ideologically, neoliberalism, which can be understood as being a model of economic and social governance (Dunn, 2017) has become so pervasive that it has been referred to as the 'neoliberal world order' (Burman, 2008, p. 5). Also conceptualised as 'the application of the economic grid to social phenomena' (Foucault, 2008, p. 240), it has been observed that as a model of economic competitiveness, neoliberalism prioritises the conferring of economic health on the corporate entity over the avoidance of deleterious effects on people or the environment (Harvey, 2007), effectively creating a binary between economy and culture (Kaplan, 2020). Further binaries arise via the ideological assumption that competitive free marketisation is good, and anything that is not subject to competitive market forces is wasteful, outmoded, woefully inefficient, and in need of restructuring (Davies & Bansel, 2007). At the heart of neoliberalism is the separation of public life which is assumed to be economically productive and private life which is assumed to be economically unproductive, and the preferential positioning of the entrepreneurial individual above what might be considered the collective or common good (Hekman, 2014). Neoliberalism has been conceptualised as everything from an economic route to egalitarian prosperity and individual freedoms to a deliberate strengthening of class divide and consolidation of power and control within a capital elite (Harvey, 2007). In economic real terms, neoliberal policy has led to a profound polarisation between the richest and the poorest on global, national, and local levels (Barkin, 2000). In other words, neoliberalism is associated with a constellation of institutionally and personally restructuring technologies of governance.

As a mode of governance, neoliberalism is a way of organising society whereby the primacy of free market forces is promoted by governmental intervention (Foucault, 2008). Neoliberal monetary policies, worked out globally and nationally by the enforced deregulation of protected markets and re-regulation of those same markets, ensure international access to asset ownership. These structural changes are justified in the name of freedom, although what that freedom entails is contested (Harvey, 2007). Ways of managing business, and words and concepts such as efficiency, productivity, audit, and outcomes, that arose in the business context are imposed on increasingly diverse areas of the social fabric, including areas that have traditionally been held as separate from the marketplace, such as health care.

In this context, even the classroom has been marketised (Hall, 2019). As more areas of society are reconceptualised in terms of private enterprise, the administrative and procedural technologies associated with finance and manufacturing are applied to them. This includes the adoption of technologies of audit, accountability, and surveillance (Shore & Wright, 1999) that owe more to Taylorism than to human relations (Knafo, Dutta, Lane, & Wyn-Jones, 2019; Moore & Robinson, 2016). This reflects a binary where from the neoliberal perspective the only acceptable model is the model of market-oriented productivity. This is a model into which people must fit like the components of a machine. In the name of freedom – by which is meant the freedom of the market – there can be only one, pre-determined, standardised, industry regulated, and easily audited way of approaching and completing any given task.

The Natures of Neoliberalism and Performativity: Performativity

The effects of this are profound. Working on the level of rhetoric as well as through economic policy and practice, those who advocate for or who speak through the discourses of neoliberal modes of governance justify the generalisation of economic policy and practice to multiplying areas of life in terms of individual freedom and economic prosperity. In this discourse environment, people performatively externalise the values of the marketplace via various embodied forms, for example through the architecture of the day (Spencer, 2016). There is increased concern with performativity which is a state of being where, because of the internalisation of prevailing discourses (Uljens & Ylimaki, 2017), individual worth becomes dependent on a self-motivated ability to perform to externally validated outcome-measures to which personal or what might be termed traditional professional values have no relevance (Ball, 2003). One effect of this is that people work harder to sustain what they perceive to be the correct image through, for example, maintaining an audit trail of good practice, at the expense of the good practice itself. There is concern with self-marketing, self-image, and self-promotion leading to increased commodification of relationships and the legitimising of using other people as a means to an end rather than seeing them as an end in themselves (Smolovic-Jones, 2017). Furthermore, because only what is measurable can exist in a performative audit culture, for people to exist, they must be measurable. To be measurable, they must be pre-recognised, for example by being identified as a member of an officially sanctioned group. If no appropriate group is available, the choices are to remain invisible or to create one. This second option results in the multiplication of ever more specific interest groups. In each case, in terms of identity, individuals are either part of an auditable group that is placed in constitutive relationship to other groups, or they are invisible and their concerns and contributions are not measured and therefore not recognised and not addressed (Hunter, 2015).

Incompatible and Competing Legislative Policy and Educational Paradigms

In education, this has worked out in the following ways: through increased managerialism; through increased top-down management; through the extension of governance to increasingly lower administrative levels so that staff, experiencing themselves as being under constant surveillance, function as if in a 'panopticon' of self-regulation (Bentham, 1791; Foucault, 1975); through the commodification of relationships and the demise of collegiality; through a concern with the extrinsic at the expense of the intrinsic benefits of education; through working to externally imposed outcome-measures at all levels resulting in the de-valuing of developmental self-actualisation in favour of easily measurable but superficial outcomes (Ball, 2008; Moos, 2017; Morales & Abegglen, 2020); through new school builds that embody in their design the ideology of value-as-commodification, for example by prioritising flow over the creation of congregational spaces (Wood, 2018); through the erosion of space in the curriculum for relationality and multiplicity despite the rhetoric of inclusion; and through carte blanch imposition by school leadership of undifferentiated, standardised, and inappropriate working and assessment practices in the interests of an easy audit (Shore & Wright, 1999). I explore the ways neoliberal technologies of governance have worked out in my school context below. The position I take, which is to offer students dramatherapeutically sensitised developmental drama, draws parallels with what is emerging globally as effective resistance (after Foucault, Deacon, 1998) to the binary performativities of neoliberal restructuring. That is, a concern with relationality, emancipation, dialogy, multiplicity, and democracy (Barkin, 2000) and a heteroglossic approach that brings multiple aspects of identity, which have themselves been contextually and relationally co-constructed, into relational dialogue (Kaplan, 2020).

The School's Built Environment

Recent research and thinking has gone some way to demonstrating the profound effects that physical spaces have on individual and group functioning (Sweeney, 2024). As an example of this, in the case of the school build in which I worked, the influence of neoliberal thinking was profoundly expressed through the school's architecture. As you read, I invite you to take the opportunity to consider what the effects are on your thinking, practice, and relationships of the built environment of your own context.

Architecture can be a concrete expression of prevailing social values, *embodying* within its structures the values and ideals that inform its designers and being a physical template or vector for those values (Spencer, 2016). The school in which I teach is a new build and, designed by architects from England, it inflects a commodified version of education to the extent that 'it deletes the very people it attempts to project forward' (Wood, 2018, p. 141).

It is a long thin building designed so that a member of staff could stand at one end of a parametrically undulating (Schumacher, 2008; Spencer, 2016) main corridor and enjoy an unobstructed panopticon view down its full length. For the staff, the staffroom is placed *in*conveniently out of the way and discourages informal congregating. There are small departmentally-based offices located near departmental teaching classrooms, but they are limited workspaces not large enough for informal socialising or formal department meetings. The building itself does not encourage the formation of collegiate relationships and supports instead the development of commodified or mercantile links between staff who now mainly only interact as a body to 'exchange information' (Ball, 2008, p. 53). There are no student socialising areas, and if students are to sit, they must sit on the floor in the deterritorialised (Spencer, 2016) stair wells. The building does not facilitate the development of congregationality and encourages 'flow' (Schumacher, 2008).

The building was designed with no teaching space for drama and no drama department office. I do my administration in a cleaner's cupboard furnished with a table and inadequate lighting. Drama-teaching takes place in the warehouse space at the back of a hall under lighting that the law deems legal for warehousing, but which is inadequate for teaching. The space is separated tangentially from the main body of the school and as few people find a need to speak to me in person, and the staff room is a long distance away, I have found it hard to create and maintain personal links with the staff who are working in the rest of the school. All this has had an impact on the ways I see myself and others, the ways other staff see Drama, and the ways students relate to the subject area. For example, in a reflection of trends in the UK where it has been demonstrated that the East-Asian population is the 'visible ethnic-minority' group (Javier, 2016, p. 227) most likely to be targeted for racially motivated abuse (Cole et al., 2009; Office for National Statistics, 2020), some young people at the school have capitalised on the isolated location of the drama room and have, on a repeating basis, used it as an opportunity to engage and express racist discourses aimed at myself as a mixed-race visibly East-Asian teacher. The school is a new build and was part of the jurisdiction's most recent round of local school development. It was designed by educational architectural consultants based in the UK, and it presumably embodied within its structure the values and ideals that informed its designers.

Resistance Is Not Futile

Nevertheless, resistance is not futile. The Crown Dependencies have had, and continue to have, a convoluted relationship with neoliberalism. At some times, some aspects of neoliberal culture have been embraced by parts of the community. At other times, aspects of neoliberal culture have been resisted. As you read, I invite you to consider what aspects of neoliberal culture are embraced, and what is resisted, in your own context.

The Crown Dependencies, well known for being centres of finance and for being among some of the world's most aggressive marketers of hedge funds (Belchem, 2001; Ogier & Chan, 2020; Oliver, 2019), are independent jurisdictions, and historically, the relationship between government, church or parish, commerce, individual benefactor, and the influence of the outside world on education has been worked out in specific ways. For example, within education policy, the Crown Dependencies have followed their own developmental trajectories albeit in relational tension to policy developments happening on the UK mainland (Crossan, 2016; Kelly, Azaola, & Schilz, n.d.). For instance, in 1872, the Isle of Man enacted an education policy that made education compulsory for all children aged 7–13. This made the Manx educational ambition more comprehensive than that of England where in line with the English Elementary Education Act of 1870, school attendance was still 'voluntary' (Little, 2022). Guernsey did not offer separate island-wide infant and secondary schooling until 1959. Furthermore, on Guernsey in the 1970s, full employment of school leavers meant that the school leaving age did not need to rise as it did in the UK, and on the Isle of Man, the school leaving age was not raised to 16 until 1986 which was a full 15 years after schooling to 16 was implemented in England.

Neither Guernsey, Jersey, nor the Isle of Man adopted the National Curriculum for England and Wales at the time of its implementation in primary schools in England and Wales in 1989. Rather, each jurisdiction developed its own bespoke curriculum. For example, in what was effectively an act of strong resistance to the imposition of neoliberal structures via the operationalisation of learning that has been prevalent in the UK since the 1970s, in 2012, Guernsey elected to move away completely from the UK National Curriculum and develop its own island curriculum which was implemented in 2016 under the title 'The Big Picture' and which had the tag line 'Promoting joyous and purposeful learning' (States of Guernsey Education Service, 2017, pp. 1–2). Likewise, the Isle of Man chose to develop their own curriculum titled 'Freedom to Flourish' which also foregrounds the whole child (Ynsee, 2006). In each case, the contexts in which their curriculums are embedded reflect aspects of educational policy in the UK; at the same time, they resist some of the values imposed by the English system. For example, whereas in England and Wales a system of league tables has given rise to a culture of inter-school competitiveness, on the Isle of Man, the necessity of school league tables has been contested (gov.im, 2017).

Nevertheless, the move from centralised control to a devolved restructuring, and neoliberal 're-regulation' of control (Ball, 2003, p. 217) that has in England been part of education since the 1970s, and at the heart of education there since the 1988 Education Act (Morales & Abegglen, 2020), has had its inevitable influence on the educational landscape. In the jurisdiction where I teach, there is as yet no exogenous privatisation of schools (Ball, 2008) apart from the use of external contractors for such as builds, additional contract cleaning, and the very limited school catering, what Ball refers to as endogenous privatisation and the 'terror of performativity' (Ball, 2003, p. 216), and what Stronach and Clarke refer to as 'paracapitalist mimicry' (Stronach & Clarke, 2011, p. 989), is becoming ever more embedded. For example, the head-teacher for whom I worked, who was also employed as an inspector for the Office for Standards in Education (OFSTED), embraced a regime of reporting 'student progress' based on target setting, with the expectation that students would make unerring, constant, and linear progression in the direction of up, and the evidence of this was published to students five times each academic year on colour-coded reports. Students were expected to gain one National Curriculum 'subgrade' every term in every subject, and no matter that they had a single lesson in any given subject once a week, or a lesson 5 times a week, the expectation was the same. Accountability and the pressure to meet externally applied targets was made public and the colour of failure was red. The head-teacher's appointments included a deputy head from England who insisted that marking and progression across school including in drama be tied to specific pre-determined criteria, and each year at results time, the staff endured a meeting where each department's examination results were publicly compared. Data crunching software such as Service for Improved Schools' Results Analysis (SISRA) (SISRA Analytics, 2021) which only accepts and gives numerical data was introduced, and its metrics were applied to staff and students. As Ball, and as Shore and Wright point out, to make like-for-like comparisons (Ball, 2008), performativity must make value of what is measurable (Shore & Wright, 1999). However, as Priestly (2017) points out, in responding, for example, to a literary text (and by extension, I suggest that this also applies to dramatic text both written and enacted), 'the individual undergoes a process of self-actualisation' (Culler, 2011, quoted in Priestly, 2017, p.45) and this cannot be measured or standardised. And if a subject such as drama is valued only in terms that can be quantified, then 'by treating literary [or dramatic] education according to this lower means of valuation, neoliberal policy corrupts the purpose of education, the purpose of literature [or dramaturgy] and by extension human selfhood, identity and existence' (Hart, 1978, in Priestly, 2017, p.45). In effect, the emphasis on 'reliable assessment' measured by often 'industry advocated' (Autio, 2017, loc.7385) testing programmes based on psychological learning theories (Uljens & Ylimaki, 2017), eclipses the validity of what is being measured (Davies, 2001, in Priestly, 2017).

Furthermore, the undermining of an approach that has as its goal the self-actualisation of the students, by the imposition of pre-determined outcome-measures based on the assumption that a market-style value-added is the only kind of value worth pursuing (Ball, 2003), changes what it means to be a teacher and necessitates a new and different relationship to the process of teaching, bringing with it a new teacher identity (Davies & Bansel, 2007). Rather than the first-order activity of teaching children, it is second-order activities such as performance management and monitoring that take the greater proportion of teacher attention, and the whole teaching experience ends up defined as a response to targets, benchmarks, indicators, and evaluations (Ball, 2016; Stronach & Clarke, 2011). Ultimately, the process of auditing and performativity turns people into self-governing subjects (Moore & Robinson, 2016) who know *how* they are teaching but not *why* they are teaching (Adams, 2011; Pinar, 2018). I suggest that in the case of Drama, we also seem to have lost sight of *what* we are teaching.

It is important to recognise that corporate culture can provide individuals with new opportunities and can be 'one of satisfaction and rewards, at least for some' (Ball, 2008, p. 51). However, the irony is that in the interests of transparency, using a culture of target-setting to define the workplace agenda, and to find out how people and the institution are performing, the reality becomes increasingly obscured (Shore & Wright, 1999). As Ball says: 'performativity produces opacity rather than transparency as individuals and organisations take ever greater care in the construction and maintenance of fabrications' (2003, p. 215). Ethics begins to take on a different meaning as the ways we represent ourselves is informed by the prevailing policy context, and effectiveness and impression management replace truthfulness as prevailing virtues (Ball, 2003). Through a process of the 'exteriorisation' of knowledge (Lyotard, 1986, p. 4), performativity changes what counts as real teaching and real learning (Stronach & Clarke, 2011). In fact,

> the first order effect of performativity is to reorient pedagogical and scholarly activities towards those which are likely to have a positive impact on measurable performance outcomes and are a deflection of attention away from aspects of social, emotional, or moral development that have no immediate measurable performative value.
>
> (Ball, 2016, p. 1054)

In my jurisdiction, the push to drive through performative measures was resisted by the majority of the teaching workforce and by some key members of the education department, and this led directly into the development of a local curriculum. The curriculum was refocussed in the ethos of the 'why' of teaching and on the whole child. The 'what' of teaching became a vehicle for enabling students to explore their relationships to the material. This curriculum offered a reaffirmation of developmental drama work in the classroom. Nevertheless, the trajectory that this curriculum has taken the educational offering, alongside other policy changes on the island such as the implementation of local management of schools and a planned restructuring of school sites in the interests of efficiency, was, and continues to be, highly contested.

A Synthesis of Marginality – Drama, Theatre, Dramatherapy, and Drama-Teaching

Historically, educational drama and dramatherapy shared ideological and practical beginnings. Both drew on a knowledge of drama and theatre, and I explore the relationship between drama and theatre shortly. Both encompassed aspects that were didactic and developmental. By didactic, I mean the imparting of concrete and abstracted ideas (knowledge) in either implicit or explicit ways (Uljens & Ylimaki, 2017). By developmental, I refer to the maturation of what Blatner refers to as meta-skills (Blatner & Blatner, 1988), and the emergence of what Elliott referred to as the necessary for 'living wisely' (Elliott, 1991, p. 148). Development is about nurturing the ability to be flexible and is a task that can continue for the whole of a person's life (Blatner & Blatner, 1988). Development is about cultivating the traits we need to maintain a sense of well-being (World Health Organisation, 2013), and those traits include 'having a positive sense of identity, the ability to manage thoughts, emotions, and to build social relationships … ultimately enabling … full active participation in society' (World Health Organisation, 2013, p. 3). However, despite their shared ancestry in both the didactic and the developmental, to *protect its status* as a profession, dramatherapy re-visioned itself as a clinical model of practice. Therefore, when dramatherapy comes into schools, it does so in the context of withdrawal or special intervention groups and is usually not accessible to most students. Furthermore, due to *policy pressures*, educational drama re-visioned itself in terms of measurable and marketable pseudo-vocational skills (Adams, 2013) so that, in effect, via the logics of governance (after Foucault, Deacon, 1998), the developmental aspect has been removed from school curriculum-drama (Elliott, 1991). I argue that a dramatherapeutically informed classroom could restore the balances between education-for-value and education-for-values, and education-for-knowledge and education-for-development, within the mainstream drama classroom.

As disciplines, drama in schools and dramatherapy also draw on practices derived from both drama and theatre, which are words often used interchangeably, but which are different words connoting different things (Schechner, 2004). One way of making the distinction between drama and theatre is to allocate to drama what is about process, and to theatre what is about product (Jones, 1996). In this way, drama comes to refer to the process of exploration, to the *doing* of role play, improvisation, and play-acting. As Jones put it, 'drama is the entry into a special state where individuals, the space they use and the things they do, exist in a pretend reality' (Jones, 1996, p. 13) and is akin to the work of self-realisation. An informal audience might watch at some stage, but it is not necessary. Theatre then refers to the crafting of a piece of work with a more formal audience in mind and is akin to performativity (Ball, 2003). Of course, the boundary between what might be drama and what might be theatre is fuzzy. Theatre can happen without technological trappings (Brook, 1996) and drama can occur with an audience in mind. In the teaching context, when showing or *doing* drama work, the benefit of the performance or *doing* is to validate the child, and although the benefit can be described, it cannot be measured because the benefit is a result of the interaction between the child in their context and the material, and as explained earlier, that cannot be pre-determined because the benefits are emergent (Hart, 1978, in Priestly,

2017). Theatre on the other hand is about the crafting of work for the benefit of an audience using a variety of theatrical conventions and skills, the learning of which teachers can facilitate through a didactic model which is in some ways, though not entirely, more amenable to standardised assessment. In the classroom, the work becomes theatrical when we start to think about the effects the use of specific skills and conventions might have on an audience. The boundary between what might be considered drama and what might be considered theatre is fuzzy, especially in schools, where what is moving towards looking like theatre must also validate the child. In schools, the point at which the balance is to be struck between working with students in a drama (or process) mode and working with them in a theatre (or product-oriented) mode has been contested (Michael, 2005). Although there is a balance to be struck, in my practice, I see drama as developmental and chose to orient the students' classroom experience mainly, though not exclusively, to the process-mode style of drama.

My orientation to a process-mode style of drama-teaching practice is not exclusive, because historically, theatre *qua* theatre has also synthesised aspects of the didactic and the developmental. Although the roots of theatre go back over 20,000 years to the Palaeolithic and Neolithic ages (Schechner, 2004) and are said to have had different beginnings in different places arising for example from the rituals of ancient Egypt, or from Sanskrit drama in India (Edwards, 1976; Schneider, 2014), the start point of modern *Western* theatre is usually taken to be the theatre of Ancient Greece. The theatre of Ancient Greece provides a useful example of the intersection of development and education. In the theatre of Ancient Greece were dramatised the great ethical and moral debates of the day, played out in the presence of the community and in relational positioning to different perspectives of community opinion as spoken by the 'voice' (or voices) of the chorus. Furthermore, it was the spectators' collective experience of catharsis at those performances, which happened in the context of religious festivals, that enabled Aristotle to develop a theory of cathartic healing which described the cleansing process by which individuals emerged from their theatrical experience renewed. Later, the Medieval Church in England used the ritual *performance* of the Christian Mass to educate their congregations, including having priests adopt the roles of characters who figured in significant stories (Edwards, 1976; Grainger, 1990). Furthermore, as church ritual-performance developed into Medieval Theatre, in the blurring of boundaries between actor and spectator, and between church ritual, education, and popular entertainment, and with the concretisation of iconic images such as the 'Mouth of Hell', the theatre of Medieval England provides another example of the intersection of the developmental and the educational (Rossmeisl, 2012). From its earliest roots, theatre involved didactic education, supported developmental growth and healing, facilitated exploration of values and ethics, and taught and explored cultural values. However, in the context of drama in schools, due to current globalised and neoliberal policies that include an international competition-based curriculum structured by a homogenised, psychologised, dislocated, and commodified educational framework, and the pressure of commodifiable outcome-measures, the developmental aspects of both drama and theatre have, for the most part, been side-lined, and that is the topic of the next paragraphs.

Historically, the value of active play and its connection to the developmental has been acknowledged in school practice and policy. For example, the 1931 Hadow report (Hadow, 1931) recommended that education should focus on 'activity and experience' which was a phrase that repeated 8 times in the report. In 1967, in acknowledgement of the contribution that drama as a play-based, active, and experiential pursuit could make, the Plowden report advocated a more 'progressive' approach and referred to the value of 'spontaneous' acting out and moral explorations such as making up and acting in a drama that pitted good against evil (Plowden, 1967, p. 19 ff). This was very much a developmental, exploratory, experiential vision for drama in schools which held in balance the didactic and the developmental, and for which there was historical precedence. For example, early 20th-century educationalist Harriet Finlay Johnson believed that everything in the curriculum could be adapted and taught via dramatic action, Caldwell Cook wanted to bring the acting back into Shakespeare, and to enable his students to develop a mastery of the craft of drama, and Joan Gilpin tried to make the performance of plays the core of the work of schools (Bolton, 1984). But, Harriet Finley Johnson also believed in the child's natural dramatic instinct, that the process was more important than the product, that both improvised and scripted work were valid, that an audience was irrelevant, and that the happiness of the children was a priority (ibid.). Likewise, after Montessori, Caldwell Cook stressed the 'fundamental' role of play in children's learning (Cook, 1919, p. 8) and emphasised the benefit of drama to the 'health and well-being' of students (ibid., p. 18). Others, such as Chris Parry, emphasised the developmental value of 'engagement' (Parry, 1972, p. 31). However, with its emphasis on the concrete and commodifiable, and with the dislocation between local values on one hand and the Organisation for Economic Cooperation and Development (OECD) and Program for International Student Assessment (PISA) agendas that are centred on creating a homogenised assessment platform that is not rooted in the values of the local community (Moos, 2017) on the other, recent policy has side-lined the developmental and de-valued the emergent aspects of the work, in favour of more easily standardised and pre-determinable outcome-measures. For example, the National Curriculum for England and Wales, which was introduced in 1989, initiated new requirements for subject-specific teaching and, in the UK, this led to the decline of exploratory and developmental drama (Baldwin, 2007; Elliott, 1991). Following this, in England and Wales, Drama was subsumed into English and then further side-lined as for several years English, under the auspices of the National Literacy Strategy, was defined only in terms of reading and writing (Baldwin, 2007). In addition, drama teacher-training courses in the UK became less available, and drama in schools adapted in an effort to comply with National Curriculum and emerging educational requirements (ibid.). In other words, the developmental aspects of the subject were de-valued, and in terms of assessment, despite marketing rhetoric to the contrary, drama was recognised primarily in terms of its didactic and skills subject content (Baldwin, 2007; Department for Education and Skills, 2003). In the jurisdiction where I taught the picture was more positive, however, changes in the UK eventually affected the outlook for drama for my students because inevitably, as a subject, it had to fall in with the pedagogical and administrative demands being imported from the mainland.

In contrast to this, despite the demonstrable links between what happens in a drama classroom, and what happens in a dramatherapy session (Holmwood, 2016), dramatherapy has maintained its strong link with development but lost its connection with educational drama and the mainstream classroom. For example, at the time of writing, the World Alliance of Drama Therapy defined dramatherapy variously. It used quotes from eminent dramatherapists from round the world to capture the different ways dramatherapy was being realised. Each quote referred to play, to being active, and to inviting participants to engage in a change-process towards greater relationality, role flexibility, and behavioural choice (World Alliance of Dramatherapy, 2023). That change-process, in dramatherapy, is often conceptualised in terms of 'core processes' which, following Jones, are dramatic projection, playing, role, embodiment, empathy and distancing, active witnessing, life-drama connection, transformation, and triangular relationships (Jones, 1991, 1996; Mayor & Frydman, 2021). These core change-processes underpin the key concepts of dramatherapy which are to do with story-telling, problem solving, expressing feelings, and exploration of the inner and social self, which parallel closely the aims of personal development as envisioned by Blatner (Blatner & Blatner, 1988) and the World Health Organization (2013). In other words, dramatherapy is about using the tools of drama and theatre to support the development of personal identity, to facilitate engagement in values-based ethical negotiation, and foster the development of an enhanced role repertoire. This kind of dramatherapy approach could help students resist an uncritical acceptance of the value, not values-based, culture of neoliberalism, and the development of an enhanced role repertoire could better equip them to navigate the demands of performativity (Edmiston & Towler-Evans, 2022). However, although dramatherapy maintained its strong link with the developmental aspects of drama, its educational application was side-lined because dramatherapy as a profession withdrew from mainstream schools and established itself as a clinical profession located within the context of mental health institutions (O'Toole, Stinson, & Moore, 2009). Therefore, when practitioners of dramatherapy, in line with exogenic neoliberalism, are bought into schools as a commodity, they tend to offer withdrawal groups or special initiatives and the developmental benefits of dramatherapy are not made available to the student body as a whole.

For example, a scrutiny, involving a search for studies situated in the mainstream school context, in the dramatherapy journal *Dramatherapy*, revealed many articles and studies undertaken in a school context over the past several years. However, they tended to focus on groups of students who had been withdrawn from their mainstream class (Dix, 2015; Dyer, 2017; Godfrey & Haythorne, 2013). Or, the study took place in the context of special or additional needs, and despite that the key word 'education' cropped up repeatedly, this did not refer to mainstream education (Dawson, 1994; Payne, 1981). On the contrary, it was more likely that the work had been done in the context of 'profound and multiple learning difficulties' (Ellinor, 2019) or be targeted at groups of school-aged adolescents who had 'self-withdrawn' from mainstream schooling (Millbrook, 2019, p. 28). Vicky Karkou edited a volume titled 'Arts therapies in schools: Research and practice' (Karkou, 2010). The section in that volume that was devoted to the use of Arts Therapies in the mainstream setting included no offerings from dramatherapists working in mainstream classrooms. Rather, one was located within a 'school-based student-support unit' (Christensen, 2010, p. 85), the second used the building of a mainstream school and worked with the cooperation and participation of staff and students but involved only a withdrawal group that was selected as a result of specific referral criteria (Smyth, 2010), and the third was 'small-group work with disaffected students' (Quibell, 2010, p. 115).

Jennings (2011) and Holmwood (2016) offered notable exceptions to this trend. Jennings offered a developmental model of drama that could appropriately be applied in a mainstream context. Her model is based on a proposed developmental progression from a drama to a theatre process (Jennings, 2011), so that bodies on stage (signs) are given signification (Sajnani, 2012) with increasing levels of awareness in order that form is brought to chaos (Miller, 1995). In other words, students move on a trajectory that starts with free play and moves towards crafted drama where they use their bodies in three-dimensional stage space in increasingly intentional ways to create or reflect meaning. Holmwood conducted research within mainstream schools that explored the relationships between dramatherapy and drama-teaching, although he kept the two practices separate (Holmwood, 2016). However, apart from these exceptions, and despite Holmwood's observation that 'simple constructions that aim to determine what is drama and what is dramatherapy will be difficult to make' (Holmwood, 2016, p. 118), what is not happening is a meeting of the developmental, which has become the domain of dramatherapy, and the didactic, which has become the priority of classroom drama, in the mainstream educational classroom context. In line with the work of Edminston and Towler-Evans on the potential for collaborative dramatic inquiry to rehumanise education (Edmiston & Towler-Evans, 2022), this polarisation between the developmental and the didactic is a concern I am interested to rectify through my own work by developing what I refer to as a dramatherapeutically informed classroom.

What do I mean by a dramatherapeutically informed classroom? It would clearly not be appropriate to undertake clinical or psychological therapeutic intervention in the context of a mainstream curriculum-drama class. However, there are models of dramatherapy practice that are not necessarily interpretation based (Mitchell, 1994) and which have the potential to be more developmental than clinical (Jennings, 2011). It is to this end of the dramatherapy spectrum that the work in a mainstream classroom needs to orient. There needs to be a place where the didactic and the developmental aspects of drama are held in knowing balance. By a dramatherapeutically informed classroom, I am specifically referring to bringing a dramatherapy sensibility to the mainstream curriculum for the teaching of drama in timetabled classes. This does not imply introducing a different set of activities or conventions to the classroom. Rather, it requires that the classroom teacher: be explicitly aware that work in drama is intricately bound up with the development of individual (Jones, 1996) and group identity and well-being (Grainger, 1990; Jennings, 1987); facilitate choice (Cattanach, 1992) and be sensitive to the developmental needs of individual students (Grimshaw, 1995); use their facility to manage the learning and experiential environment of the children structurally (Jennings & Gersie, 1987), technically (Holmes & Karp, 1991), and relationally (Grimshaw, 1995) within a cross modal (Jennings, 2011; O'Toole et al., 2009; Slade, 1977) and interpretational (Jones, 1996) framework. The teacher should be both audience and witness (Cattanach, 1992) as students develop their drama skills and knowledge (Jennings, 1990) and develop as people (Landy, 1993). It means that, following educator Heathcote and therapists Cox and Thielgaard, there has to be space allowed in the classroom for flexibility and the freedom to work with and through metaphor and symbolism (Cox & Theilgaard, 1997). It means that the teacher must understand the self-actualisation process and how that relates to the drama-process (Jennings, 2011) and to play. The teacher should be aware of the concept and importance of aesthetic distance, which is the idea that individuals must be able to maintain a safe affective/cognitive distance from challenging material in order to be able to engage with it (Jones, 1991) (see Chapter 7). The teacher should also be cognisant of the importance of allowing students to enter a 'heightened play' space which is unstructured and experimental (Mayor & Frydman, 2021, p. 8). As Jones stated: 'One of the simplest definitions of therapy is that it is a form of intervention aiming to bring about personal change' (Jones, 1996, p. 11). It is about new ways of telling, and relating to, who we are (Jones, 1996) and creating for ourselves new roles and ways of being (Pendzik, Emunah, & Johnson, 2016), and although not necessarily the stated aim of all dramatherapists, it is my position that the opportunity to develop greater role flexibility will better equip students to resist, and to engage in, the performative aspects of neoliberal society. A dramatherapeutically informed classroom is, in short, about valuing the developmental aspects of the work, asserting a democratising re-valuing of values, promoting ethical exploration, and offering students an opportunity to negotiate a more critical position in relation to their context.

Conclusion

As jurisdictions independent from England, the Crown Dependencies have been able to take from UK educational policy only that which their communities felt best suited their needs. However, inevitably what is in the best interests of children, and where the balance should be between an educational model based on discourses associated with advanced global capitalism, i.e., neoliberalism, and resistance to it, continues to be contested. As part of this contestation, in my context, the development of a local curriculum for schools offered a revalidation of a developmental style of classroom drama, one informed by dramatherapy sensibilities. Key to the identity-work done in the dramatherapeutically sensitised drama classroom is the concept of the situated mindbody, and it is to an exploration of this that I turn in the next chapter.

References

Adams, J. (2011). The degradation of the arts in education. *International Journal of Art & Design Education, 30*(2), 156–160. doi:10.1111/j.1476-8070.2011.01704.x

Adams, J. (2013). The Artful Dodger: Creative resistance to neoliberalism in education. *Education, Review of Education, Pedagogy, and Cultural Studies, 35*(4), 242–255. doi:10.1080/10714413.2013.819726

Autio, T. (2017). Curriculum theory in contestation? American curriculum, European didaktik, and Chinese wisdom traditions as hybrid platforms for educational leadership. In M. Uljins & R. M. Ylimaki (Eds.), *Bridging educational leadership, curriculum theory and didaktik, educational governance research* 5 (Kindle ed., Vol. 5, pp. 7193–7788). Switzerland: Springer Open.

Baldwin, P. (2007). *With drama in mind: Real learning in imagined worlds.* London: Network Continuum.

Ball, S. (2003). The teacher's soul and the terrors of performativity. *Journal of Education Policy, 18*(2), 215–228. doi:10.1080/0268093022000043065

Ball, S. (2008). Performativity, privatisation, professionals and the state. In B. Cunningham (Ed.), *Exploring professionalism* (pp. 50). London: The Institute of Education, University of London.

Ball, S. (2016). Neoliberal education? Confronting the slouching beast. *Policy Futures in Education, 14*(8), 1046–1059. doi:10.1177/1478210316664259

Barkin, D. (2000). Overcoming the neoliberal paradigm: Sustainable popular development. *Journal of Developing Societies, 16*(1), 163–180.

Belchem, J. (2001). *A new history of the Isle of Man, Vol. 5: The modern period, 1830–1999.* Liverpool, UK: Liverpool University Press.

Bentham, J. (1791). *Panopticon: The inspection house* (2017 reprint ed.). Dumfries and Galloway: Anodos Books: Candida Casa.

Blatner, A., & Blatner, A. (1988). *Foundations of psychodrama: History, theory and practice* (3rd ed.). New York: Springer Publishing Company.

Bolton, G. (1984). *Drama as education: An argument for placing drama at the centre of the curriculum.* Durham England: Longman.

Brook, P. (1996). *The empty space.* New York: Simon and Schuster.

Burman, E. (2008). *Developments: Child, image, nation.* London and New York: Routledge.

Cattanach, A. (1992). *Play therapy with abused children.* London: Jessica Kingsley.

Christensen, J. (2010). Making space inside: The experience of dramatherapy within a school based support unit. In V. Karkou (Ed.), *Arts therapies in schools: Research and practice* (Kindle ed., pp. 90–101). London: Jessica Kingsley.

Cole, B., Adamson, S., Craig, G., Hussain, B., Smith, L., Law, I., … Cheung, T. (2009). *Hidden from public view: Racism against UK Chinese* (T. M. Group., Trans.). Sheffield University Research Archive: Sheffield Hallam University.

Cook, C. (1919). *The play way: An essay in educational method* (2015 ed.). New York: Frederick A. Stokes Company.

Cox, M., & Theilgaard, A. (1997). *Mutative metaphors in psychotherapy: The Aeolian mode.* London: Jessica Kingsley.

Crossan, R.-M. (2016). *The states and secondary education 1560–1970.* Guernsey: Melody Press.

Davies, B., & Bansel, P. (2007). Neoliberalism and education. *International Journal of Qualitative Studies in Education (QSE), 20*(3), 247–259. doi:10.1080/09518390701281751

Dawson, A. (1994). Dramatherapy and movement therapy in special education. *Dramatherapy, 16*(1), 2–7. doi:10.1080/02630672.1994.9689368

Deacon, R. (1998). Strategies of governance: Michel Foucault on power. *Theoria: A Journal of Social and Political Theory, 92*, 113–148. doi:10.3167/004058198782485966

Department for Education and Skills. (2003). *Key stage 3 national strategy drama objectives bank.* London: Department for Education and Skills.

Dix, A. (2015). Telling stories: Dramatherapy and theatre in education with boys who have experienced parental domestic violence. *Dramatherapy, 37*(1), 15–27. doi:10.1080/02630672.2015.1055778

Dunn, B. (2017). Against neoliberalism as a concept. *Capital & Class, 41*(3), 435–454. doi:10.1177/0309816816678583

Dyer, N. (2017). Behold the tree: An exploration of the social integration of boys on the autistic spectrum in a mainstream primary school through a dramatherapy intervention. *Dramatherapy, 38*(2–3), 80–93. doi:10.1080/02630672.2017.1329845

Edmiston, B., & Towler-Evans, I. (2022). *Humanizing education with dramatic inquiry: In dialogue with Dorothy Heathcote's transformative pedagogy.* New York and London: Routledge.

Edwards, F. (1976). *Ritual and drama: The Medieval theatre.* Guildford and London: Lutterworth Press.

Ellinor, J. (2019). It's the 'group' that matters: Dramatherapy working with a group of parents and their children who have profound and multiple learning difficulties. *Dramatherapy: Official Journal of the British Association of Dramatherapists, 40.* doi:10.1177/0263067219834697

Elliott, J. (1991). *Action research for educational change.* Milton Keynes: Open University Press.

Foucault, M. (1975). *Discipline and punish: The birth of the prison* (A. Sheridan, Trans.). London, UK: Penguin Random House.

Foucault, M. (2008). *The birth of biopolitics: Lectures at the College de France, 1978–1979.* London, UK: Palgrave Macmillan.

Godfrey, E., & Haythorne, D. (2013). Benefits of dramatherapy for autism spectrum disorder: A qualitative analysis of feedback from parents and teachers of clients attending Roundabout Dramatherapy sessions in schools. *Dramatherapy, 35*(1), 20–28. doi:10.1080/02630672.2013.773131

gov.im. (2017). Arguments against league tables – November 2017. Retrieved from www.gov.im/media/1359585/arguments-against-league-tables-december-2017.pdf

Grainger, R. (1990). *Drama and healing: The roots of dramatherapy.* London: Jessica Kingsley.

Grimshaw, D. (1995). Shall I be mother? The development of the role of the dramatherapist and reflections on transference/countertransference. In S. Jennings (Ed.), *Dramatherapy with children and adolescents* (pp. 189–209). London: Routledge.

Hadow, W. H. (1931). *Report of the consultative committee on the primary school.* London: His Majesty's Stationery Office.

Hall, R. (2019). Neoliberalism and primary education: Impacts of neoliberal policy on the lived experiences of primary school communities. *Power and Education, 11*(3). doi:10.1177/1757743819877344

Harvey, D. (2007). *A brief history of neoliberalism.* Oxford: Oxford University Press.

Hekman, S. J. (2014). *The feminine subject.* Cambridge, UK: Polity.

Holmes, P., & Karp, M. (1991). Inspiration and technique. In P. Holmes & M. Karp (Eds.), *Psychodrama: Inspiration and technique* (pp. 1–6). London: Routledge.

Holmwood, C. (2016). *Drama education and dramatherapy: Exploring the space between disciplines.* London: Routledge.

Hunter, S. (2015). *Power, politics and the emotions: Impossible governance?* London, UK: Taylor & Francis Group.

Javier, E. (2016). 'Almost' native speakers: The experiences of visible ethnic-minority native English-speaking teachers. In F. Copland, S. Garton, & S. Mann (Eds.), *LETs and NESTs: Voices, views and vignettes* (pp. 227–239). London: British Council.

Jennings, S. (1987). Dramatherapy and groups. In S. Jennings (Ed.), *Dramatherapy: Theory and practice for teachers and clinicians* (pp. 1–18). London: Routledge.

Jennings, S. (1990). *Waiting in the wings: Dramatherapy with families, groups and individuals.* London: Jessica Kingsley.

Jennings, S. (2011). *Healthy attachments and neuro-dramatic play* (Kindle ed.). London: Jessica Kingsley.

Jennings, S., & Gersie, A. (1987). Dramatherapy with disturbed adolescents. In S. Jennings (Ed.), *Dramatherapy: Theory and practice for teachers and clinicians* (pp. 162–182). London: Routledge.

Jones, P. (1991). Dramatherapy: Five core processes. *Dramatherapy, 14*(1), 8–15. doi:10.1080/02630672.1991.9689804

Jones, P. (1996). *Drama as therapy: Theatre as living.* London and New York: Routledge.

Kaplan, J. (2020). Against economy–culture dualism: An argument from raced economies. *Feminist Theory, 22*(3), 381–403. doi:10.1177/1464700120975699

Karkou, V. (Ed.) (2010). *Arts therapies in schools: Research and practice* (Kindle ed.). London and Philadelphia: Jessica Kingsley Publishers.

Kelly, A., Azaola, M. C., & Schilz, J. (n.d.). *Island voices: Choice, equity and opportunity in Jersey schools.* Retrieved from: https://eprints.soton.ac.uk/430131/1/Island_Voices.pdf

Knafo, S., Dutta, S. J., Lane, R., & Wyn-Jones, S. (2019). The managerial lineages of neoliberalism. *New Political Economy, 24*(2), 235–251. doi:10.1080/13563467.2018.1431621

Landy, R. (1993). *Persona and performance: The meaning of role in drama, therapy, and everyday life*. New York, London: Guildford Press.

Little, A. (2022). *150 years of 'education for all' on the Isle of Man: Context, resistance and resolution*. Retrieved from Isle of Man: https://culturevannin.im/media//Resources/150YearsOfEducationForAll_030322.pdf

Lyotard, J.-F. (1986). *The postmodern condition: A report on knowledge* (2001 reprint ed.). Manchester, UK: Manchester University Press.

Mayor, C., & Frydman, J. S. (2021). Understanding school-based drama therapy through the core processes: An analysis of intervention vignettes. *The Arts in Psychotherapy, 73*. doi:10.1016/j.aip.2021.101766

Michael, A. (2005). New stages: Challenges for teaching the aesthetics of drama online. *Journal of Aesthetic Education, 39*(4), 119–131. doi:10.1353/jae.2005.0035

Millbrook, A. (2019). Digital storymaking: Dramatherapy with young people online. *Dramatherapy: Official Journal of the British Association of Dramatherapists, 40*. doi:10.1177/0263067218817296

Miller, A. (1995). *Pictures of a childhood: Sixty-six watercolours and an essay* (H. Hunnum, Trans.). New York: Meridian.

Mitchell, S. (1994). The theatre of self expression: A 'therapeutic theatre' model of dramatherapy. In S. Jennings (Ed.), *The handbook of dramatherapy* (pp. 20–29). London: Routledge.

Moore, P., & Robinson, A. (2016). The quantified self: What counts in the neoliberal workplace. *New Media and Society, 18*(11), 2774–2792. doi:10.1177/1461444815604328

Moos, L. (2017). Neo-liberal governance leads education and educational leadership astray. In M. Uljens & R. M. Ylimaki (Eds.), *Bridging educational leadership, curriculum theory and didaktik, educational governance research 5* (Kindle ed., Vol. 5, pp. 4425–5252). Switzerland: Springer Open.

Morales, J. B., & Abegglen, S. (Eds.). (2020). *Understanding education and economics: Key debates and critical perspectives*. London and New York: Routledge.

Office for National Statistics. (2020). *Crime in England and Wales: Year ending June 2020*. England: Office for National Statistics Retrieved from www.ons.gov.uk/peoplepopulationandcommunity/crimeandjustice/bulletins/crimeinenglandandwales/yearendingjune2020

Ogier & Chan, C. (2020). *Hedge funds jurisdictional comparisons (Offshore jurisdictions) 2014*. London: Thomson Reuters Westlaw Books.

Oliver, M. (2019). A small island territory moving down the 'development ladder'?: A case study of Jersey. *Open Research Online*. Retrieved from www.um.edu.mt/library/oar/handle/123456789/44944

O'Toole, J., Stinson, M., & Moore, T. (Eds.). (2009). *Drama and curriculum: A giant at the door* (Vol. 6). Dordrecht: Springer.

Parry, C. (1972). *English through drama: A way of teaching* (Digitised by the Internet Archive ed.). Cambridge: Cambridge University Press.

Payne, H. (1981). Movement therapy in a special education setting. *Dramatherapy, 4*(3), 17–22. doi:10.1080/02630672.1981.9689225

Pendzik, S., Emunah, R., & Johnson, D. R. (2016). *The self in performance*. New York: Palgrave.

Pinar, W. F. (2018). Foreword: Educational governance research. In L. Moos & S. Carney (Eds.), *Bridging educational leadership, curriculum theory and didaktik: Non affirmative theory of education* (pp. 7–12). Switzerland: Springer Open.
Plowden, J. P. (1967). *Children and their schools volume 1* (Vol. 1). London: Her Majesty's Stationery Office.
Priestly, M. (2017). '...two decades of neoliberal policy have generated a cupboard-full of troubles' (Ryan, 2012, p.23). *The STeP Journal: Student Teacher Perspectives 4*(3), 42–49.
Quibell, T. (2010). The searching drama of disaffection: Dramatherapy groups in a whole school context. In V. Karkou (Ed.), *Arts therapies in schools: Research and practice* (pp. 114–128). London: Jessica Kingsley.
Rossmeisl, R. (2012). *Encountering the embodied mouth of hell: The play of oppositions in religious vernacular theatre* (Masters Degree). The University of British Columbia, Vancouver.
Sajnani, N. (2012). The implicated witness: Towards a relational aesthetic in dramatherapy. *Dramatherapy, 34*(March 2012), 6–21. doi:10.1080/02630672.2012.657944
Schechner, R. (2004). *Performance theory*. London and New York: Routledge.
Schneider, R. (2014). *Theatre and history*. London: Palgrave Macmillan.
Schumacher, P. (2008). Parametricism – A new global style for architecture and urban design. *Architectural Design – Digital Cities, 79*. https://doi.org/10.1002/ad.912]
Shore, C., & Wright, S. (1999). Audit culture and anthropology: Neo liberalism in British higher education. *The Journal of the Royal Anthropological Institute, 5*, 557–575. https://doi.org/10.2307/2661148
SISRA Analytics. (2021). SISRA Home Page. Retrieved from www.sisra.com
Slade, P. (1977). Aspects of drama in remedial education. *Dramatherapy, 1*(2), 1–3. doi:10.1080/02630672.1977.9689106
Smolovic-Jones, O. (2017). *B100 Block 6 business ethics* (2nd ed.). Milton Keynes: The Open University.
Smyth, G. (2010). Solution-focused brief dramatherapy group work: Working with children in mainstream education in Sri Lanka. In V. Karkou (Ed.), *Arts therapies in schools: Research and practice* (pp. 97–113). London: Jessica Kingsley Publishers.
Spencer, D. (2016). *The architecture of neoliberalism: How contemporary architecture became an instrument of control and compliance*. New York: Bloomsbury Academic.
States of Guernsey Education Service. (2017). *The Bailiwick of Guernsey curriculum: Teacher handbook* (2nd ed.). Guernsey: States of Guernsey Education Service.
Stronach, I., & Clarke, J. (2011). Eight contentions for an educational future: Timely rules for unruly times. *Qualitative Inquiry, 17*(10), 986–996. doi:10.1177/1077800411425155
Sweeney, E. (Ed.) (2024). *Space, place and dramatherapy: International perspectives*. London and New York: Routledge.
Uljens, M., & Ylimaki, R. M. (Eds.). (2017). *Bridging educational leadership, curriculum theory and didaktik: Non-affirmative theory of education* (1 ed. Vol. 5). Cham: Springer International Publishing.
Wood, A. (2018). Economies of school-building: The selling of architectural and educational features. *Ardeth Online, 3*. doi:10.17454/ARDETH03.08
World Alliance of Dramatherapy. (2023). World Alliance of Dramatherapy. Retrieved from www.worldallianceofdramatherapy.com

World Health Organisation. (2013). *Comprehensive mental health action plan 2013–2020* (Agenda item 13.3). Retrieved from https://apps.who.int/gb/ebwha/pdf_files/WHA66/A66_R8-en.pdf?ua=1
Ynsee, R. (2006). Freedom to flourish: A curriculum for learning and achievement. Retrieved from www.gov.im/media/186468/curriculumlearnachieveapr06_1_.pdf

3 The Situated Mindbody

Embodied Psychosocial Relationality

As explained in Chapter 1, this book is about the processes involved when students do identity-work in a dramatherapeutically informed drama classroom. Chapter 2 suggested that neoliberal technologies of governance, despite the ways they have been resisted locally, have had a significant impact on educational policy and practice. The current chapter explores what a fluid identity looks like in the context of neoliberalism. I include reference to: the ways that identity comes about relationally, including through the impact of others and cyclical feedback, and in relationship to dominant discourses (Bowlby, 1988; Hunter, 2015b; Sluss & Ashforth, 2007); the relevance of roles and the ability to adopt a wide variety of roles in different contexts (Elliott & Lemert, 2009); the performative nature of identity (Butler, 2006); the relationships between performance and critiques of neoliberal performativity, with reference to the young people with whom I work, who are no longer young children but who are transitioning into adulthood (Curran & Hill, 2019); the implications of the necessity to, and our ability to, story and re-story our lives and to re-position or reinvent ourselves, or to be re-visioned, or reproduced as our life contexts change (Hollway, 2005; Wrenn, 2014); and the importance of embodiment (Haraway & Wolfe, 2016; Strathern & Stewart, 2008). I also suggest that identity is rooted in the ability to make values-based ethical choices, and this is important in a context where individuals are required to make decisions in the absence of moral certainties (Gergen, 2000; Hollway, 2005). The chapter goes on to explore the ways that drama is made up of roles, performances, and stories and makes the argument that drama is a container for ethical negotiations. I link the component parts of drama which are role, performance, and story to an embodied psychosocial relational understanding of identity. I introduce the idea that identity is enacted relative to normative social discourses and explore some of the more powerful constituting discourses, including the ways that enlightenment thinking still strongly influences how gender is perceived today. I consider the ongoing legacy of psychodynamic theory, including attachment theory. I explore the ways that the introduction of the concept of intersectionality effects how we think about marginalisation,

DOI: 10.4324/9781003464532-3

and what is meant by psychosocial relationality, performativity, and embodiment, and how these concepts change how we think about identity.

The Situated Mindbody: Embodied Psychosocial Relationality

I would like to draw out several strands of thinking that are crucial to understanding identity as conceptualised in this book. The first is that discourse is constituted (van Dijk, 2002) *and* constituting (Burman & Parker, 2017). Discourse is a means through which formal and informal groups, and individuals relative to those groups, construct and share social meanings, and a way by which formal and informal groups, and individuals relative to those groups, constitute and maintain power relationships (Foucault & Nazzaro, 1972). Discourses are based on shared understandings, relationships, and practices and tell us something about normative positioning. In other words, they form and express truth-claims (Hook, 2001). For this project, the term discourse refers 'beyond language to sets of organised meanings (which can include images as well as words) on a given theme' (Hollway & Jefferson, 2013, p. 13) and concerns 'all the ways in which people actively produce social and psychological realities' (Davies & Harré, 2011, p. 45) (see also Chapter 4). Discourses are embodied and enacted through power dynamics that are embedded in and utilise context; theme; proximal relationship; physical, visual, and vocal cues; and use of speech (van Dijk, 2011). Discourses work in relationship to and are part of the subtle and complex interweaving of the embodied, the psychological, and the social through which identity is constituted (Gee, 2014; Hollway & Jefferson, 2013). Social discourses reflect and create the thinking that is prevalent in a society. The thinking relevant to this thesis includes: the influence of the Cartesian *cogito*; the influence of psychotherapeutic theory and practice; the concept of intersectionality; the perspective of psychosocial relationality; and the concepts of performativity and embodiment. These lineages of thought help me to think about identity. That includes my thinking about race and gender which are bracketed aspects of identity that are currently politically significant and that feel particularly salient to my own experience.

One kind of thinking-about-identity, underpinned by the concept of the Cartesian *cogito*, is the fundamental idea that there is an independent and pre-existing I-as-subject that sits in relationship to a constituting other or object. In this lineage of thinking, sometimes, the individual has been conceptualised as constituting societal discourses and structures. Sometimes, societies' discourses and structures have been conceptualised as constituting the individual. Often, it has been stated that identity is carved out in the relationship or dialectic between the individual on the one hand and societal discourses and structures on the other. However, this fundamental framework rests on an unproblematised inner/outer Cartesian binary (Walkerdine, 2005). Dependent on an ontological and epistemological foundation of a binary or dualistic relationship between society/person, structure/agency, cultural/

individual, subject/object (Henriques, Hollway, Urwin, Venn, & Walkerdine, 1998), this strand of thinking is important because it influences social discourse and frames the ways we are able to think about ourselves and others, including, but not limited to, the ways we think about our relationships to the socio-political context, the ways we think about race, and the ways we think about gender. Discourses arising from binary thinking about race and binary thinking about gender overlap considerably (McRobbie, 2008). For example, the neoliberal discourse that promotes resilience as both important and marketable (Webster & Rivers, 2019) rests on the liberal assumption of the independent self that is conceptualised as hegemonically male (Higgins, 2004). That hegemonic masculinity derives from the liberal binary of the independent man whose natural domain is the public sphere, whereas the natural place for women is sequestered in the privacy of the home (Brown, 1995). Other neoliberal discourses include those to do with white male superordination, the responsibilisation of the individual and family, the ascendency of neo-traditional family values, and lack of trust in social, i.e., relational/welfare/care institutions (Brown, 2019; Hekman, 2014). The alt-right provides an extreme expression of neo-traditional values (Dignam & Rohlinger, 2019). Furthermore, our life contexts include structures such as global social media (Elliott & Lemert, 2009) and the technologies that have given rise to the 'selfie generation' (Eler, 2017, p. 393) that feeds from and into them. Global social media perpetuate dominant identity discourses about, for example, the way men and women should be. This extends to discourses about the way differently raced women should be. Although these discourses can be challenged (Francis, 1998), they perpetuate 'larger culture' (Wharton, 2012, p.68) stories. Those stories include the infantilisation and hyper-sexualisation (Shimizu, 2007) of East-Asian women. They perpetuate the belief that men are more aggressive and dangerous than women (Wharton, 2012), which is part of the stereotype that suggests that girls are 'sugar and spice' whereas boys are 'puppy dogs tails' (Francis, 1998), and that girls should be quieter than or less intelligent than boys (Oakley, 1986).

Conceptualising identity in terms of a normative, subjectivised self, positioned in a binary relationship to an objectified other, has not only framed much thinking about identity but also, by extension, of marginalisation (Henriques et al., 1998; Walkerdine & Jimenez, 2012). It has, for example, framed the possibilities of self-stereotyping behaviours (Eagly & Wood, 2017) that make it difficult for marginalised groups or individuals to construe their own sense of selfhood in discourse-terms other than as the object of the dominant subjectivity. This effectively positions the marginalised individual as having no voice of their own. This includes but is not limited to those experiencing marginalisation or oppression as a consequence of their gender or race. They are disallowed the position of subject and faced with the necessity of locating their identity in terms of the object of dominant social discourse (Henriques et al., 1998). Gilligan suggests that when girls come into conflict with male-centred definitions of what constitues the norm, this is experienced as a profound psychological loss as they realise that their own knowledges are marginalised (Hekman, 2014). Some societal discourses subject individuals, and particularly women, in certain contexts such as the context of being dependent on welfare (Esping-Anderson, 2012), or because they are identified with an ethnic minority (Cole et al., 2009), to stigmatisation.

A further kind of thinking about identity comes from the field of psychoanalysis. Psychoanalytic theorising regarding the importance of the relationships between infants and early care-givers is important because it explores the foundations of the deep roots that relationality and contextuality have in the formation of selfhood and identity. Melanie Klein and the Object Relations school (Klein, 1932), and others such as Bowlby (1988) and Winnicott (1971), are credited with formulating the ways in which infants' contexts, which are supposedly experienced by infants entirely in terms of their relationships with early care-givers, facilitate and shape intrapsychic and interpsychic processes. Out of those relational processes emerge a sense of self. Those early relationships determine the ways in which people structure their relationships with their contexts, including their relational contexts, as they move into adulthood. For example, early relationships including family 'scripts' (Byng-Hall, 1985, p. 301) influence the ways children relate to people who share physical racial characteristics or don't share them (Paujer, 2021). People are relational beings, constituted in and through relational contextuality.

Identity can be conceptualised in terms of intersectionality, which was a term coined by law professor Kimberlé Crenshaw to refer to the ways different discriminations combine (Losleben & Musubika, 2023), and which has been further conceptualised as a 'relational choreography' (Hunter, 2015a, p. 43) that describes the ways that relational dynamics of oppression of all kinds work out in multiple and fluctuating ways for different people. Personal narratives arise from the confluence of intersectionalities that are particular to each person, and life stories capture the multiplicities, inventions, and interpretations that are part of personal identity (after Gilligan, Hekman, 2014). The idea that people make sense of their lives by telling stories about themselves is an understanding shared by narrative and dramatherapists (Sepinuck, 2023). This thread of thinking about identity is important because the de-essentialisation of identity, and an acknowledgement of the ways the different situated multiple influences on identity interrelate, is crucial to a conceptualisation of identity as situated, multiple, and re-constitutive and represents a challenge to the binary and essentialising dualism that underpins neoliberal discourse.

Drawing together threads from the above thinking on identity, a psychosocial relational approach is a way of understanding the contradictions, the reproductions, and the re-creations inherent in human experience by attempting to step outside of the binary; to dissolve subject/object dualism; and to understand society, culture, agency, acquiescence, and experiencing individuals as relationally, contextually, and narratively co-invoking. It places the negotiated *psychosocial* (both personal to self and in interaction with the social context) *relationality* (Burman, 2012; Hunter, 2008, 2015b; Sluss & Ashforth, 2007) at the heart of identity.

The final thread contributing to the conceptualisation of identity relative to this book draws in the embodied human being via the concepts of embodiment and performativity. Embodiment and the concept of mindbody (van der Kolk, 1977) has been suggested as an alternative to inner/outer, subject/object dualism (Strathern & Stewart, 2008). Influenced by phenomenology (Merleau-Ponty, 1945), feminist theory pointed out that bodies are central to identity. Feminist theory avoided the essentialising determinism of the *cogito* by acknowledging the body's situatedness as contextualised embodiment (Hekman, 2014). The concept of performativity in two of its incarnations, i.e., as a critique of neoliberal façade, and as referring to the performed nature of identity, has been addressed earlier as part of my discussion of neoliberalism in the context of this book (see Chapter 2). Here, I would like to re-emphasise the second of those aspects, i.e., the aspect of performativity that is to do with the embodied performance of identity, including 'self-aestheticization' (McRobbie, 2008, p. 541), staging, physical display, facial expression, tension, costume, gesture, stance, rhythm, and so on, i.e., everything to do with how we negotiate between what is imposed and what-we-can-chose to be our physical embodied performance, of ourselves, in the three-dimensional world (Gregg, 2012). By drawing the threads of psychosocial relationality and embodiment together to align them with the embodied, relational, and contextual focus of this study, it is possible to think of the situated mindbody and of embodied psychosocial relational identity. So, gender and racialised identities, and all other identities and aspects of identity, are co-evolved in embodied, emotional, and social ways with others. This means that embodied relationship is constitutive and re-constitutive of self, and self only has meaning in relationship, including relationship to story, relationship within story, and relationship to environment, including the non-human and technical environment (Haraway, 2016). Embodied relationality constructs gender identities, racialised identities, and all identities and aspects of identities. Haraway refers to this embodiment as a process of the 'flesh' and comments that 'there is no becoming, there is only becoming-with' (Haraway & Wolfe, 2016, p. 221). In other words, identity is embodied, psychosocial, and relational and this is the perspective taken in this book.

The Dramatic Elements of Role, Performance, and Story Are Inherent in a Psychosocial Relational Conceptualisation of Identity

Role, performance, and story are central to drama. There is a relationship between embodied psychosocial relational identity and dramatic role, performance, and story in that the roles we play in life as well as in fiction are relationally and contextually mediated. Additionally, audience/witness-oriented performance and performativity are central to self-presentation in life as well as in drama. Furthermore, stories are about characters who relationally enact roles in contexts. It is in the synthesis between the processes of taking on roles, enacting performances, and narrating stories in drama and the links between role, performance, story, and identity that the theoretical and applied foundations of this book rest. Through drama, students story themselves as they engage in the storying of the characters they create. They work towards a sense of identity coherence, and at the same time, they explore multiple roles. I will explore each of these elements and their relationships to an embodied psychosocial relational conceptualisation of identity in turn.

Role

The dramatic term 'role', which derives from the rolled up scrolls on which actors of antiquity recorded their parts (Landy, 1993), has been associated with identity because it has been noted that in life as well as in the theatre, identity is constituted in the performance of roles (Sluss & Ashforth, 2007). The concept of role is important enough that several dramatherapy theorists have attempted to classify the roles people play. For example, Moreno suggested three domains of roles: the psychosomatic, the psychodramatic, and the social (Moreno, 1960, in Landy, 1992). Landy offered six role domains: somatic, cognitive, affective, social, spiritual, and aesthetic (Landy, 1993). In line with dramatherapy role theory, Meldrum suggested that it is a person's role repertoire that creates the individual's sense of identity (Meldrum, 1994), and Jones suggested that 'an individual's identity is seen as constructed through the roles they perform in various contexts' (Jones, 1996c, p.196). It has been suggested that the concept not only of role but also of 'role relationship[s]' (Sluss & Ashforth, 2007, p.9) is fundamental in the ongoing expression and structuring of identity and self (Blatner, 1997; Landy, 1993). Role repertoires and role relationships, and therefore identities, are not fixed, they are flexible and can be increased, and become more nuanced, and dramatherapist Emunah saw the task of dramatherapy, in part, as being to help people expand their repertory of role and role relationships (Landy, 1990). Indeed, in the present mobile global climate (Elliott & Urry, 2010) where the corporate emphasis is on 'polyvalence', 'flexibility', and on 'the ability to learn and to adapt to new functions' (Elliott & Lemert, 2009, p. 19), the ability to recreate yourself by invoking an expanded repertoire of role and role relationship is considered an increasingly crucial and marketable skill. As Wilshire commented, 'One *is* one's 'roles' but not *just* one's 'roles', for one is also an unobjectifiable consciousness of 'roles' actual and possible – even roles as yet unimagined' (Wilshire, 1982, p. 227).

Performance

Goffman (1959) and Landy (1993) have pointed out that like dramatic roles, life roles are performed and can therefore be crafted and rehearsed. Brook, and Elliot and Lemert, pointed out that performance is an embodied psychosocial relational process that can only occur in the context of audience (Brook, 1996) or witness, including self-as-witness (Elliott & Lemert, 2009) (see Chapter 8 for discussion of the dialogue between audience and witness processes). It has been theorised that it is in experiencing ourselves being witnessed by significant others that our identities are constituted and that the psychological formation of identity begins in relationship with the audience of our primary care-givers, the establishment of 'object relations' (Winnicott, 1971), and the development of the 'secure base' that people require in infancy to develop healthy identity functions in adulthood (Bowlby, 1988). Processes that are to do with our perceptions of how significant others receive us have an impact on the ways we see ourselves which in turn provide a personal internal context from which to move out into the world. That internal context has an impact on the flavour of our relationships with and our experiences of the world. In other words, as our agency meets a variety of physical and social structures, our identities arise in the tensions between the context, including prior learning (Vygotsky, 1978), our 'deep stories' (Yam, 2018, p. 1), the social 'memes' that influence us (Hess, 2015, p. 326), prior expectations (Zvelc, 2009), group dynamics (Shapiro, 2010), and the invitation to genuine expression and relationality (Rogers, 1961).

The performer/audience relationship is embodied, psychosocial, and dialectic (Jones, 1996a), and this encounter (Mayor & Frydman, 2021), which is a process central to drama, theatre, and dramatherapy (Sajnani, 2012), as well as to identity-work, can be instrumentalised to facilitate positive change (Mayor & Frydman, 2021). The performer/audience relationship can be used to consolidate latent competencies, including role competency (Emunah, 2020), and it can deepen relationships (Sajnani, 2012). Related to, but not the same as, the performer/audience relationship is the performer/witness relationship (see Chapter 7). In the classroom, witnessing is recognised as being a crucial part of facilitating a positive, caring, and effective learning environment (Lumpkin, 2007) and is worked out in practice as the need to give positive regard (Mihalas, Morse, Allsopp, & McHatton, 2009) and to see from the perspective of the students (Vansteenkiste et al., 2012).

An important aspect of performance, including identity-performance, is embodiment. Identity-performance and embodiment are inextricably linked because performance implies doing something for a communicative purpose, and that purpose is often best served through an embodied representation, including, for example, the clothes we choose to wear (Strathern & Stewart, 2008). It is possible in our embodied performance to choose to simultaneously refer, consciously or unconsciously, by imitation or opposition, to multiple competing or complementary familial, social, and cultural discourses, including those to do with gender and race (Josselson & Harway, 2012). Van der Kolk (2005) highlighted the relationship between embodiment and identity: firstly from the biological perspective, there are neural carriers that determine some identity-forming behaviours; secondly real, embodied, others influence the basic internalised introjects that build selfhood. In other words, people, who are physically around us, define our identities by imposing or supporting the social circumstances and norms that young children are unable to escape. Those norms form our 'deep stories' and become internalised.

What is the relationship between performance and performativity? As explained in Chapter 2, the concept of performativity has been used by some as a critique of the personal and corporate masquerade created by the technologies of governance and discourses to do with neoliberalism (Ball, 2008). This takes the form of a critique about the emptiness of action, where, for example, the seeming of good practice has become more important than good practice, and genuine relationality (Rogers, 1961) has been replaced by the commodification of relationships (Hess, 2015). Furthermore, in today's world of mobility and social media, our potential audience is vast and varied (Elliott & Lemert, 2009), and this can exert significant pressure on the individual (Curran & Hill, 2019) to perform to increasingly perfectionist standards (Ball, 2008). In effect, by the process of adapting our performances of self to the structures and discourses of society, we are, as it were, performed by our contexts (Butler, 2015). However, performativity as conceptualised throughout this book refers to the process whereby lives are created, meanings expressed, and relationships negotiated through doing and being. It is to do with how embodied performance, display, semiotics, and proximity in three-dimensional space not only expresses but also encodes (see Chapter 5) the relational negotiations with whoever and whatever else is in – and by implication not in – that space (Butler, 2015). Those performances emerge as crafted-and-experienced, in relation to our embodied psychosocial relational context. Inevitably, as it would in any context, in the context of advanced capitalism, what is being performed and the meanings those performances create adapts and changes to reflect the prevailing mechanisms of governance and dominant social discourses (Brown, 2019).

Story

Dramatic stories, as do life-autobiographical stories, feature characters who enact roles in social contexts. In both drama and real life, those stories represent important identity-work for the characters – or people – who feature in them because those stories explain past behaviour (for example, as retrospective excuses and justification) and act as possible guides for the future (Presser and Sandberg, 2015, in van Hulst, 2019). As van Hulst pointed out, 'stories construct the identity of people in them' (van Hulst, 2019, p. 3). It has been suggested that it is the function of stories to be a bridge between self, ethics, and identity (Bhaumik, Dash, & Kakkar, 2020; Hess, 2015). In that respect, in order to maintain a sense of personal coherency in an environment where identity can seem fragmented, distributed, and increasingly 'mobile' (Elliott & Lemert, 2009, p. 19), one way to do this is through the narratives, that is through the stories, that we create to explain ourselves to ourselves. In other words, if we can create and maintain coherent-enough (Winnicott,

1971) self-narratives, we are more likely to experience well-being. However, many people have life stories that contain within them competing multiple and unresolved voices, and therefore, the challenge is to find self-stories that give a coherent-enough sense of identity (Dimaggio & Semerari, 2004, in McAdams, 2006).

Based on the idea that narrative story-telling is the primary way that people construct and reconstruct their personal identities, one key strand of research into the storying of identity has been based on an exploration of autobiographical life story. In contrast to this, drama and dramatherapy often focus not on the autobiographical 'real-life' story but on the fictional created stories of individuals and groups. The rationale for foregrounding the fictional comes from the idea that people project self into their fictionally created stories by working on the level of symbol and metaphor. This is supported by research into not only the six-part story structure and BASIC-Ph analytical tool of Lahad (Lahad, 2013) but also into other projective modalities such as thematic apperception tests (Morgan, 1995). Projection, which is usually an unconscious process (Jung, 1991; Yalom, 1985), is 'the placing of aspects of ourselves or our feelings into other people or things' and is a normal part of everyday life (Jones, 1996b, loc.3012). It is often the starting point for creative endeavour and creates a strong relationship between what is emotionally real for a person, and, for example, the drama that they create (Jones, 1996b). Importantly, through the dramatic process, projection becomes 'expressive rather than being primarily defensive' (Jones, 1996b, loc.3070), so that the enactment of a dramatic fiction becomes a vehicle for the exploration of self.

In other words, story is central to identity. Stories can be changed and the corollary of that is that our identity can be re-storied. In other words, storied identities are not fixed but are relationally negotiated. Stories are part of a projective process that works on the level of symbol and metaphor. Stories are ethically rooted because the stories we tell about ourselves influence our behaviour. When individuals relationally and dialogically engage with the stories of others, this gives rise to 'epistemic suspicion' and subsequent re-positioning (John, 2018, p. 647). If we, as a result of that re-positioning, change our self-stories, we change our identity and vice versa. This is not about a dualistic tension between story structure and lived experience. It is about a multifaceted relationship between story structure and lived experience.

Role, Performance, and Story

The theoretical and applied foundation of this book rests in the links between role, performance, story, and identity. Through drama, students story themselves as they engage in the storying of the characters they create, explore multiple roles, and work towards a sense of identity coherence. Even though some of what is experienced remains contained within the 'discrepant communication' of the fiction (Sajnani, 2012, p. 17), this opens up possibilities (Blair, 2009; Fauconnier & Turner, 2002). For example, students experience themselves making choices. They identify with or disassociate from the results of those choices. They explore ways of discovering, or creating, who they are or who they would like to be and move closer to, or come to terms with, their sense of idealised-or-not personal identity (Rogers, 1961). Identity-work is done in the dynamic between the metaphoric and the real-worlds (Ouellette, 2012). Using that dynamic, students explore the ethical implications of being a global citizen (Bhaumik et al., 2020), in their own individual and social context, which is currently influenced by neoliberal socio-political discourse (see Chapter 2). In the embodied psychosocial relational context of the drama, students interactively and experientially put off and take on, or encode (see Chapter 5), a range of roles in various story contexts. Because the ways in which people orient themselves to context, or are oriented by context, position them, students find that they must, in the midst of the drama-process, make situated ethical choices (Figure 3.1).

Therefore, my position on identity and drama-based identity-work is that identity is the result of the embodied psychosocial relationally negotiated synthesis of drama-processes associated with role, performance, and story. Role implies both biological and social multiplicity, as well as a 'meta-role' function, flexibility, and choice (Blatner, 2006). Performance implies something created with an 'other' in mind (Bakhtin, 1994). This other might be self as witness, the significant other, or the social other (Shelton, 2019). There is an embodied as well as an internalised and projected reciprocal influence between performer

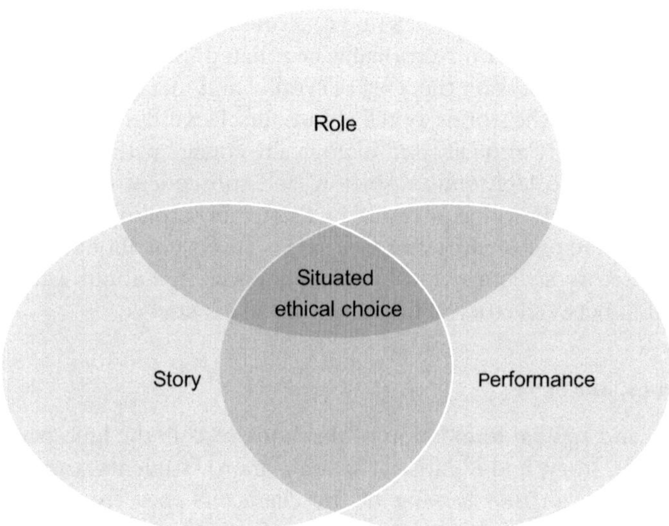

Figure 3.1 The relationally negotiated synthesis of identity-processes to do with role, performance, and story creates a crucible within which ethical choices (values-based choices) can be enacted in both fictional and real-life contexts.

and audience (Bakhtin, 1994). Stories are the primary means through which individuals and groups create their identities (Ernst, 2012; Gubrium & Holstein, in van Hulst, 2019). Those identity stories are co-created, mutable, and work on the level of projection, symbol, and metaphor. Referring to the link between the crucible of role, performance, and story that is drama, and identity, Landy said, 'If I can know my actual and fictional role models, then I can have a good idea of what I value and who I am' (Landy, 1992, p. 441), and Wiltshire commented, 'Let us commit ourselves ... to a very broad and flexible notion: all our mimetic involvements and individuations within the world, sequential or simultaneous, pertain to our identity as self' (Wilshire, 1982, p. 231).

We are as much defined by others as we are by ourselves, and identity is linked in fundamental ways to power, entitlement, emancipation, and choice. From this perspective, identity is a 'profoundly political issue ... steeped in issues of power, oppression, justice, fairness' (Chandler, 2016, p. 9). Drama, as a container for role, performance, and story, provides a context wherein students can conjointly explore behavioural and values-based choices, as characters-in-roles, in the context of the given circumstances as defined by the story and dramatic structure, in the validating – or not – context of an audience. That creative, exploratory, educational, and emancipatory process offers students the opportunity to develop more flexibility in terms of how they position themselves in their context (Blatner, 2006; Chandler, 2016; Jennings, 1987; Jones, 1996c; Landy, 1993; Wilshire, 1982). The double benefit of this in the context of neoliberalism is that through doing drama students engage in values explorations that help them to critically examine their positioning relative to prevailing discourses, and they develop an expanded role repertoire (see Chapters 5, 6, and 7). This helps students develop the skills needed for coping with performativity and mobility and allows students to explore prevailing and counter-market discourses through the safety of a fiction, in a context-embedded, relational, and embodied way.

Conclusion

Drama has often been used as an emancipatory modality. The Theatre for Social Justice movement seeks to be emancipatory in a political sense, and many dramatherapists hope to facilitate the kind of emancipation that comes from personal, relational, and community healing, by helping clients find a better balance between holding and change. I locate my practice at the confluence of these orientations. For me, the dramatherapeutically sensitised classroom, existing within the contested logics of governance between encroaching managerialism and resistance to it (see Chapter 2), offers the possibility of allowing students to explore personal and group identities. They can explore their personal and group identities by placing themselves bodily, psychosocially, and relationally, in characters-in-roles inside stories. At the same time, the dramatherapeutically sensitised classroom facilitates exploration by holding students within the safety of the one-remove of fiction. It facilitates skills development that gives more choice over mode of expression. With choice comes control. How might it be possible to take those philosophical, sociological, psychological, relational, and pedagogical principles and implement a sustainable, embodied, emancipatory intervention within the strictures of the school drama curriculum?

Of particular interest to this question is the work that Dr Clive Holmwood has done on the overlaps between drama-teaching and dramatherapy. Holmwood explored the relationships and overlaps between dramatherapy and drama-teaching in mainstream schools (Holmwood, 2016). He used a dramatherapy sensibility to see the therapeutic moments happening in the dramatic play of children in school and to acknowledge the therapeutic aspects inherent in the dramatic form. He situated his work in the context of interviews from eminent dramatherapists, including Dr Sue Jennings, Dr Phil Jones, and David Read Johnson who each opined that the strict professional boundaries that have been drawn between the two professions of drama-teaching and dramatherapy might be artificial and unhelpful. Holmwood delivered a dramatherapy intervention to a group of gifted students in one school, and he worked as a class teacher in another. From his experiences, he looked at the overlaps and differences in practice and student experience. My aim, however, is to explore a dramatherapeutically informed curriculum-drama, and I build on his work by bringing together the knowledges and practices of drama-teaching and dramatherapy into one space. Through drama, students story themselves as they engage in the storying of the characters they create, explore multiple roles, and work towards a sense of contextually situated identity coherence. Focussed by my commitment to working within mainstream curriculum-drama and precipitated by the current global and local political and legislative context, the work described in this book has been driven by my interest in drama as both education and development. It is underpinned by the conjoined roots, practices, and insights of drama in education and dramatherapy. These pages hold within them the pain of struggling to work between incompatible and competing legislative policies and educational paradigms as I search for ways to help the students I teach explore their place in a complex socio-political world. It is the embodied psychosocial and relational processes that underpin the work in the drama classroom, which is identity-work, in the tension created by the current policy climate of encroaching managerialism where the teaching of curriculum-drama in schools has been de-valued by being reduced to a skills/outcomes-based pseudo-academic subject because there is no longer room for developmental or exploratory drama within the curriculum, that this book explores.

References

Bakhtin, M. (1994). *The Bakhtin reader: Selected writings of Bakhtin, Medvedev, and Voloshinov*. London, New York: E. Arnold.

Ball, S. (2008). Performativity, privatisation, professionals and the state. In B. Cunningham (Ed.), *Exploring professionalism* (pp. 50). London: The Institute of Education, University of London.

Bhaumik, S., Dash, S., & Kakkar, K. (2020). Moral philosophy, pragmatism, and the larger cause: Why 'war' metaphors are needed during pandemics. *Indian Journal of Medical Ethics, 3*. doi:10.20529/IJME.2020.067

Blair, R. (2009). Cognitive neuroscience and acting: Imagination, conceptual blending, and empathy. *The Drama Review, 53*(4), 93–103. doi:10.1162/dram.2009.53.4.93

Blatner, A. (1997). *Acting in: Practical applications of psychodramatic methods* (3rd ed.). London: Free Association Books.

Blatner, A. (2006). The choosing self: Developing the meta-role functions. Retrieved from www.blatner.com/adam/psyntbk/choosingself.html

Bowlby, J. (1988). *A secure base: Clinical applications of attachment theory*. London: Routledge.

Brook, P. (1996). *The empty space*. New York: Simon and Schuster.

Brown, W. (1995). *States of injury*. Princeton, NJ: Princeton University Press.

Brown, W. (2019). *In the ruins of neoliberalism: The rise of antidemocractic politics in the West*. New York: Columbia University Press.

Burman, E. (2012). Deconstructing neoliberal childhood: Towards a feminist antipsychological approach. *Childhood, 19*(4), 423–438. doi:10.1177/0907568211430767

Burman, E., & Parker, I. (Eds.). (2017). *Discourse analytic research: Repertoires and readings of texts in action*. London and New York: Routledge.

Butler, J. (2006). *Gender trouble* (1st ed.). New York and London: Routledge.

Butler, J. (2015). *Notes towards a performative theory of assembly* (Kindle ed.). Cambridge: Harvard University Press.

Byng-Hall, J. (1985). The family script: A useful bridge between theory and practice. *Journal of Family Therapy, 7*(3), 301–305. doi:10.1046/j..1985.00688.x

Chandler, J. (2016). *Identity at work*. Oxon: Routledge.

Cole, B., Adamson, S., Craig, G., Hussain, B., Smith, L., Law, I., ... Cheung, T. (2009). *Hidden from public view: Racism against UK Chinese* (T. M. Group., Trans.). Sheffield University Research Archive: Sheffield Hallam University.

Curran, T., & Hill, A. P. (2019). Perfectionism is increasing over time: A meta-analysis of birth cohort differences from 1989 to 2016. *Psychological Bulletin, 145*(4), 410–429. doi:10.1037/bul0000138

Davies, B., & Harré, R. (2011). Positioning: The discursive production of selves. In M. Wetherell, S. Taylor, & S. Yates (Eds.), *Discourse theory and practice* (pp. 261–271). Los Angeles and London: SAGE in Association with The Open University.

Dignam, P. A., & Rohlinger, D. A. (2019). Misogynistic men online: How the red pill helped elect Trump. *Signs: Journal of Women in Culture and Society, 44*(Spring 2019). doi:10.1086/701155

Dijk, T. V. (2002). Discourse and racism. In D. T. Goldberg & J. Solomons (Eds.), *A companion to racial and ethnic studies* (pp. 145–159). Malden, MA and Oxford, UK: Blackwell Publishing.

Dijk, T. V. (2011). Discourse studies and hermeneutics. *Discourse Studies, 1*, 1–13. doi:10.1177/1461445611412762

Eagly, A., & Wood, W. (2017). Gender identity: Nature and nurture working together. *Evolutionary Studies in Imaginative Culture, 1*, 59. doi:10.26613/esic/1.1.10

Eler, A. (2017). *The selfie generation: How our self images are changing our notions of privacy, sex, consent, and culture*. New York: Skyhorse Publishing.
Elliott, A., & Lemert, C. (2009). *The new individualism: The emotional costs of globalization* (Revised ed.). New York and Oxon: Routledge.
Elliott, A., & Urry, J. (2010). *Mobile lives*. London and New York: Routledge.
Emunah, R. (2020). *Acting for real: Drama therapy process, technique, and performance* (2nd ed.). New York and London: Routledge.
Ernst, S. (2012). Evaluation of cultural and linguistic practices: Constructing Finnish-German identities in narrative research interviews. In R. Josselson & M. Harway (Eds.), *Navigating multiple identities: Race, gender, culture, nationality, and roles* (pp. 207–226). Oxford and New York: Oxford University Press.
Esping-Anderson, G. (2012). *The three worlds of welfare capitalism*. Cambridge, UK: Polity Press.
Fauconnier, G., & Turner, M. (2002). *The way we think: Conceptual blending and the mind's hidden complexities*. New York: Perseus Books Group.
Foucault, M., & Nazzaro, A. (1972). History, discourse and discontinuity. *Psychological Man: Approaches to an Emergent Social Type, 20*(Summer/Fall), 225–248.
Francis, B. (1998). Oppositional positions: Children's construction of gender in talk and role plays based on adult occupation. *Educational Researcher, 40*, 31–43. doi:10.1080/0013188980400103
Gee, J. P. (2014). *An introduction to discourse analysis: Theory and method*. London: Routledge.
Gergen, K. J. (2000). *The saturated self: Dilemmas of identity in contemporary life*. New York: Perseus Books.
Goffman, E. (1959). *The presentation of self in everyday life*. New York: Anchor Books.
Gregg, G. (2012). Multiple identities and their organisation. In R. Josselson & M. Harway (Eds.), *Navigating multiple identities: Race, gender, culture, nationality, and roles* (pp. 13–51). Oxford and New York: Oxford University Press.
Haraway, D. (2016). *A cyborg manifesto* (ProQuest Ebook Central ed.). Minneapolis, MN: University of Minnesota Press.
Haraway, D., & Wolfe, C. (2016). *Manifestly Haraway*. Minneapolis, MN: University of Minnesota Press.
Hekman, S. J. (2014). *The feminine subject*. Cambridge, UK: Polity.
Henriques, J., Hollway, W., Urwin, C., Venn, C., & Walkerdine, V. (1998). *Changing the Subject: Psychology, social regulation and subjectivity* (J. Henriques, W. Hollway, C. Urwin, C. Venn, & V. Walkerdine Eds. 2005 ed.). London and New York: Routledge.
Hess, K. (2015). Metaphors matter: Ethics and the memes of the market. *Georgetown Journal of Law and Public Policy, 13*, 321–336.
Higgins, T. (2004). Gender, why feminists can't (or shouldn't) be liberals. *Fordham Law Review, 72*(5), 1628–1641.
Hollway, W. (2005). Gender difference and the production of subjectivity. In *Changing the subject: Psychology, social regulation and subjectivity* (pp. 227–263). London and New York: Routledge.
Hollway, W., & Jefferson, T. (2013). *Doing qualitative research differently* (K. Metzier Ed. 2013 ed.). London: SAGE.
Holmwood, C. (2016). *Drama education and dramatherapy: Exploring the space between disciplines*. London: Routledge.

Hook, D. (2001). Discourse, knowledge, materiality, history; Foucault and discourse analysis. *Theory and Psychology, 11*(Online), 521–547. doi:10.1177/0959354301114006

Hunter, S. (2008). Living documents: A feminist psychosocial approach to the relational politics of policy documentation. *Critical Social Policy, 28*(4), 506–528. doi:10.1177/0261018308095300

Hunter, S. (2015a). Being called to 'By the Rivers of Birminam': The relational choreography of white looking. *Critical Arts, 29*(1), 43–57. doi:10.1080/02560046.2015.1102250

Hunter, S. (2015b). *Power, politics and the emotions: Impossible governance?* London, UK: Taylor & Francis Group.

Jennings, S. (Ed.) (1987). *Dramatherapy theory and practice for teachers and clinicians.* Kent: Routledge.

John, E. (2018). Allegory and ethical education: Stories for people who know too many stories. *Journal of Philosophy of Education, 52.* doi:10.1111/1467-9752.12327

Jones, P. (1996a). The active witness: The acquisition of meaning in dramatherapy. In H. Payne (Ed.), *Handbook of inquiry in the arts therapies: One river many currents* (pp. 41–55). London: Jessica Kingsley.

Jones, P. (1996b). *Drama as therapy volume 1: Theory, practice and research* (2nd ed.). London and New York: Routledge.

Jones, P. (1996c). *Drama as therapy: Theatre as living.* London and New York: Routledge.

Josselson, R., & Harway, M. (2012). The challenges of multiple identity. In R. Josselson & M. Harway (Eds.), *Navigating multiple identities: Race, gender, culture, nationality, and roles* (pp. 3–14). Oxford and New York: Oxford University Press.

Jung, C. G. (1991). *The archetypes and the collective unconscious* (R. F. C. Hull, Trans. 2nd ed.). London and New York: Routledge.

Klein, M. (1932). *The psycho-analysis of children* (A. Strachey, Trans.). London: Random House Vintage.

Lahad, M. (2013). Six part story revisited: The seven levels of assessment drawn from the 6PSM. In M. Lahad, M. Shacham, & O. Ayalon (Eds.), *The 'BASIC PH' model of coping and resiliency: Theory, research and cross-cultural application* (pp. 121–147). London and Philadelphia: Jessica Kingsley.

Landy, R. (1990). The concept of role in dramatherapy. *The Arts in Psychotherapy, 17*, 223–230. doi:10.1016/0197-4556(90)90005-B

Landy, R. (1992). A taxonomy of roles: A blueprint for the possibilities of being. *The Arts in Psychotherapy, 18*, 419–431. doi:10.1016/0197-4556(91)90054-E

Landy, R. (1993). *Persona and performance: The meaning of role in drama, therapy, and everyday life.* New York and London: Guildford Press.

Losleben, L., & Musubika, S. (2023). Intersectionality. In M. Duarte, K. Loslleben, & K. Fjørtoft (Eds.), *Gender diversity, equity, and inclusion in academia: A conceptual framework for sustainable transformation.* London, UK: Routledge.

Lumpkin, A. (2007). Caring teachers: The key to student learning. *Kappa Delta Pi Record, 43*(4), 158–160. doi:10.1080/00228958.2007.10516474

Mayor, C., & Frydman, J. S. (2021). Understanding school-based drama therapy through the core processes: An analysis of intervention vignettes. *The Arts in Psychotherapy, 73.* doi:10.1016/j.aip.2021.101766

McAdams, D. P. (2006). The problem of narrative coherence. *Journal of Constructivist Psychology, 19*(2), 109. doi:10.1080/10720530500508720

McRobbie, A. (2008). Young women and consumer culture. *Cultural Studies, 22*(5), 531–550. doi:10.1080/09502380802245803

Meldrum, B. (1994). A role model of dramatherapy and its application with individuals and groups. In S. Jennings, A. Cattanach, S. Mitchell, A. Chesner, & B. Meldrum (Eds.), *The handbook of dramatherapy* (pp. 36–45). London: Routledge.

Merleau-Ponty, M. (1945). *Phenomenology of perception* (D. A. Landes, Trans. 2012 Reprint ed.). London and New York: Routledge.

Mihalas, S., Morse, W. C., Allsopp, D. H., & McHatton, P. (2009). Cultivating caring relationships between teachers and secondary students with emotional and behavioral disorders: Implications for research and practice. *Remedial and Special Education, 30*(2), 108–125. doi:10.1177/0741932508315950

Morgan, W. G. (1995). Origin and history of the thematic apperception test images. *Journal of Personality Assessment, 65*(2), 237. doi:10.1207/s15327752jpa6502_2

Oakley, A. (1986). *Taking it like a woman.* London: Collins Publishing Group.

Ouellette, S. C. (2012). A garden for many identities. In R. Josselson & M. Harway (Eds.), *Navigating multiple identities: Race, gender, culture, nationality, and roles* (pp. 129–142). Oxford and New York: Oxford University Press.

Paujer, K. (2021). Ending racism starting with kids. Retrieved from www.hawaii-can.org/keikitalkracism_recording]

Rogers, C. (1961). *On becoming a person: A therapist's view of psychotherapy.* Boston: Houghton Mifflin Company.

Sajnani, N. (2012). The implicated witness: Towards a relational aesthetic in dramatherapy. *Dramatherapy, 34*(March 2012), 6–21. doi:10.1080/02630672.2012.657944

Sepinuck, T. (2023). *We are the ripple effect: Theatre of witness in Northern Ireland.* Northern Ireland: NI Community Relations Council.

Shapiro, D. L. (2010). Relational identity theory: A systematic approach for transforming the emotional dimension of conflict. *The American Psychologist, 65*(7), 634–645. doi:10.1037/a0020004

Shelton, L. G. (2019). *The Bronfenbrenner primer: A guide to develecology.* London: Routledge.

Shimizu, C. P. (2007). *The hypersexuality of race: Performing Asian/American women on screen and scene.* Durham and London: Duke University Press.

Sluss, D. M., & Ashforth, B. E. (2007). Relational identity and identification: Defining ourselves through work relationships. *Academy of Management Review, 32*(1), 9–32. doi:10.5465/AMR.2007.23463672

Strathern, A., & Stewart, P. (2008). Embodiment theory in performance and performativity. *Journal of Ritual Studies, 22*(1), 67–71.

van der Kolk, B. (1977). *The body keeps the score: Brain, mind, and body in the healing of trauma.* New York: Penguin.

van der Kolk, B. (2005). Developmental trauma disorder: Towards a rational diagnosis for children with complex trauma histories. *APA Psycnet Psychiatric Annals, 35*(5), 401–408. doi:10.3928/00485713-20050501-06

van Hulst, M. (2019). Ethnography and narrative. *Policing and Society,* 1–18. doi:10.1080/10439463.2019.1646259

Vansteenkiste, M., Sierens, E., Goossens, L., Soenens, B., Dochy, F., Mouratidis, A., … Beyers, W. (2012). Identifying configurations of perceived teacher autonomy support and structure: Associations with self-regulated learning, motivation and problem behavior. *Learning and Instruction, 22*(6), 431–439. doi:10.1016/j.learninstruc.2012.04.002

Vygotsky, L. (1978). *Mind in society: The development of higher psychological processes.* Cambridge, MA: Harvard University Press.

Walkerdine, V. (2005). Developmental psychology and the child-centred pedagogy: The insertion of Piaget into early education. In J. Henriques, W. Hollway, C. Urwin, C. Venn, & V. Walkerdine (Eds.), *Changing the subject: Psychology, social regulation and subjectivity* (pp. 153–202). London and New York: Routledge.

Walkerdine, V., & Jimenez, L. (2012). *Gender, work and community after de-industrialisation [electronic resource]: A psychosocial approach to affect.* Basingstoke: Palgrave Macmillan.

Webster, D., & Rivers, N. (2019). Resisting resilience: Disrupting discourses of self-efficacy. *Pedagogy, Culture and Society, 27*(4), 523–535. doi:10.1080/14681366.2018.1534261

Wharton, A. (2012). *The sociology of gender: An introduction to theory and research* (2nd ed.). Chichester, West Sussex: Wiley-Blackwell.

Wilshire, B. (1982). *Role playing and identity: The limits of theatre as metaphor.* Bloomington: Indiana University Press.

Winnicott, D. (1971). *Playing and reality* (2009 reprint ed.). London and New York: Routledge.

Wrenn, M. (2014). Identity, identity politics, and neoliberalism. *Panoeconomicus, 61*(4), 503–515. doi:10.2298/PAN1404503W

Yalom, I. D. (1985). *The theory and practice of group psychotherapy* (3rd ed.). New York: Basic Books.

Yam, S. (2018). Interrogating the 'deep story': Storytelling and narratives in the rhetoric classroom. *Composition Forum, 40.* doi:ISSN-1522-7502

Zvelc, G. (2009). Between self and others: Relational schemas as an integrating construct in psychotherapy. *Transactional Analysis Journal, 39*(1), 22.

4 Bridging the Theory/ Practice Divide

What Is Actually Going On Inside the Classroom and How Do We Know?

The Pedagogic Landscape

Education is a discipline beset with contestation. Competing policies make their demands. Initiatives that derive from opposing ideological and pedagogical positions are imposed simultaneously. Tension is generated. Tension is generated when school mission statements claim that their education prepares young people to take a full and active social and economic role in society when in reality the critical thinking that underpins a person's ability to fully engage in democratic debate has been squeezed out of the curriculum. There is a mismatch between the expectation that education will help young people to develop into creative problem solvers who are able to work cooperatively as well as on their own initiative and the imposition of pre-determined outcome-measures that encourage a 'there is only one right answer' approach to learning. This disparity between policy and some practices is a tension that needs managing in the classroom.

In addition, there is a tension between the enlightenment desire for a 'liberal' education, the aim of which is to develop the individual as a whole person, versus the push for schools to deliver a 'vocational' or 'skills-based' training. This tension is mirrored in the tension that exists between the pseudo-vocational skills-based delivery of drama in schools versus the exploratory and self-actualising use of drama that now remains for the most part the domain of the dramatherapist working with withdrawal groups or in clinical settings. The result is that what is considered educationally valid, and what is considered dramatherapeutically valid, is contested.

Furthermore, the local social-political context of the school site where the young people with whom I worked lived and went to school was a site of contestation. Some local factions pushed for a more neoliberalised, skills-based, and outcome-measures/audit approach within education. Other factions resisted with some considerable success the drift towards increasing managerialism. This is, no doubt, a pattern that is widely recognised.

Finally, as a drama practitioner, I work in the overlapping multiplicities of realities that are fictions and fictions that are realities. What is fictional and what is real is consciously interwoven and relationally negotiated in the construction

DOI: 10.4324/9781003464532-4

of meaning or in pursuit of 'truth' (Lehleiter, 2016). I work between the physical realities of stagecraft, and the fictional realities it supports, and between the embodied realities of student-actors, and the imaginative realities in which they become immersed. In and through drama, the 'now' and the 'then' overlap, as do the 'here' and the 'there', and the 'me' and the 'you'. There exists in balance the reality of what is happening on stage and the willing suspension of disbelief of the audience (Coleridge, 1847).

How is it possible to make sense of all this? A useful place to start is to move away from the empirical assumption that the physical, emotional, and social landscape has meaning in and of itself and to move towards the assumption that the meanings ascribed to the physical, emotional, and social landscape are relationally negotiated. In this way, it is possible to consider the ways students navigate the contestable nature of their work. Students negotiate the meanings of their drama as they go along. As the drama develops, the relationships of one student to another shifts, and so the meanings of the drama shift, and vice versa. Therefore, it is important to recognise that at any given point in time when observing, or working with, young people in the drama context, what is being experienced is an in-the-moment snap-shot, or series of moments, accompanied by a narrative that pertains to the moment, accepting that on another day, the work might seem to mean something entirely different (Larkin, Watts, & Clifton, 2006).

Classroom Practice as Research Landscape: Practice into Research

It is typical for a teacher to use the formula 'plan-do-review' as the basis for practice. It is usual to plan for what a lesson will look like and to plan what it is hoped the students will learn or experience. Once the lesson has been delivered, it is reviewed, and formal or personal assessments are made about how far the lesson aims were met. As part of that review, it is usual to plan adjustments to take forward so that any next lesson is 'better'. To look with more rigour at the meanings that are being made in the classroom, and at the processes that are taking place, what is needed is an approach that formalises the 'plan-do-review' format while still sitting naturally within the classroom environment. The methodology of 'practitioner enquiry' is one such approach.

Within practitioner enquiry, there is no set method of data collection. Rather, the research process follows the teaching rhythm of plan-do-review, and the research intervention follows classroom practice. Other than a formalisation of the plan-do-review protocol so that classroom practice is deliberately contextualised in the wider literature, no additional layers are required (Vivienne Baumfield, Elaine Hall, & Kate Wall, 2013). Therefore, the method of data collection for this project started with the school context. In this case, students agreed to help generate and record two strands of data. Those two strands were firstly, an iPad record of the stories that they created and secondly, an iPad recording of their rehearsals. For 39 lessons, students made recordings of their stories and their rehearsals which they passed to me for transcribing and analysis. Students had a drama lesson once every week, and the lessons were 55 minutes long. In the lessons, the students worked in small groups; the size of which resulted in an average of five groups in the class. Therefore, the data sample comprised 195 recordings.

A reflection process, including journaling, has been demonstrated to promote interactional learning and re-learning (Costello, 2011); therefore, I created a third strand of data that comprised my own reflections on the classroom and the research. This third strand was a record of my own thinking and planning. To capture my thinking and planning, I kept a written journal for the duration of the project. This strand of data began as a record of my responses to what I saw emerging from the transcribing, coding, and early analysis of the first two strands of data. However, those reflections immediately became part of the data itself as reflections fed into practice. Therefore, in a cyclical process typical of practitioner research, my practice influenced the practical work of the students and their practical work influenced my practice (Kizilcik & Daloglu, 2018).

Practitioner enquiry starts with the relationships between classroom practice and student learning experience (Murray & Lawrence, 2000), and it explores the impact teachers have on the learning of their students (Gilchrist, 2018). Classroom practice starts with personal and pedagogic orientation, and therefore for me, working with these students, some reflection on my own personal and pedagogic orientation seemed a good place to begin. In turn, pedagogical orientation is informed by the way a sense of being embodied, and what that means, works out in everyday choices and practices. It is also informed by the ways ethical, conceptual or theoretical, and procedural knowledges are worked out through quotidian choices and practices. It is those everyday choices and practices that comprise my teaching practice. That teaching practice becomes part of the educational landscape. As this was also a research project, teaching practice as worked out through pedagogy in practice and as informed and underpinned by embodied ethical conceptual and procedural knowledges, also became the research landscape (see Figure 4.1).

In line with the pedagogical underpinnings of the project, I chose to step away from a dynamic where, by asserting my power as teacher and researcher, I pursued pre-validated outcomes. Instead, I elected to enter a space where what was judged 'good' could be contested (Powell & Smith, 2009) and so

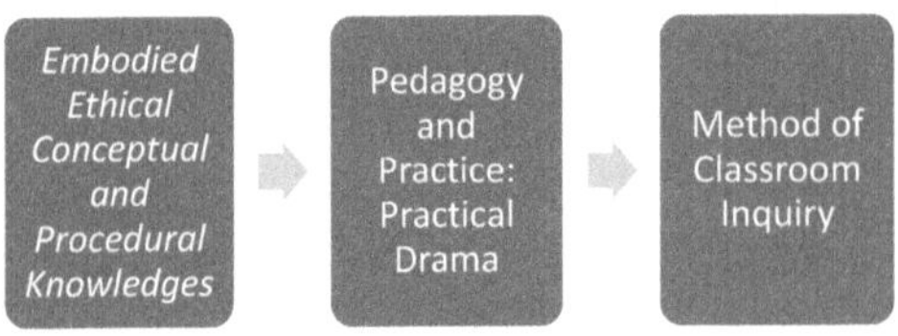

Figure 4.1 Pedagogy into practice.

I worked with one mixed ability year-9 class with a wide range of aptitudes and styles of engagement who would challenge myself and the teaching material robustly, be more determining of the classroom environment, and demand from me a searching dialogue with the meanings that they created within and through their work. Although some students had additional needs, they were all accommodated within mainstream provision. The class's form-teacher supported the project and devoted tutor-time to supporting my initial approach to the students. This included allowing students to use tutor-time to choose their own pseudonyms for the project, which in line with the pedagogical and epistemological orientations of the project was considered part of their identity-work.

A Very Personal Journey

My personal orientation as theatre practitioner, drama teacher, and dramatherapist means that I tend to assume that the meanings we ascribe to our various realities are negotiated and that the fictional, because it has been brought into being, is also a reality (Lehleiter, 2016). I also tend to assume that it is possible to see the world from a variety of points of view through drama. Furthermore, my understanding is that meanings are negotiated on the level of projection, symbol, and metaphor (Lengelle, Meijers, & Hughes, 2016; Wilshire, 1982). All this implies that several processes are happening simultaneously. For example, a negotiation between a person's inner voices, including their habitual and novel thoughts, attitudes, and internal positions, becomes over-layered with a person-to-person negotiation that is to do with interpersonal, relational, and social dynamics. Moreover, 'inner voice' to 'other person' negotiation takes place, as does the negotiation that happens as individuals and groups position themselves and others relative to symbolic material (Barthes, 2009; Jones, 1991). In the theatre, this implies a multi-level relationship between the audience and the different aspects of production and a conscious or unconscious assumption that everything on stage can be granted meaning (Elam, 1987).

These assumptions and understandings, which are to do with the constructed nature of reality, self-realisation, open-endedness, embodiment, and exploration, permeate my teaching practice. They inform my pedagogical understanding that important learning arises from the processes and activities that happen when young people physically engage in fictional, practical drama. In classroom terms, this means that I invite students to show me, not tell me. Drama conventions such as freeze framing and slow motion, changing the way a character walks by manipulating rhythm, pace, and tension, or by placing characters in different places on the stage, give students a chance to explore their experience of embodiment in the context of the embodiment of their characters and of the embodiment of other characters who share the space. Therefore, to understand what is going on in the classroom, I need to look in three places. Firstly, I need a record of the embodied interactions of the students as they conduct their drama. In this project, the students created this record by sharing with me iPad recordings of their rehearsals. Secondly, I need a record of the stories that are generated. In this project, this was extracted from the students' iPad recordings. Thirdly, I need a record of my own reflections on the drama and future planning. I created this by keeping a reflective journal.

As part of my usual practice, to help me navigate my own part in the complex web of meanings generated in the classroom, and in line with dramatherapy ethical and professional practice, and good practice for teachers (Kelly & Bruck, 2012), I built reflective dialogue (Hollway & Jefferson, 2013; Kizilcik & Daloglu, 2018) into my teaching practice via a weekly meeting with a clinical supervisor. This weekly meeting offered me, in the context of another professionally trained person, the space to reflect on my responses to work the students did and to my relationships with them and to school policy. If I felt stuck, or if the classroom relationships or rehearsals did not go well, my clinical supervisor was the person with whom I could talk things through confidentially as we searched for a way forward together. My clinical supervisor took the role of 'critical friend' (Gilchrist, 2018, p. 25) who helped me see, explore, and make explicit my own biases, as I worked towards 'relative neutrality and reasonable freedom from unacknowledged researcher biases' (Miles & Huberman, 1994, p. 278). With her, I was able to voice and test out reflections, have them corroborated or challenged, and explore alternative points of view. This kind of reflection helped generate insights into the process of negotiation by which student reflection that was an inherent part of the rehearsal process, and teacher reflection, came into dialogue (Hollway & Jefferson, 2013). This process of reflection also provided direction that helped determine a trajectory for further interaction and intervention (Kizilcik & Daloglu, 2018). Reflecting in this way gave me an opportunity to consider the ways that my own responses to the students, whether that was the warmth of recognition or a disconnect of some kind, was part of what I contributed to creating those students' identities (see, for example, my discussion of the work of Peter First in Chapter 7) (Hollway & Jefferson, 2013).

I used a three-column format for the reflective journal. For an excerpt from the three-column reflective journal, see Figure 4.2. From left to right, the first column details my initial response to the material. If I had no clear thoughts, this column might take the form of questions, or be a narrative record of what I noticed. The second column was a record of my response to the comments in the first column. I used the third column to embed my thoughts in a wider context by making links to research and to literature, and to draw out exploratory thematic links. The three columns capture my effort to deepen and broaden my reflections and to see from different perspectives (Sherin & van Es, 2005; Vicary, Young, & Hicks, 2017), in other words, to move from a first-order to a second-order analysis (Larkin et al., 2006). Initially, I used this reflective process to create a way into analysis of the material rather than to plan. Nevertheless, the reflective process had a

Thoughts	*Second Thoughts*	*Third Thoughts*
Walton Hero. Who was Walton today? He was the trusted and competent leader.	Dynamic. Very much the one in charge. The other boys know where they are with him.	This relates to work by Pellegrini - suggests for boys, that when used in conjunction with relational skill, conflict builds peer groups (Pellegrini 2009).
Justin Soft – a performer. Loved just standing in the lights and declaiming. Was very emotionally engaged in the distress of his character. Walton found this difficult. I wonder what this was raising for Walton?	Dynamic. Was happier after he had accepted that he had lost the power struggle with Walton that has been going on for a few lessons. Distance. I wonder what the distressed bemoaning represented for Justin. He was really into it and did it really well. It was also very sustained.	I love how he just wants to perform. I do get that. I also note the link between catharsis, humour, and resistance (Willett 2019).

Figure 4.2 Three-column reflective journal.

significant impact on my planning because the understandings and insights I created as I journaled was a major determinant of the ways I viewed the students' work, the ways I understood students' relationships to their work, and possible meanings I ascribed to their work. The reflective process also helped me to create, deepen, and enrich my response to their work, and this in turn informed the ways I related to the students about their work, and it informed the suggestions I made as possible ways forward with the rehearsal process (Figure 4.2).

What We Did Together

My students and I completed three projects together. The students worked in groups of between two and six and as part of their normal curriculum-drama took part in one text-based and two devised-based projects. This translated into a research design that included two different kinds, or modes, of drama, which were devising work and text-based work. They did this in the context of a stable structuring framework (Guba, 1981, in Kivunja & Kuyini, 2017).

Each project was structured as follows:

- Pre-planning: negotiate choices of topics.
- Planning: explore initial and potential ideas for drama.

- Exploration: learn new skills and conduct initial practical experimentation.
- Iterative rehearsal process: including negotiated teacher response and feedback, choosing and engaging rehearsal conventions, and taking responsibility for the direction of the drama.
- Perform and reflect.

Written down like that or presented as a diagram (Figure 4.3), those teaching phases seem well organised and clear and appear to represent a definite learning trajectory. In practice, the five phases had fuzzy boundaries, and elements of the phases worked in tandem throughout every phase and lesson. This approach mirrored an open interview style associated with interpretivist and qualitative research. It facilitated the gathering of naturalistic data that showed me what was of interest to the young people. It also created a vast volume of diverse and open-ended data which needed a lot of processing.

Over three classroom drama projects, the students and I addressed educational aims that included: how to use a range of drama conventions to develop character and story; exploring character, role, and plot using improvised drama; and rehearsing to performance. In developing the work, I collaborated with a colleague from a neighbouring school (Roberts & Walters, 2018a, 2018b,

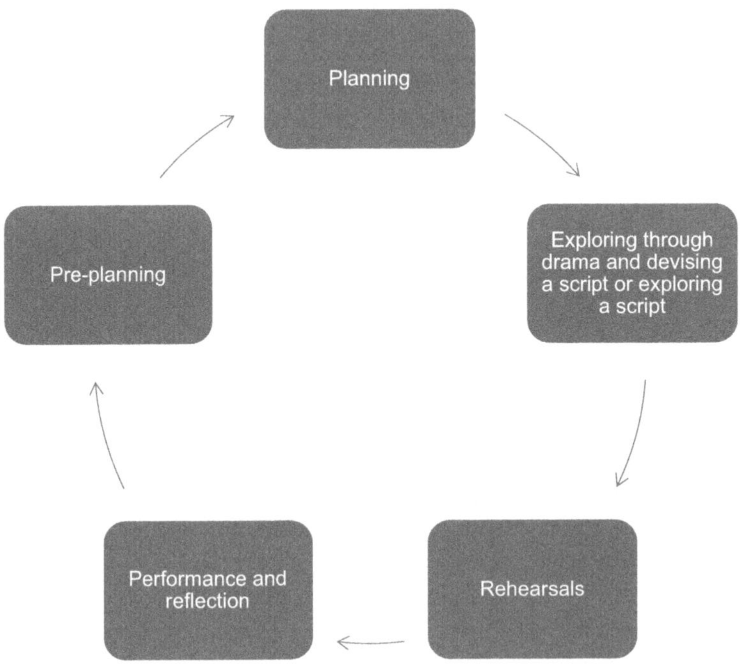

Figure 4.3 The five phases of the drama projects.

2018c). Initial lessons were teacher-led and enabled the students to generate a foundational structure for their work that was based in the conventions of drama and not in the conventions of literature. Those initial lessons centred around use of freeze frames, physical exploration, improvisation, and work in three-dimensional stage space. In subsequent lessons, students were invited to rehearse more independently supported by a 'levelling up' skills-list that offered guidance regarding the kinds of skills and conventions they could include in their work that would demonstrate 'progression' and approximate the kind of vertical integration and deliberate re-visiting of content-learning required by the 'deep dive' model of curriculum scrutiny. Those 'skills' included reference to drama 'basics' such as speaking confidently and clearly, taking turns, facing the audience and use of the '4th wall', as well as reference to a variety of conventions including: mime, freeze frame, role reversing, hot seating, developing storyboards, using costume and set, and so on. The progression elicited in the skills sheet was technical progression and fulfilled the school's requirement to demonstrate pre-determined learning outcomes. In response to the material and to the relational themes the students explored in our second project, I judiciously selected a range of texts for inclusion in our third project (Cox & Theilgaard, 1997). The texts offered a range of difficulties and styles and were drawn from a standard corpus of texts used in schools. The final week of each project was formal reflection. This reflection did not remain focussed on theatrical merit but instead invited students to consider their positioning to the identities of the characters and the situations they had created (Bastemur & Bras, 2021).

The embodied nature of the work meant that, in practice, the students required more physical space than there was in my drama-teaching classroom. Therefore, when I taught older students, who required more space than younger ones, my practice was to allow them to disperse to various locations round the school to rehearse independently. I conducted remote supervision by circulating. Typically, with the participant class, I was able to visit each group three or four times a lesson. I spent more time with the groups who needed me more and less time with groups who needed me less and for whom my proximity was an impediment to their working dynamic. Although this meant that I did not spend equal times with each group, the guiding principle was not the structural imperative of, for example, ten minutes per group but the relational and ethical imperatives of what do you need from me right now, and how can I best support you. The reality is that some students require more teacher-time than others.

Each lesson started and ended with the same ritualised protocols. At the start: students lined up outside the drama studio, then filed in; I stood by the door, greeted students, and took the lesson register. At the end: everyone returned to the drama studio from wherever they had been rehearsing; students uploaded their rehearsal recordings or handed in their iPad and other equipment; and we addressed issues arising from the rehearsals. Endings to lessons often felt chaotic because some students returned to the studio sooner, and some later, and each group arrived with a different agenda. Sometimes, students had equipment to process, including props, costumes, and items of 'set' that needed storing, and this required supervision. Students who did not need so much attention milled about and waited more-or-less impatiently for the bell that signalled the start of their break time. Often, the situation was further complicated because one or more of the groups would want to stay in over break to conduct further rehearsals or to show me something they had done. Inevitably, they were joined by friends and peers from the wider school community who also wanted to take advantage of the drama-room space for their own extra rehearsals.

In my typical teaching practice, the middle sections of the lesson included a stage where I introduced new vocabulary or concepts, such as 'blocking' or 'proxemics', and set the focus of the lesson. For the participating class, this meant that in the early stages of the projects, this was a simple matter of saying that the rehearsal was to be about 'blocking', or 'a read through', or 'vocal characterisation', or 'physical characterisation', or 'proxemics'. However, in later rehearsals, as students in the different groups started to need different interventions, I had to address each group individually to provide each group with a bespoke focus for rehearsal. Therefore, I adopted the pragmatic of preparing a written sheet for each group based on the transcriptions of the previous week's recordings, with suggestions for a rehearsal focus, and this was a

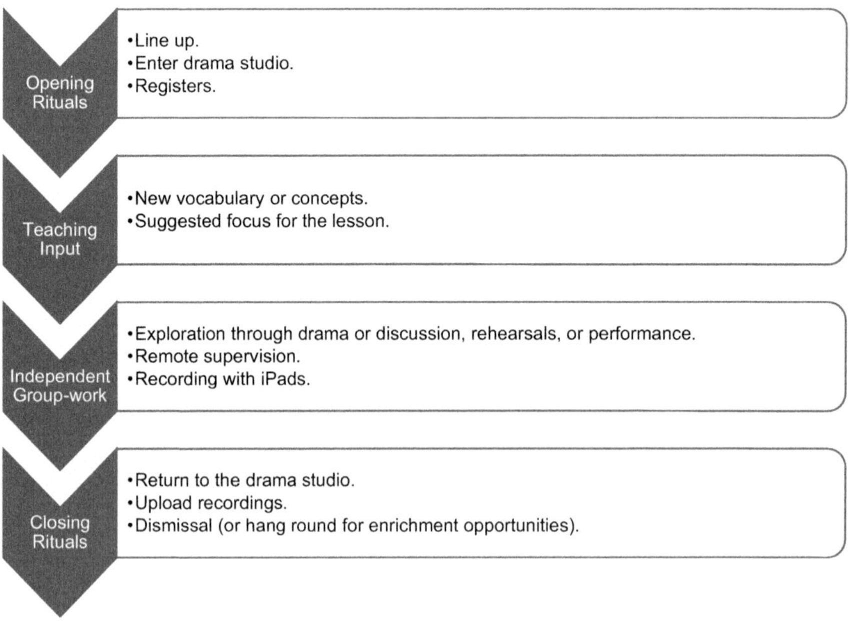

Figure 4.4 Typical lesson framework.

practice that I adopted in my teaching practice across my full teaching timetable. The sheet formed the basis of a negotiation and was either adopted or adapted by each group. In my typical teaching practice, the other middle section was when students went independently to locations around the school to do rehearsal work. For the participating class, it was during this phase of the lesson that students took recordings of their work. This lesson routine offered a stable and predictable framework around which the work of the students could coalesce (Corsaro, 2018) (see Figure 4.4).

But What Does It All Mean?

To start to make sense of what I was seeing, I used three approaches. I started in the first project by placing the stories the young people created against the six-part story structure of Gersie and Lahad (Lahad & Dent Brown, 2012). The six-part story structure is a projective tool (ibid.) conceived in a dramatherapy context. Gersie and Lahad took story elements reportedly found in all mythic stories (von Franz, 1991) and synthesised them into a structure for story-making (Lahad & Dent Brown, 2012). Lahad later integrated the structure into his PhD work on coping styles. The six-part story structure in conjunction with the BASIC-Ph coping analysis has become a diagnostic tool which has been demonstrated to be reliable in determining individual coping strategy and resilience (Lahad & Dent Brown, 2012), and which has been used with people living with high levels of stress. However, in my context, I soon found that the six-part story framework did not capture the complexity of the students' embodied interactions. Therefore, in the second project, I added a coding and categorising approach based on the 'grounded theory' of Glaser and Strauss (2017) (see Figure 4.5).

In brief, the grounded theory approach requires that the researcher:

- Codes transcripts of the student's work. This represents a first attempt to categorise the data.
- Recodes the transcripts whilst looking for relationships between the categories. The aim is to create meta categories.
- Repeats the process until one category emerges which links all the other categories. This then becomes the 'core variable' to which the other categories now become sub-categories.
- Throughout, in the margins of the work, records practitioner reflections and insights.
- Allows the coding process and practitioner reflections to direct the research gaze moving forward.

I tried to approach the analysis of the material with an open mind, though not an 'empty head' (Thornberg, 2012, p. 9). For example, dramatherapy knowledges informed my understanding that the fictional stories created by the students were related to student identity formation (Jones, 1991).

<table>
<tr><td rowspan="11">• Ethics (what is the right thing to do?) and identity work.
• In role (implies formal audience).
• Out of role (implies informal audience).
• In and out of role at the same time.
• Encoded work (both conscious and unconscious embodied engagement with a role.</td><td rowspan="8">Group Dynamic
Relating to my group – one's place within the group.</td><td rowspan="4">Status and hierarchy.</td><td>Physical.</td><td>• Roughhousing.
• Weapons (distanced).
• Possession of things/ resources.</td></tr>
<tr><td>Language.</td><td>• Implied physical.
• Other insults.</td></tr>
<tr><td>Knowledge.</td><td>• Knowledge.
• Skill.</td></tr>
<tr><td>Association.</td><td>• By association (seconding).</td></tr>
<tr><td rowspan="4">Bonding.</td><td>Physical.</td><td>• Care.
• Sharing.</td></tr>
<tr><td>Language.</td><td>• Compliments.</td></tr>
<tr><td>Knowledge.</td><td>• Help.</td></tr>
<tr><td>Association.</td><td>• Imitation (Actions, Clothes, Attitudes).</td></tr>
<tr><td rowspan="3">Idealised/ shadow self – the kind of person I am.
Relating to the wider society.</td><td colspan="2">Framing: strong or lose framing.
Scripted or improvised.</td><td>• Making a choice.
• Following a rule.</td></tr>
<tr><td colspan="2">Resources (What do I have that positions me to others in the wider society?).</td><td>• Physical strength.
• Commodities.
• Knowledge/ skill.
• Belief (the supernatural).
• Agency (freedom).
• Network.</td></tr>
<tr><td colspan="2">Image management.</td><td>• External display – what I look like. Dialogue with 'out there'.
• Internal – hiding–dialogue within me.</td></tr>
</table>

Figure 4.5 Conceptual coding matrix with the core variable on the far left.

However, it was as I observed the ways the students related to each other inside the fictions that I was able to notice the ways in which these students, with these stories, negotiated their identity-work. Moreover, my initial reaction to some of the students' drama and conduct, informed as it was by my own cultural expectations, became tempered and transformed via close, and open minded, scrutiny of and reflection on their work. This altered my relationship to their work and changed the basis of the relationship between the student and myself, and this altered the meanings that became ascribed to their drama in the classroom. In fact, in practical terms, the teaching intervention for each week was entirely dependent on the drama the students had created the week before. This was not something that could be planned in advance because it was dependent on ongoing reflection and negotiation (Costello, 2011).

On the far right is the initial list of behaviours that I observed from the students' iPad recordings. Moving from right to left, the way the behaviours have been categorised takes an increasingly distanced perspective so that the second left column ascribes all the students' behaviours to one of the following five categories: to do with status and hierarchy; to do with bonding; to do with choices that gave an indication of whether the students preferred working with strong boundaries such as those provided by use of a text, or preferred to be left to experiment and explore; to do with the meanings the young people ascribed to the resources they had to hand; and to do with image management. These five categories were then reconceptualised into two. One category comprised all the behaviours that were explicitly about the group managing its dynamic. The other category comprised all the behaviours that represented a negotiation between an idealised self and a shadow self. The core variable of ethical negotiation arose as a meta category into which interactions to do with the group dynamic and those to do with the negotiation between the shadow and the idealised self could be subsumed. What had emerged was a framework where at the heart of all the work that the young people did, and at the heart of all their interactions, was an ethical negotiation.

The coding process that I applied as we worked through the second project gave me a model for understanding what was happening in the classroom. However, I was still curious about how it was happening. Therefore, moving into our third project, I conducted a discourse-level analysis. In this book, discourse is understood to be a way through which formal and informal groups, and individuals relative to those groups, construct and share social meanings, and a way by which formal and informal groups, and individuals relative to those groups, constitute and maintain power relationships, because discourses constitute groups through power and agency (Foucault & Nazzaro, 1972). In other words, discourses are ways of understanding relationships, and practices, and tell us something about normative positioning. In short, discourses form and express truth-claims (Hook, 2001). For this project, the term discourse refers 'beyond language to sets of organised meanings (which can include images as well as words) on a given theme' (Hollway & Jefferson, 2013, p. 13) and concerns 'all the ways in which people actively produce social and psychological realities' (Davies & Harré, 2011, p. 262). Discourses are embodied and are enacted through power dynamics that are embedded in and utilise context; theme; proximal relationship; physical, visual, and vocal cues; and use of speech (van Dijk, 2011). Discourses work in relationship to and are part of the subtle and complex interweaving of the embodied, the psychological, and the social through which identity is constituted (Gee, 2014b; Hollway & Jefferson, 2013). In this project, it was allowed that elements of the fiction, such as the characters portrayed by students, took on communicative intent. They were therefore considered constitutive of and constituted by discourses (Gee, 2014a), as were the situating elements of discourse, including socio-cognitive, social, and political context (van Dijk, 2011); intonation and implication (Bakhtin, 2008; Holquist, 2008); and relationality, time, and place (van Dijk, 2011). This brings a broad understanding to the definition of discourse which comes to refer to the embodied communicative landscape, which is actively, materially, and relationally produced (Gee, 2014b).

Discourse analysis is a method of analysing text, which as a unit of analysis has been variously conceptualised along a continuum that ranges from spoken or written 'language material', such as letters, diaries, or transcripts of talk (Taylor, 2013, p. 2), to the actions and consequences of actions of people, and to their use of 'cultural tools' (Norris & Jones, 2005, p. xi) such as use of art, narrative, or any other culturally recognised means of mediating interaction (Wertsch, 1997). In this project, text refers to anything that can be read for meaning in a systematic way (Johnstone, 2018), and this includes any form of meaning making, including the choice of an emoji as an avatar, and the drama the children devise and perform. By conceptualising text-as-a-unit-of-analysis as being the meaning-making of the students, I was able to scrutinise the discourses that constituted them (Gee, 2014b; van Dijk, 2011), in the context of the intersection of various relational and embodied social practices (Norris & Jones, 2005). This aligns discourse analysis with the embodied psychosocial relational approach used in this project (Wetherell, 2012).

For example, in common with all the participants, Drew chose his own pseudonym. In addition, Drew was one of several students who chose to add a pictorial emoji to his pseudonym (not reproduced). His choice of name plus emoji are communicative and serve to position him relative to his audience. The audience encounters this self-representation in the context of the varying discourses to do with ethnicity, gender, age, and so on that the name-plus-pictogram evoke. Those discourses will be nuanced differently for each person; their personal resonances having been relationally negotiated in terms of each person's own embodied psychosocial and relational context. Therefore, various possible and experienced meanings of the name-plus-pictogram come into dialogue, in a multivocal encounter (Bakhtin, 2008). Drew was racialised white (Morning, 2011) but the emoji he chose was a racially marked face-emoji depicting the wearing of a turban associated with Sikh communities. Drew was an outsider to the community. In terms of the focus of this project, questions that could usefully be addressed through a discourse analysis might include: On the basis of a scrutiny of his group interactions, what can be suggested about the meanings this self-representation had for Drew? Were they exploratory (Perkins, 1979) or aspirational, for example to do with making a claim to the perceived dangerousness of brown bodies (Katy, 2017), or was it about the exclusionary mocking of the less powerful by the more powerful (Dyer, 2002; Medhurst, 2007)? Alternatively, was this an expression of some ambivalence to do with his own insider/outsider position as racialised white but an incomer to the community? Other important questions to ask would include: Did Drew, or aspects of this character, feature in any of the dramas? So that, bearing in mind powerful discourses following recent terrorism that tend to demonise people with brown bodies (Abbas, 2021), in what ways might my understandings of the meanings he ascribed to this self-representation change following the observation that Drew played a version of 'the demon' for six months? Where was the discrepancy in the communication, and who was shifting their relationship to what discourse and to what effect (Gee, 2014b; Sajnani, 2012)?

The focus of this book is not an exploration of the discourses that students drew on per se. The focus is an exploration of the embodied psychosocial relational processes that facilitated negotiations within discourses and which provided the potential for changes in the discourses which informed, consciously or unconsciously, student identity-performances. As students re-positioned themselves relative to their personal and group prevailing discourses, their identity-performances changed. This was identity-work. The drama served as a container for and was facilitative of that identity-work. The point I wish to emphasis here is that although I come to the analysis of the material with an awareness of the discourses that influence the students' identity-positionings, the analysis is not focused on the exploration of those discourses per se but on the embodied psychosocial relational negotiations and how those negotiations are supported, facilitated, and contained by the group drama-processes. From a drama perspective, I looked at relationships to and within the structures and content of the fiction. From an embodied psychosocial relational perspective, I looked for the places where the students and their characters-in-roles' internal and external states coincided. What I was able to see following the application of discourse analysis to the work of the young people were the embodied psychosocial relational plays that were made as each student worked to create or to maintain their identity-performance, or to resist identities that were being imposed on them.

In practical terms, I looked at the relationships between the groups' fictions and the groups' interactions and then pulled together the learning arising from my consideration of the students' stories, the grounded theory, and the discourse analysis. To facilitate a process of synthesis, and to interrogate more rigorously my conceptualisations regarding the ways the drama effects the identity-forming processes, I cross-applied the analytical frameworks that were emerging from the analysis to my own understandings. A visual example of this process taken from work I did towards analysis of students' work in project two is provided in Figure 4.6.

I coded using colours to identify and represent the different processes I was seeing, and this revealed visually the complex and multi-layered nature

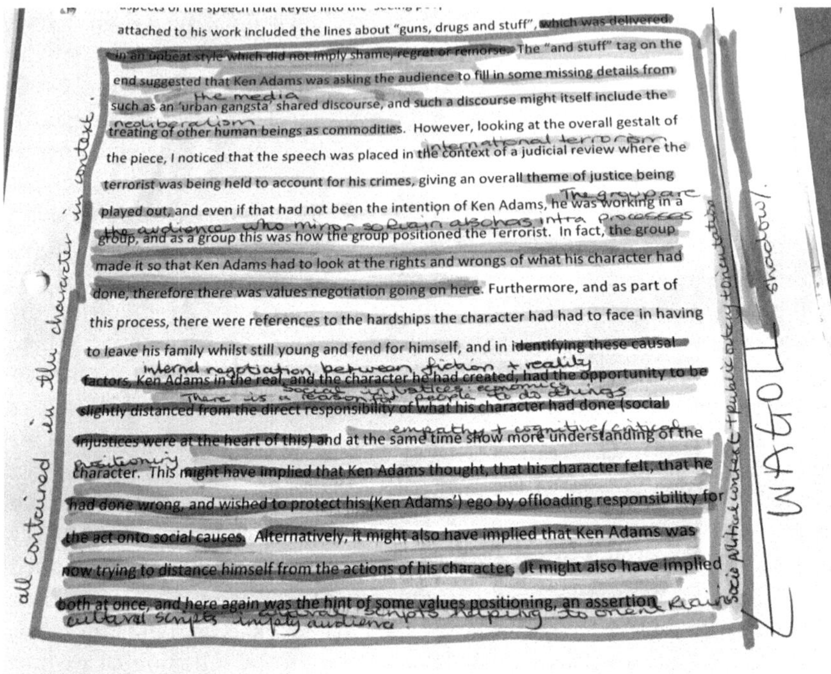
attached to his work included the lines about "guns, drugs and stuff", which was delivered in an upbeat style which did not imply shame, regret or remorse. The "and stuff" tag on the end suggested that Ken Adams was asking the audience to fill in some missing details from such as an 'urban gangsta' shared discourse, and such a discourse might itself include the treating of other human beings as commodities. However, looking at the overall gestalt of the piece, I noticed that the speech was placed in the context of a judicial review where the terrorist was being held to account for his crimes, giving an overall theme of justice being played out, and even if that had not been the intention of Ken Adams, he was working in a group, and as a group this was how the group positioned the Terrorist. In fact, the group made it so that Ken Adams had to look at the rights and wrongs of what his character had done, therefore there was values negotiation going on here. Furthermore, and as part of this process, there were references to the hardships the character had had to face in having to leave his family whilst still young and fend for himself, and in identifying these causal factors, Ken Adams in the real, and the character he had created, had the opportunity to be slightly distanced from the direct responsibility of what his character had done (social injustices were at the heart of this) and at the same time show more understanding of the character. This might have implied that Ken Adams thought, that his character felt, that he had done wrong, and wished to protect his (Ken Adams') ego by offloading responsibility for the act onto social causes. Alternatively, it might also have implied that Ken Adams was now trying to distance himself from the actions of his character. It might also have implied both at once, and here again was the hint of some values positioning, an assertion

Figure 4.6 Visual open coding applied to discourse analysis of student work.

of the active processes. For example, I used an orange to represent audience awareness, light blue to represent cultural and social scripts, pink to represent values, light green to represent aspects of the socio-political context, yellow to refer to anything that was intra or inter-personal, purple to reflect anything to do with distancing, dark green to relate specifically to the four-part structure, and brown to indicate places where there was evidence of a developmental scenario. The full range of colours identified the elements of what became the model I used to describe the processes invoked during the group dramas.

That example illustrates that processes arise relationally: all at once, and in mutual influence. A red line surrounding the whole excerpt signified 'character-in-context', and this illustrated visually that the dramatic fiction was the container for the students' identity and ethical work. The genesis of the four-part structure was in this intersection of multiple analytical frameworks. I give a fuller exposition of the four-part structure and what it says about the ways that the children worked in the next chapter.

Conclusion

The coding and inductive work based on grounded theory exposed the ethical core that lay at the heart of the work of the students. It also pointed to the relationality that underpinned the students' identity-work. The discourse analysis revealed the processes by which that relational and identity-work occurred. It also gave a sense of the movement of the relational and identity-work over time. When at the end of each project I invited students to formally reflect over their work, I found that student formal reflections often, but not always, coincided with my own. Where there was a mismatch between student perception of change, and mine, this led to further reflection regarding what I had observed of the students' drama and interactions. This often led to a re-negotiation of the rehearsal focus in the classroom between myself and the students. In either case, I was able to place my own observations and analysis in dialogic relationship to student voice, and to understand not only that students were able to make statements such as 'My self-esteem has grown through doing drama', and 'My confidence has grown through doing drama' but also why they were able to make those statements. I had developed a coherent framework of understanding.

In the next chapters, I explore the relational processes invoked in the doing of the drama. I tease out the embodied psychosocial and relational processes that are the vectors for ethical change on the one hand, and the group drama-processes that contain and facilitate those changes for individuals and groups on the other. I approach the writing of the following chapters in terms of processes that I observed when thinking horizontally across all the participants in the class, and then when thinking in vertical terms about how those processes played out for individuals. This reflects the focus of my findings in terms of the grounded theory approach which looked at the group as a whole, and then of the discourse analysis which focused on interactions between individual students in the group drama context. Therefore, in Chapter 5, I look at the relationships between students' participation in the classroom, identity expression, and the group drama-processes. This offers a horizontal perspective that explores the processes at play in the group as a whole through the lens of the four-part structure. In Chapter 6, the focus is vertical and explores those group drama-processes which contain and facilitate interactional relationships with a focus on two individual students, in their relational context. Chapter 6 explores the relationships between the emerging self-narratives of individuals and those of the group fiction. In Chapter 7, I move the focus of discussion to the teacher and explore the impact of teacher use-of-self. Throughout all three chapters, there is consideration of the embodied psychosocial and relational processes that are the vectors for ethical change and the group drama-processes that contain and facilitate them.

References

Abbas, M.-S. (2021). *Terror and the dynamism of Islamaphobia in 21st century Britain: The concentrationary Gothic*. Cham, Switzerland: Springer International Publishing.

Bakhtin, M. (2008). *The diologic imagination: Four essays by M.M. Bakhtin*. Austin: University of Texas Press.

Barthes, R. (2009). *Mythologies*. London: Vintage Books.

Bastemur, S., & Bras, E. (2021). Integration of narrative therapy with expressive arts practices. *Current Approaches in Psychiatry* (1), 146–169. doi:10.18863/pgy.771319

Baumfield, V., Hall, E., & Wall, K. (2013). *Action research in education* (2nd ed.). Los Angeles, London: SAGE.

Coleridge, S. T. (1847). *Biographia literaria 2nd edition* (Kindle 2012 ed.). London: William Pickering.

Corsaro, W. (2018). *The sociology of childhood* (5th ed.). Los Angeles, London: SAGE.

Costello, P. (2011). *Effective action research: Developing reflective thinking and practice* (2nd ed.). London, New York: Continuum.

Cox, M., & Theilgaard, A. (1997). *Mutative metaphors in psychotherapy: The Aeolian mode*. London: Jessica Kingsley.

Davies, B., & Harré, R. (2011). Positioning: The discursive production of selves. In M. Wetherell, S. Taylor, & S. Yates (Eds.), *Discourse theory and practice* (pp. 261–271). Los Angeles and London: SAGE in Association with The Open University.

Dijk, T. V. (2011). Discourse studies and hermeneutics. *Discourse Studies, 1*, 1–13. doi:10.1177/1461445611412762

Dyer, R. (2002). *The matter of images: Essays of representation* (2nd ed.). London and New York: Routledge.

Elam, K. (1987). *The semiotics of drama and theatre*. London: Routledge.

Foucault, M., & Nazzaro, A. (1972). History, discourse and discontinuity. *Psychological man: Approaches to an emergent social type, 20*(Summer/Fall), 225–248.

Gee, J. P. (2014a). *How to do discourse analysis: A tool kit* (2nd ed.). London: Routledge.

Gee, J. P. (2014b). *An introduction to discourse analysis: Theory and method*. London: Routledge.

Gilchrist, G. (2018). *Practitioner enquiry: Professional development with impact for teachers, schools and systems*. London and New York: Taylor and Francis, Routledge.

Glaser, B. G., & Strauss, A. L. (2017). *The discovery of grounded theory: Strategies for qualitative research*. New York: Routledge.

Hollway, W., & Jefferson, T. (2013). *Doing qualitative research differently* (K. Metzier Ed. 2013 ed.). London: SAGE.

Holquist, M. (2008). Introduction to the dialogic imagination: Four essays by M.M. Bakhtin (M. H. a. C. Emerson, Trans.). In M. Holquist (Ed.), *The dialogic imagination: Four essays by M.M. Bakhtin* (pp. 1–5). Austin: University of Texas Press.

Hook, D. (2001). Discourse, knowledge, materiality, history; Foucault and discourse analysis. *Theory and Psychology, 11*(Online), 521–547. doi:10.1177/0959354301114006

Johnstone, B. (2018). *Discourse analysis*. Newark, NJ: John Wiley & Sons, Incorporated.

Jones, P. (1991). Dramatherapy: Five core processes. *Dramatherapy, 14*(1), 8–15. doi:10.1080/02630672.1991.9689804

Katy, P. S. (2017). Surveillance, Islamophobia, and Sikh bodies in the war on terror. *Islamophobia Studies Journal, 4*(1), 37–52. doi:10.13169/islastudj.4.1.0037

Kelly, C., & Bruck, T. (2012). Staff sharing: An integrative approach to peer supervision. In L. Leigh, I. Gersch, A. Dix, & D. Haythorne (Eds.), *Dramatherapy with children, young people and schools: Enabling creativity, sociability, communication and learning* (pp. 163–171). London: Routledge.

Kivunja, C., & Kuyini, A. B. (2017). Understanding and applying research paradigms in educational contexts. *International Journal of Higher Education, 6*, 26–41. doi:10.5430/ijhe.v6n5p26

Kizilcik, H., & Daloglu, A. (2018). Implementing an interactive reflection model in EAP: Optimising student and teacher learning through action research. *Australian Journal of Teacher Education, 43*(9). doi:10.14221/ajte.2018v43n9.1

Lahad, M., & Dent Brown, K. (2012). Six-piece story-making revisited: The Seven levels of assessment and the clinical assessment. In D. Johnson, S. Pendzik, & S. Snow (Eds.), *Assessment in drama therapy* (1st ed., Vol. January 2012, pp. 121–147). Springfield, IL: Charles C Thomas.

Larkin, M., Watts, S., & Clifton, E. (2006). Giving voice and making sense in interpretative phenomenological analysis. *Qualitative Research in Psychology, 3*(2), 102–120. doi:10.1191/1478088706qp062oa

Lehleiter, C. (Ed.) (2016). *Fact and fiction: Literary and scientific cultures in Germany and Britain.* Toronto, Buffalo, London: University of Toronto Press.

Lengelle, R., Meijers, F., & Hughes, D. (2016). Creative writing for life design: Reflexivity, metaphor and change processes through narrative. *Journal of Vocational Behavior, 97*, 60–67. doi:10.1016/j.jvnglish07.012

Medhurst, A. (2007). *A national joke: Popular comedy and English cultural identities.* London and New York: Routledge.

Miles, M. B., & Huberman, A. M. (1994). *Qualitative data analysis* (2nd ed.). London: SAGE.

Morning, A. (2011). *The nature of race: How scientists think and teach about human difference.* Berkley, Los Angeles, London: University of California Press.

Murray, L., & Lawrence, B. (2000). *Practitioner-based enquiry: Principles for postgraduate research* (Professor Roberts G Burgess Ed.). London and New York: Falmer Press.

Norris, S., & Jones, R. (2005). Introduction to discourse in action: Introducing mediated discourse analysis. In S. Norris & R. Jones (Eds.), *Discourse in action: Introducing mediated discourse analysis* (pp. 3–14). London and New York: Routledge.

Pellegrini, A. (2009). *The role of play in human development.* Oxford: Oxford University Press.

Perkins, T. (1979). Rethinking stereotypes. In M. Barrett, P. Corrigan, A. Kuhn, & J. Wolff (Eds.), *Ideology and cultural production* (pp. 135–159). London: Routledge.

Powell, M. A., & Smith, A. B. (2009). Children's participation rights in research. *Childhood, 16*(1), 124–142. doi:10.1177/0907568208101694

Roberts, J., & Walters, M. (2018a). Cross school collaborative projects for year 9. In J. Roberts (Ed.). The Crown Dependencies: Private.

Roberts, J., & Walters, M. (2018b). Devising project scheme of work. In J. Roberts (Ed). The Crown Dependencies: Private.

Roberts, J., & Walters, M. (2018c). Text-based scheme of work. In J. Roberts (Ed). The Crown Dependencies: Private.

Sajnani, N. (2012). The implicated witness: Towards a relational aesthetic in dramatherapy. *Dramatherapy, 34*(March 2012), 6–21. doi:10.1080/02630672.2012.657944

Sherin, M., & van Es, E. (2005). Using video to support teachers' ability to notice classroom interactions. *Journal of Technology and Teacher Education, 13*(3). doi:ISSN1059-7069

Taylor, S. (2013). *What is discourse analysis.* London: Bloomsbury Academic.

Thornberg, R. (2012). Informed grounded theory. *Scandinavian Journal of Educational Research, 56*, 243–249. doi:10.1080/00313831.2022.2115135

van Dijk, T. (Ed.) (2011). *Discourse studies: A multidisciplinary introduction* (2nd ed.). London: SAGE.

Vicary, S., Young, A., & Hicks, S. (2017). A reflective journal as learning process and contribution to quality and validity in interpretative phenomenological analysis. *Qualitative Social Work, 16*(4), 550–565. doi:10.1177/1473325016635244
von Franz, M.-L. (1991). *Individuation in fairy tales.* Boston: Shambala.
Wertsch, J. (1997). *Mind as action* (2012 ed.). Online Edition: Oxford University Press.
Wetherell, M. (2012). *Affect and emotion: A new social science understanding.* Los Angeles and London: SAGE.
Willett, C., & Willett, J. (2019). *Uproarious: How feminists and other subversive comics speak truth.* Minneapolis and London: University of Minnesota Press.
Wilshire, B. (1982). *Role playing and identity: The limits of theatre as metaphor.* Bloomington: Indiana University Press.

5 Group Drama

Trust the Process

Students Multirole: Character-in-role as a Functional Device for Exploring a Situation

Group stories are created by negotiation in relationship with others. In group drama, students encode parts of themselves as single or multiple protagonists, develop a fictional context, explore ethical issues, and reflect formally and informally. To do so, they play and dialogue with character and genre, follow developmental scenarios, and position and re-position themselves and each other to a range of social discourses. The choices made by the teacher and the responses of the teacher are part of that relational dynamic. All the processes are co-evoking.

At Box 5.1 is the story that one group of all boys created (Box 5.1).

Group drama is a relational process, and in group drama, students encode into single or multiple protagonists. From the outset, this group elected to each play multiple characters. This was a decision based on the demands of the plot (Box 5.2).

This kind of multi-roling provides increased opportunities for dialogue. It gives rise to character-to-character dialogue as well as character-to-student dialogue. For example, in this case, Peter First played the terrorist, an aeroplane, and later a paramedic. In rehearsal, he had to switch between these characters-in-roles and to navigate their juxtaposing actions and attitudes.

Group drama participants develop a fictional context including a plot, in part, from an intersection of character and their character's roles, and genre. In this case, these students were as happy playing planes and buildings as they were playing human beings, whether dead or alive. Some characters, such as a dead body, were cameos or 'actants' (Tesniere, 2015, p. 100), or like the pilot had a mainly functional-role in the drama. These students mainly used a genre where they embodied their characters and anthropomorphised aspects of the play's context such as the buildings and the aeroplane. However, in the early stages of the work, one member of the group, Jent le Manx, recorded a scene on his iPad, where he used as a puppet his foot to represent one of the buildings that was destroyed by the terrorist attack. The double distance achieved by placing himself behind the screen of the iPad in this way kept

DOI: 10.4324/9781003464532-5

Box 5.1 The story one group of all boys created

A hijacked aeroplane is deliberately crashed into a building by a terrorist. The scene shifts to the devastation on the ground as paramedics search for survivors. Another scene shift takes us to a courtroom where the terrorist is put on trial. Following the trial, the condemned man tries to flee and is gunned down by security forces.

Box 5.2 Students negotiate towards a more crafted drama

SoundBloke: I'm going to be one of the buildings.
Peter First: You're tower one. You're tower two.
Jent le Manx: (*Indicates* Peter First *and* SoundBloke). They're the planes. (*Indicates* Peter First). And he's the terrorist and a plane.
SoundBloke: He's plane one and he's plane two.
SoundBloke: And then we're all people that are sad at the end.

Box 5.3 Using recording and puppet work to achieve double distance

Jent le Manx: (*Recording on iPad – Close up of foot*). I'm the tower. I was made in the … er … in the city. (*Vocal sound effect of aeroplane divebombing into the tower. The foot falls sideways*). We got crushed.
(*Camera shot zooms in and out of the shoe. Sounds of distress and cries*).

him out of the audience gaze and allowed him to inhabit a watching position that offered a kind of anonymity that in the early stages of the work he felt he needed (Box 5.3).

Students develop and craft a fictional context and use that context to be a vector through which to explore ethical issues. As part of the crafting process, the students dialogue with and re-position themselves to a range of dominant social discourses. In this example, the group decided that in their play they would place the terrorist in a court room for questioning, to explore his motivations (Box 5.4). This gave rise to a group negotiation that catalysed

Box 5.4 Students use a court scene to explore the motivations of the terrorist

Jent le Manx: Why are you a terrorist?
Peter First: (*Pause to think*). I'm getting to that point .... 'cos I had to get money somehow, you know.
Nulch Ap: Why did you decide to be a terrorist though?
Peter First: Because, well, I wasn't really a terror-
Jent le Manx: Why did you join the cartel?
Peter First: Easy money I suppose.
Jent le Manx: There's other ways of getting money than being a bad boy.

Box 5.5 Peter First's peers repeat their questions

Jent le Manx: Why are you a terrorist?
Peter First: I had to get money somehow, *you know*.
Nulch Ap: Why did you decide to be a terrorist though?

Box 5.6 Peter First becomes less sure

Peter First: Because, well, I wasn't really a terror ......

a change of identity-positioning relative to a 'bad-boy' discourse, for one of their group members.

In the fictional context of the courtroom, Peter First, as character-in-role, was asked by the group to justify the actions of his character-in-role. The group did not accept his justifications and showed their rejection by repeating their questions more emphatically (Box 5.5).

Furthermore, the questioning was taken up by more than one of his peers: this was a group initiative. This insistent questioning by his peers started to loosen the allegiance Peter First had to the actions of his character-in-role, and this had the effect that the character-in-role also became more tentative and less sure (Box 5.6).

Peter First, as character-in-role *and* as Peter First, started to distance himself from the actions and choices of this character-in-role.

The group drama-processes are co-evoking, and the ethical exploration, the development of character, the use of genre, and the movement of the plot cannot be separated out because the way each element is realised is dependent on the tension it holds with the others. For example, in this case, after his peers had challenged him about his character's motivations, Peter First crafted a cheerful song into his performance (Box 5.7).

The singing seemed to have been a response to the insistent grilling his character had been given by his peers, which had forced Peter First to confront the human consequences of the terrorist's acts. After the grilling, it seemed that Peter First had to work harder to perform a character that was impervious to the reality of the human cost of their choices, whereas, if Peter First had lacked empathy, he would not have been affected by this confrontation. I concluded that Peter First was reconsidering his ethical position and using a distancing genre as a protective which enabled him to continue to perform the material at all (Jones, 1991).

The fiction is also developed, explored, and crafted relative to developmental scenario such as the developmental scenario explored by SoundBloke that consolidated his leadership and directorial skills. For example, Peter First found it hard to self-regulate, tended to be rough, and to be at the same time both physically under-distanced from his material and emotionally over-distanced from it. However, in the midst of this, SoundBloke modelled a slower, more expressive pace, and at one point, demonstrated how to kneel, feel for a pulse, check for breathing, and administer cardiopulmonary resuscitation. In another moment, when Peter First found it difficult to focus on anything on stage, SoundBloke guided Peter First's attention to the body that was lying there. Then, when Peter First found it difficult to disengage from some repetitive action he was doing on stage, SoundBloke led him away. Using their fictional-roles as a vector, and by invoking the functional-role of director, SoundBloke was able to help Peter First access increased role flexibility and a greater role repertoire in a kind of embodied reflective practice.

Formal reflection space at the end of the project provided an opportunity for students to re-visit and re-consider characters-in-roles that had been 'abandoned' in the fiction. For example, one character-in-role that had been 'left' in the drama was the airline pilot. This character-in-role, in terms of the story, was incidental and functional: an 'actant', there to facilitate the hijack. However, in their formal reflection lesson, this character-in-role became the

Box 5.7 Peter First adds a cheerful song

Peter First:	(*Clambers onto the stage block where* SoundBloke *is*). Give me the plane! (*Sits in the pilot seat and starts to fly the plane, holding the control wheel in his hands, and jiggling up and down and side to side*).
Peter First:	(*Singing*). so long, sooo long ....

Box 5.8 The responsibility of being a pilot

Jent le Manx: I wouldn't be a pilot. I wouldn't like to have that much responsibility of looking after other people's lives.
SoundBloke: I wouldn't be a pilot as well because I would want to see my family and I wouldn't want to take all my time flying.

Box 5.9 Constant encoding and deroling

(Peter First *enters behind* SoundBloke *and throttles him. Many choking sound effects.* SoundBloke *is wrestled to the floor*).
SoundBloke: OK, stop there. Stop there.
Peter First: (*Singing out loud ostensibly to himself*).
SoundBloke: Stop there, Peter First you don't throw me off I just fall off, right? Jent le Manx?
Jent le Manx: Yeah.
Peter First: Maybe we should move them further apart.
Jent le Manx: No, we've swapped now, 'cos I fall off the stage so it's easier if I'm on this side.
(Peter First *as the terrorist strangles and kills* SoundBloke *the pilot*).
Peter First: (*Stands up, out of role, to* Jent le Manx). And then, just, just duck dead.
(Peter First *sits back down and becomes the terrorist piloting the plane*).

basis for significant values reflection. For example, Jent le Manx reflected on the nature of the emotional toll exacted on the pilot from the point of view of his responsibility to the passengers onboard his plane. SoundBloke agreed that being a pilot would not be the ideal job but for a different reason: because it would mean too much time away from family (Box 5.8).

Deroling and reflection is usually conceptualised as something that happens at the end of a session. However, in reality, participants not only de-role formally at the end of the session but de-role and re-encode repeatedly throughout the rehearsal process, swapping repeatedly between the frame of the real and the frame of the fiction, and this rhythm of deroling, reflection, and re-encoding is an important part of the development and exploration of the material (Box 5.9).

Reconsidering, and crafting the way a movement happens, implies consideration of characters' intentions, abilities, the situation, and the specifics of the relationships between the characters that participants are trying to relate.

Box 5.10 Excerpt from reflective journal. I am troubled by Peter First's performance

In role as 'the one who delays the lesson by demonstrating how clever he is by pretending to be daft'. A version of 'class fool'. Mr. 'I Don't Understand' is a role that this student plays often and well. Mr. 'I Don't Understand' is a made-up persona. What that persona is hiding is a question worthy of some contemplation. But, what Mr. 'I Don't Understand' doesn't do is to not understand. He understands perfectly well. I don't like Mr. 'I Don't Understand' because I feel manipulated by him, controlled, played with, humiliated. I need to take this to supervision.

The choices made by the teacher, and the teachers' responses, are an important aspect of the relational environment. For example, in this case, what is not apparent from the examples above is what I experienced as the bad-boy terrorist performance that Peter First often enacted in the context of my classroom in the frame of the real. I reflect on it in my journal during the early days of the project (Box 5.10).

This personal reaction to his actions was a perspective based on the intersections of my own 'deep stories' (Yam, 2018, p. 1), the influence of professional training, wider discourses, and the evolving dynamic within the classroom. As the teacher in the classroom, I recognised that I do not sit outside the relational dynamic. Understanding that this needed exploring, I chose to take this to 'supervision', i.e., to talk this over with my critical friend. This choice was an expression of my own teacher use-of-self. To my mind, there were aspects of this 'terrorism' that paralleled the terrorism enacted in his fiction. It was as if Peter First encoded aspects of self into the character-in-role and in the safety of the fiction exposed those 'bad-boy' aspects to trial by jury of his peers.

Students Use a Single Role Each: Character Represents Me in the Given Circumstances

A second group of young people created a drama where they each played one role and the plot was contained in the relationships between the characters. This led to, and was a result of, greater individual investment in those characters. Again, the processes include encoding, although in this case each student encodes into a single character. The students also develop a fictional context, they explore ethical issues, and they make use of formal and informal de-roling, reflection, and re-encoding. When scrutinising this drama, it is possible to see: the ways that students use puppet and prop to create safe access to the drama space; the ways that character and context evolve together; the ways the fictional context creates the need to make ethical and values-based choices; the ways that some aspects of real-life identity are stepped away from whereas some aspects are embraced; the ways the teachers' choices can facilitate development of the functional-, fictional-, and relational-roles; and how in some cases it is better to allow the drama to speak for itself. The key take-aways are that: identity-work is framed by relational processes, including audience/witness processes; content is important but not as important as the participants' relationships to that content; and the dramatherapy 'core processes' are vectors for embodied psychosocial relational processes, but it is the embodied psychosocial processes that effect change.

At Box 5.11 is the story that this group created (Box 5.11).

From the outset, this group elected to encode as one character each and to use their own names which gave the feel of a role-play (Box 5.12).

None of these students put on an accent or changed the way they walked or stood when they were in the fiction. They were themselves, albeit, a version of themselves that they were able to disown if need be, because they were in a drama and therefore only pretending (Jones, 1996b). The nature of their encoding was embodied, and their preferred genre was empathic. This emphasised and increased the investment of each student into their character-in-role. Although it started as a 'not knowing' response, as the weeks progressed, it began to connote and reflect a strong sense of identity, i.e., a lack of aesthetic distance (Dent-Brown & Wang, 2006) between themselves and the characters-in-roles they were playing.

Kelly Burk also encoded by extending her body using a paper axe she crafted, and which functioned as a mask, or a puppet which she could use to

Box 5.11 The story created by a mixed group of three

A group of friends flee an invasion of alien spores. They take refuge in an old mine; race against time to find clean air, food, and water; and dig an escape tunnel, which leads them under the ocean and to safety.

Box 5.12 Students use their own names

Leven Baker: So, Kelly Burk, what is the name of your character, if it has one?

Kelly Burk: I don't know.

Leven Baker: OK, I think we were all just using our own names for our characters.

foreground aspects of herself. In particular, although usually very quiet, when armed with her axe, she was able to assert herself (Box 5.13).

For each student, their own character was the main protagonist. The students developed and crafted the fictional context week by week. The context contained and shaped the plot. The plot and the characters were evolved together (Box 5.14).

Week by week the students gradually built an environment that had strong limits and which forced the characters-in-roles to make values choices and take up values positionings. The parameters were set by an external danger, and the restricting of fundamental resources including water and air. The characters-in-roles had to work against the clock. It became apparent that just as role and theme were interrelated, so were context and values positionings. They co-arose in the fiction in the same ways they co-arise in the 'real' world, where our contexts force us to take positions that reveal and shape our values (Eagly & Wood, 2017; Mitchell, 2014). The questions that arose were to do with: who will decide who is entitled to what; who will share; how much will be shared; who will be selfish; will the students/characters-in-roles work together or will they turn on one another; who will choose to act for the common good; and who will choose to work for self alone (Box 5.15).

Not only was there the potential for values negotiations and positioning to occur between the roles into which the students had encoded, they were also able to explore a values negotiation between a position they might occupy in the real-world and a position they might adopt in the fiction. For example, in the real-world, Bright Spark was occasionally marginalised because he was new to the school and was of mixed race (Cole et al., 2009). On the other hand, Leven Baker was well established at the school, and an army cadet trained first aider. In line with the idea that our identities are a self-construction that

Box 5.13 Kelly is able to assert herself when armed with her axe

Kelly Burk: *(Screams and starts to attack an alien that is on the floor with her pick axe).*
Leven Baker: OK, OK, guys, guys, guys, I think it's dead.
Kelly Burk: I wanted to assert dominance.

Box 5.14 Plot and character evolve together

Kelly Burk: So are there any other bits to your personality or persona or you would like to add some more?
Leven Baker: Not yet. I'm hoping it will all evolve as we go along. When challenges come up we can, I can adapt to the situation.

Box 5.15 Ethical choices

Bright Spark: (*He has returned with drinks and hands them out*). Here's a bottle of water for you, and a bottle of water for you. And a bottle of Gin for me (Bright Spark *drinks greedily*).
Leven Baker: Don't drink it all we could use it for first aid. Also, when we're probably going to be digging a tunnel, we don't need you drunk.
(Bright Spark *drinks his Gin*).
Kelly Burk: Deaf Bright Spark.

Box 5.16 The weapons master

(Leven Baker *and* Bright Spark *run in,* Bright Spark *now has a gun in his hand*).
Bright Spark: I've got gin, and I've found a gun.
Leven Baker: Great.

arise in the dialogue between stories that are imposed and those that are chosen (Josselson & Harway, 2012b), both boys brought their knowledges, experiences, and real-world identities into the fiction in some way, making choices about what to bring in from the outside and to build into the fiction, and what to use the frame of fiction to try to step away from (Jones, 1996a).

Invoking a shadow scenario, Bright Spark made some progress in stepping away from his marginalisation and explored memes informed by dominant discourses to do with hyper-masculinised behaviours such as bad-boy drinker, and as part of an aspirational scenario, he explored the identity of weapons master (Box 5.16).

On the other hand, invoking a consolidatory scenario, Leven Baker, who outside of school was proud to be an army cadet first aider, incorporated parts of his identity into the fiction. Via the relational-roles that invoke the processes of audience and witnessing, Leven Baker used his real-world identity to validate the fictional values choices that he made, and at the same time, he used the fictional world to validate his real-world identity as man of science and man of knowledge (Box 5.17).

Over the course of the project, Leven Baker experienced increased role repertoire, adding the functional-roles of director and technician to his initial preference for acting. He began to make decisions, mediate the ideas of the others, and solve technical problems as the group negotiated the crafting of their drama ready for sharing with a more formal audience. This role was

Box 5.17 The man of science

Leven Baker: OK, so the oxygen filters are working with about six months left in them. The system that will tell us if they are going to go off line is of course not working. The bunker's about two years old. Not everything's on line. I wonder if they've reported about the aliens. (*Listens to the radio*). London's on fire. Donald Trump is dead.

Box 5.18 Increased role repertoire

Leven Baker: So, we walk in, we'll do it on a red (*presses the red lighting pre-set*) then once we're in and we close the door we'll probably be on alert so we'll probably set it to orange (*presses the orange lighting pre-set*).

facilitated by the teacher's use-of-self choice to act as quartermaster and give access to the drama department's theatre technology (Box 5.18).

Regarding de-roling and reflection, in the formal reflection stage, Bright Spark's earlier efforts to redefine himself through the drama were contested. So, when, invoking an aspirational scenario, Bright Spark resisted parts of his real-world identity by trying to invoke the identity of a scientist and inventor, Leven Baker denied him this identity by appropriating it for the group and by reducing the inventing to 'Alien goo'. When Bright Spark tried to re-invoke the masculine identity of a weapons man, Leven Baker denied Bright Spark this status by laughing. When Bright Spark tried to invoke the identity of a man of knowledge, Leven Baker denied Bright Spark this identity by reducing him to a 'repair man' (Box 5.19).

In each case, Bright Spark tried but was unable to distance himself from his identity as outsider in the school, and from dominant discourse stereotypes imposed on him by Leven Baker, including that East-Asian men are not masculine, they are the legitimate object of fun, and they are best limited to low status jobs that service the white hegemony, as in the radio repair man. In this case, the process of formal de-roling did not have the emancipatory effect that I had hoped for and undermined the work that had been done in the practical drama. In other words, there was a change-process inherent in the embodied drama that was independent of the talking that happened afterwards. It was in the functional actor-role that Bright Spark had been able to explore an

Box 5.19 Leven Baker resists Bright Spark's self-definitions

Leven Baker: Erm, Bright Spark, life story of your character?
Bright Spark: Erm, Scientist. Wanting to invent things.
Leven Baker: Alien stuff. Alien goo. I think that's basically all of us.
Kelly Burk: Yeah. Please tell me a story that shows your character's greatest strength.
Bright Spark: Erm, possibly, weapons.
Leven Baker: (*Laughing*) Oh, yeah, with the guns.
Bright Spark: Erm, I mean, I'm not sure about strengths. I suppose, strength in knowledge.
Kelly Burk: Yeah, like knowing how you did the door.
Bright Spark: Yeah.
Kelly Burk: And the radio.
Leven Baker: So, you're like a repair man almost.

increased role repertoire. This implies that it is neither always necessary, nor desirable to formally reflect on the drama by talking about it.

The Group-drama-processes

Encoding

Encoding is the embodied taking on of a fictional character-in-role. The term connotes the foregrounding-for-processing that happens when students take on a dramatic role. The concept of encoding does not negate the established knowledges of dramatherapy that being in a role, or behind a mask, involves elements of both hiding and revealing (Landy, 1986). Rather, it offers a different way of thinking about the process of taking on a character-in-role that invites the attention to be drawn to the positive act of foregrounding, as opposed to the passive act of revealing. The concept of encoding applies only to the fictional characters-in-roles that students create and accords to those roles a special status to do with the protective 'one-remove' of dramatic fiction.

Functional-, Relational-, and Fictional-roles

The functional-roles of actor, director, and technician represent the baseline orientations the students bring with them to the drama. Fictional-roles mediate participant relations to self and to each other (Elliott & Lemert, 2009). Relational-roles represent the bridge between the functional- and the fictional-roles and provide the context for constant informal and formal crafted performance of self-as-self and self-as-other to validating – or not – self and peers. In the audience/witness relational-role context, students perform their critically considered, situated, and contingent relational ethical positions in the virtual-reality space of fictional drama. They do this individually and collectively, and the audience processes that are invoked in each given circumstance (Stanislavski, 1980) involve both the intra- and inter-personal which in turn are also influenced by social and familial contexts (Gandesha, 2020; Teo, 2018; Twenge, 2006). I explore the relationship between the functional-, relational-, and fictional-roles more fully in Chapter 6. Audience/witness processes, which are inherent in the concept of relational-role, are central to identity-work, and I explore the audience/witnessing process more fully in Chapter 7. Functional-, relational-, and fictional-roles map directly onto the elements of the drama crucible of role, performance, and story that was introduced in Chapter 3.

Character-in-context and Character-in-role

In practice, fictional-roles, and themes, cannot be separated from each other because they co-arise in mutual dependence. Therefore, it is useful to conceptualise the fictional aspects of the process as the composite 'Fictional Role: Character-in-context'. This conceptualisation accommodates the idea that a student plays a character that is embedded in a context, that is, a story. Therefore, in a dramatic fiction as opposed to a 'role play', it is the character that plays the role, whereas the student plays the character.

Ethical Negotiation

Students explore the moral and ethical implications of the fictional contexts they create. They negotiate between the idealised or aspirational-self and the shadow-self (Rogers, 1961). As an example, the fictional contexts – the stories – generated by the students I worked with centred round: the environment, gender, survival, power, and relationships (Figure 5.1). By encoding as a character-in-role to navigate a fictional-context, students can search for the scope of choice within the constraints of a given structure. In other words, the drama-process invites students to make situated ethical choices. Inherent in each fictional context are parameters and expectations to do with the intersections of social norms, i.e., structure, and individual choice, i.e., agency. In other words the stories that the students create reflect or resist cultural as well as personal norms and expectations. Furthermore, the themes embedded within the fictional contexts do not exist in isolation from each other. This is important to note because it illustrates the complexity of the intersectional nature of the students' ethical and identity-work. Figure 5.2 shows the nature of the intersectionality of the themes as explored by the students I worked with. The primary themes stand alone on the perimeter of the figure and were environment, gender, survival, power, and relationships. However, within the fictions, there were moments when the primary themes overlapped, where

Figure 5.1 Visual representation of the ethical dimension in the student work.

the groups explored intersections between, for example, the environment and gender, gender and survival, and power and survival. In addition, there were moments when the intersecting of themes was even more complex and comprehensive, comprising combinations such as power-survival-relationship and power-environment-relationship. At the core of this complexity was an ethical negotiation.

Developmental Scenario

However, the primary interest of this book is not the themes *per se* but the ways students use their relationships to those themes to explore ethics and identity. The students with whom I worked explored using four non-discrete, intersecting, and overlapping basic formats or developmental scenarios: consolidatory, aspirational, shadow, and exploratory/emancipatory (Figure 5.3).

- **Consolidatory**: A participant encodes into a character-in-role that reinforces an already established individual identity within the group. For

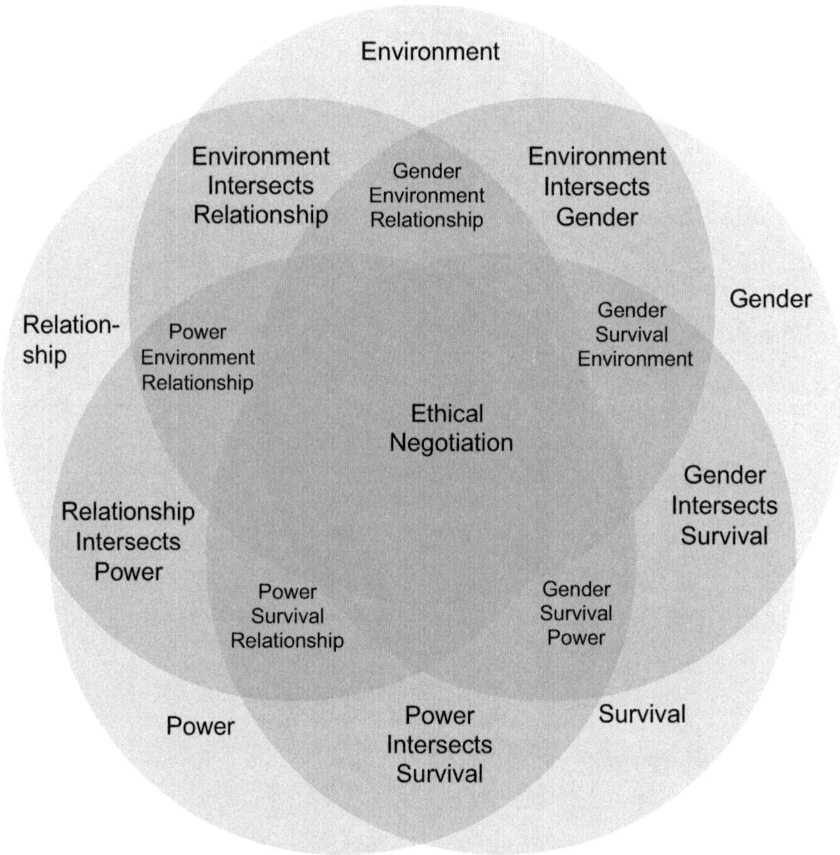

Figure 5.2 The complexity of the intersectional nature of the students' ethical and identity-work.

example, when SoundBloke used the drama to consolidate his leadership position within the group.

- **Aspirational**: A participant encodes into an idealised version of self. For example, when Bright Spark encoded as a weapons expert and scientist.
- **Shadow**: A participant explores a shadow aspect of self by encoding as a character-in-role that explores something forbidden or unpleasant. For example, when Peter First encoded as the terrorist.
- **Exploratory/emancipatory**: A participant encodes into a character-in-role that opens-up new behavioural and attitudinal possibilities. For example, when Peter First enacted a wider range of caring behaviours and expressive rhythms.

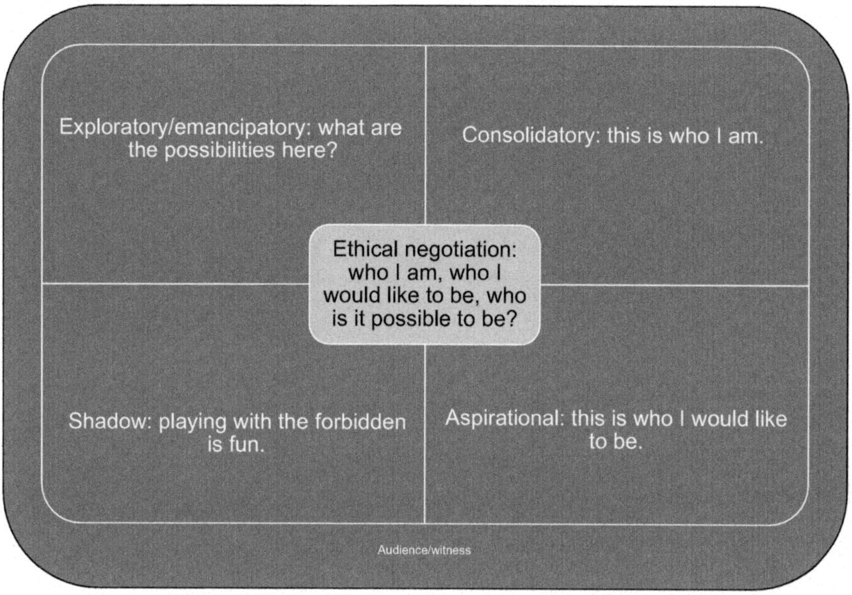

Figure 5.3 Four developmental scenarios in the context of audience/witness with a core of ethical negotiation.

The relationship between self-narrative and group fiction is never static. For example, Peter First constantly shifted his self-position relative to the group fiction.

Distancing and Aesthetics: The Qualities of the Drama

Aesthetic choices are not simply stylistic performance choices. They are part of the embodied psychosocial relational process, and participants manage their own and their group's tensions to do with regulating their distance from and engagement with their material by applying a range of aesthetic responses. These aesthetic choices can be read as being the 'qualities' of the work and spread across the whole psychosocial relational basis of identity and across all the drama-processes. Distancing responses include: ironic acting, laughter, breaking out of role, use of narrator or meta view, short-handing, lack of affect, observer point of view, use of stereotype or caricature, projection onto objects, the play within a play, not allowing the work to settle, over control, and disregard. Responses that indicate less distance include: flow, imitation, affect, development, and physical engagement. Distance and engagement are held in tension (Figure 5.4).

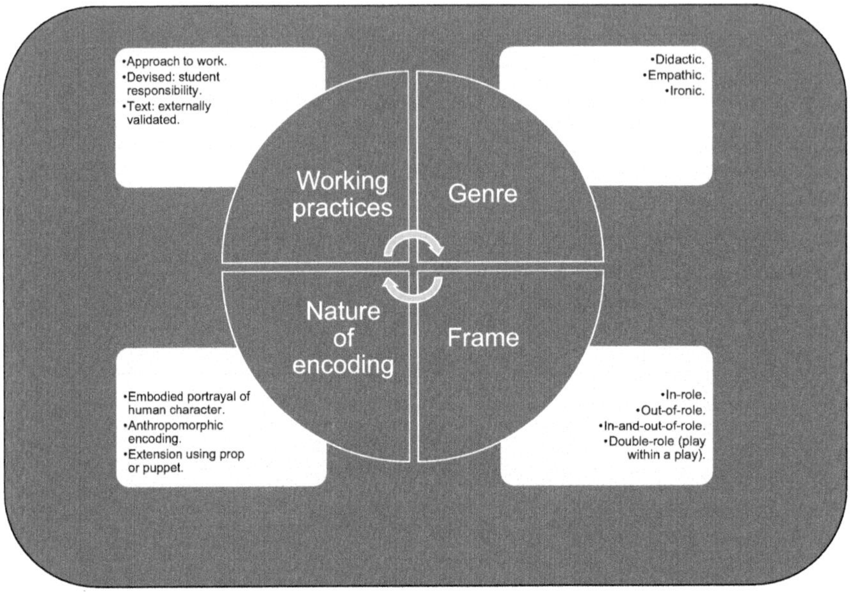

Figure 5.4 Visual representation of the four dimensions along which students managed distance. The work happens in the context of audience/witness.

- **Genre**: Whether the material configures as didactic/explanatory, as empathic/emotionally engaged, or as ironic/self-consciously distanced.
- **Frame**: The relationship or position a participant takes to the material and to the work. This includes whether students are in or out of role, both in and out of role at the same time, or double-roled as in a 'play within a play'. It includes whether participants are in the frame of the real which is what people would ordinarily construe as 'real life', or the frame of the fiction, which is what people would ordinarily refer to as 'made-up'.
- **Nature of Encoding**: The characters-in-roles encoded by the students vary in articulation and nature from loosely figured animal, object, or symbolic roles to more, or less, fully realised human roles. The students with whom I worked explored three modalities of encoding: embodied portrayals of human characters, anthropomorphised objects such as buildings and aeroplanes, and extending the reach of their body by creating and using props as puppets.
- **Group Working Practices**: Whether participants feel more comfortable when able to take more responsibility for their material, for example by creating devised work, or whether they feel more comfortable when working within the safety of externally validated material, for example by working from a published text.

As with themes, it is not the distancing strategies per se, but how the students use genre, the nature of encoding, and group working practices to manage and manipulate distance that is of interest. It is a mainstay of dramatherapy theory that being able to maintain a safe distance from challenging material enables individuals and groups to approach it in ways that do not overwhelm (Jones, 1991; van der Kolk, 2005), so it is not surprising to see these process at work for students. Distancing processes both arise from, and invoke, dialogically mediated tensions between group participants' diverse working and relational styles and artistic choices.

Crafting

The exploration and rehearsal process is iterative. There is both repetition and development. The iterative rehearsal structure acts as a container in which to invent, explore, craft, and share the material used for ethical negotiation and identity-work. With continued exploration comes familiarity and then summation, as the students take shortcuts, use shorthand, truncate, and condense their ideas in anticipation of performing to an audience and as part of the process of crafting their work. For more discussion about the implications of the crafting process, see Chapter 7.

Outcomes: Increased Role Repertoire and Greater Flexibility

Ethical negotiation and identity-work occurs in the negotiation between identity with and distance from the material, mediated by audience/witness processes. As a result, participants develop greater role flexibility and a broader in-role and out-of-role repertoire. This equips participants to both more skilfully navigate the performative aspects of neoliberal cultures and to resist it.

The Four-part Structure

The four-part structure makes visible the processes of identity-work and therefore fits well with educational claims that one main goal of education is to educate young people for citizenship. By making the processes that effect identity and values-based change visible, it becomes possible to see what practices, policy contexts, and physical and relational environments must be established and maintained to facilitate the kind of relational work that fits young people for active involvement in a valid democratic society.

Encoding as Multiple Protagonists

'Encoding as multiple protagonists' makes the object of exploratory focus not the story-as-a-thing but the inter-relatedness of the students and their multiple characters. Group drama is developed not by one story-teller but relationally, by way of interactive decisions (Bryant, 1997), in the context of group working processes. Each student is the main protagonist from their own perspective, and even though a student may play an 'actant' in terms of the 'story', this is their main character-in-role, which could have significance over and above its significance in the story, for that student. The nature of the encoding as embodied, anthropomorphised, or extended also has a bearing on, and reflects something of, the relationships between the students and their characters-in-roles.

Developing the Fictional Context

Participants co-construct a context for their characters, in the drama, over time. The context might include a 'task', an 'obstacle', and a 'helper' (Lahad, Shacham, & Ayalon, 2013), but those elements do not arise discretely, but in relational tension to other elements of context such as things, place, and time, and cannot be separated from the aesthetic qualities and processes of the drama.

Identity-work: Values Exploration and Negotiation

Participants use the drama to position and re-position themselves, to adopt alternative identities, and to pose and explore values-based questions. The use of the terms 'Exploration' and 'Negotiation' is important. They capture the idea that the drama is an exploration and, when they start out, neither the students nor the teacher knows where they will end up. They capture the idea that where the students do end up is a result of the inter-relational negotiation happening between them as a group, and between them and their immediate and wider contexts, in other words, as a result of embodied psychosocial relationality.

Cyclical De-roling and Reflection

De-roling and reflection does not happen only at the end of the work, it happens throughout the rehearsal process, and there is a cyclic process that includes both encoding and de-roling. For example, participants de-role, enter the frame of the real, talk about their characters-in-roles as 'other' to themselves, and then re-engage the frame of the fiction and re-encode into their characters-in-roles. Many of these conversations consider ideas for how better to realise characters-in-roles the next time round. Frame and relationality, de-roling, and encoding are related and form a pattern of informal reflection that happens spontaneously as part of the group process over and above any formal reflection process that is built into a teaching scheme of work.

The four-part structure as described above captures the embodied psychosocial and relational processes of participants as they engage in embodied dialogy towards values and identity re/forming work. Groups, made up of individuals with various levels of group affiliation including similarities and differences (Methot, Rosado-Solomon, & Allen, 2018; Sluss & Ashforth, 2007), negotiate the fiction, and the fiction reflects the direction of group thought. Although some individuals have greater influence on the direction of the developing fiction than others (Zvelc, 2009), the group fiction becomes a container for multiple and sometimes competing discourses. The end-result is a co-created co-owned piece of drama that represents the voices of all the group members to different extents. This mirrors the process that Hunter describes in her work on how policy documents are developed, but in this case, the student drama becomes the 'policy document', 'to be worked on, redrafted and continually re-enacted' (Hunter, 2015, p. 177).

A Dynamic Process

Occasionally, an individual participant wants to move the drama in a different direction to that which it seems to be taking as steered by the dominant feelings within their group. A good example of this was when Bright Spark wanted to re-define the genre of his group's work and develop a more 'action-sequence' piece of drama so that he could encode into a more stereotypically masculinised character-in-role (Brah & Phoenix, 2004; Burman, 2008; Butler, 2006; Eagly & Wood, 2017; Josselson & Harway, 2012a). In those cases, the group must find a way to resolve what presents as a conflict. In Bright Spark's group, they did this by accommodating the disharmonious element within their drama. There was tempering of the behaviour of the person who was out of step, plus accommodation of alternative discourses by others in the group.

The focus of this book is how the dramatic processes are a vehicle for participant ethical positioning and identity-work. Nevertheless, the substantive material also has its direct influence and leaves its mark. A good example of this was the 'Terrorist' drama explored by Peter First's group (see above) where students evolved personally in relationship to the globally themed material for example by showing more contained or caring behaviours, and at the same time, they explored their attitudes to the actual substantive material, for example by determining that the terrorist had committed a criminal act.

Conclusion

The four-part structure (Figure 5.5) makes visible the opportunities participants take to develop what is necessary for 'living wisely' (Elliott, 1991, p. 148), which as explained in Chapter 2 is the element of drama that has been largely excluded from the drama curriculum in recent years. Where drama and theatre denote quite different processes (Jones, 1996b; Schechner, 2004), the four-part structure makes clear the identity-work that happens at the interface between drama and theatre (Brook, 1996), where what is done for the self and what is done for the audience work in relationship. In that both are concerned with development, the work also takes place at the interface of the

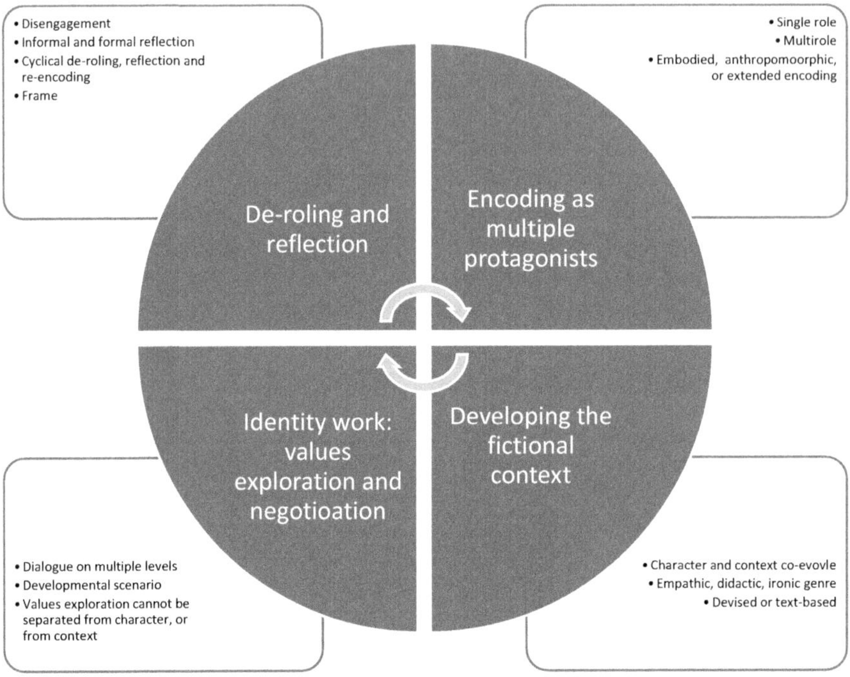

Figure 5.5 The four-part structure.

dramatherapeutic and the drama-educational, in the models of dramatherapy that are non-interpretive and non-clinical (Jennings, 2011; Mitchell, 1994) and where the educational agenda includes the development of the whole child (Bolton, 1984; Cook, 1919; Hadow, 1931; Heathcote & Herbert, 1985; Parry, 1972; Plowden, 1967) in the modern context (Baldwin, 2007). This work does not fit well with neoliberal structures because although in practicing multi-roling students are rehearsing the rigours of role fluidity that is expected of the modern workforce (Elliott & Lemert, 2009), what arises from this kind of work cannot be pre-determined, because as explained in Chapter 2, the benefits are emergent (Hart, 1978, in Prieslty, 2017). Also, as explained in Chapter 2, in being offered the opportunity to explore their values and identities in relationship to others and to their wider context, students are being given the tools of critical thinking to resist the uncritical adoption of externally imposed values that are often, but not exclusively, neoliberal in origin, by holding up for comparison and exploration the memes that influence them, including both 'market' and 'counter-market' memes (Hess, 2015, pp. 321–335). The experience of the heteroglossia that is inherent in group drama of this sort is democratising (Hirschkop, 1999) and equips students to both adapt to the neoliberalised state, and potentially, to resist it.

References

Baldwin, P. (2007). *With drama in mind: Real learning in imagined worlds.* Great Britain: Network Continuum.

Bolton, G. (1984). *Drama as education: An argument for placing drama at the centre of the curriculum.* Durham England: Longman.

Brah, A., & Phoenix, A. (2004). Ain't I a woman? Revisiting intersectionality. *Journal of International Women's Studies, 5,* 75.

Brook, P. (1996). *The empty space.* New York: Simon and Schuster.

Bryant, J. (1997). The plot thickens: Understanding interaction through the metaphor of drama. *Omega (Oxford), 25*(3), 255–266. doi:10.1016/S0305-0483(96)00062-X

Burman, E. (2008). *Developments: Child, image, nation.* London and New York: Routledge.

Butler, J. (2006). *Gender trouble* (1st ed.). New York and London: Routledge.

Cole, B., Adamson, S., Craig, G., Hussain, B., Smith, L., Law, I., … Cheung, T. (2009). *Hidden from public view: Racism against UK Chinese* (T. M. Group., Trans.). Sheffield University Research Archive: Sheffield Hallam University.

Cook, C. (1919). *The play way: An essay in educational method* (2015 ed.). New York: Frederick A. Stokes Company.

Dent-Brown, K., & Wang, M. (2006). The mechanism of storymaking: A grounded theory study of the 6-Part story method. *The Arts in Psychotherapy, 33*(4), 316–330. doi:10.1016/j.aip.2006.04.002

Eagly, A., & Wood, W. (2017). Gender identity: Nature and nurture working together. *Evolutionary Studies in Imaginative Culture, 1,* 59. doi:10.26613/esic/1.1.10

Elliott, A., & Lemert, C. (2009). *The new individualism: The emotional costs of globalization* (Revised ed.). New York and Oxon: Routledge.

Elliott, J. (1991). *Action research for educational change.* Milton Keynes: Open University Press.

Gandesha, S. (2020). The neoliberal personality. *Logos: A Journal of Modern Society and Culture, Spring 2020.* Retrieved from https://logosjournal.com/article/the-neoliberal-personality/

Hadow, W. H. (1931). *Report of the consultative committee on the primary school.* London: His Majesty's Stationery Office.

Heathcote, D., & Herbert, P. (1985). A drama of learning: Mantle of the expert. *Theory Into Practice, 24*(3), 173–180. doi:10.1080/00405848509543169

Hess, K. (2015). Metaphors matter: Ethics and the memes of the market. *Georgetown Journal of Law and Public Policy, 13,* 321–336.

Hirschkop, K. (1999). *Mikhail Bakhtin: An aesthetic for democracy.* Oxford: Oxford University Press.

Hunter, S. (2015). *Power, politics and the emotions: Impossible governance?* London, UK: Taylor & Francis Group.

Jennings, S. (2011). *Healthy attachments and neuro-dramatic play* (Kindle ed.). London: Jessica Kingsley.

Jones, P. (1991). Dramatherapy: Five core processes. *Dramatherapy, 14*(1), 8–15. doi:10.1080/02630672.1991.9689804

Jones, P. (1996a). *Drama as therapy volume 1: Theory, practice and research* (2nd ed.). London and New York: Routledge.

Jones, P. (1996b). *Drama as therapy: Theatre as living.* London and New York: Routledge.

Josselson, R., & Harway, M. (2012a). The challenges of multiple identity. In R. Josselson & M. Harway (Eds.), *Navigating multiple identities: Race, gender, culture, nationality, and roles* (pp. 3–14). Oxford and New York: Oxford University Press.

Josselson, R., & Harway, M. (Eds.). (2012b). *Navigating multiple identities: Race, gender, culture, nationality, and roles.* Oxford: Oxford University Press.

Lahad, M., Shacham, M., & Ayalon, O. (Eds.). (2013). *The 'BASIC PH' model of coping and resiliency: Theory, research and cross-cultural application.* London and Philadelphia: Jessica Kingsley.

Landy, R. (1986). *Drama therapy: Concepts and practices.* Springfield, IL: CC Thomas.

Methot, J. R., Rosado-Solomon, E. H., & Allen, D. G. (2018). The network architecture of human capital: A relational identity perspective. *Academy of Management Review, 43*(4), 723–748. doi:10.5465/amr.2016.0338

Mitchell, S. (1994). The theatre of self expression: A 'therapeutic theatre' model of dramatherapy. In S. Jennings (Ed.), *The handbook of dramatherapy* (pp. 20–29). London: Routledge.

Mitchell, S. A. (2014). *Relationality: From attachment to intersubjectivity* (Kindle ed. Vol. 20). New York and London: Psychology Press.

Morales, J. B., & Abegglen, S. (Eds.). (2020). *Understanding education and economics: Key debates and critical perspectives.* London and New York: Routledge.

Parry, C. (1972). *English through drama: A way of teaching* (Digitised by the Internet Archive ed.). Cambridge: Cambridge University Press.

Plowden, J. P. (1967). *Children and their schools volume 1* (Vol. 1). London: Her Majesty's Stationery Office.

Rogers, C. (1961). *On becoming a person: A therapist's view of psychotherapy.* Boston: Houghton Mifflin Company.

Schechner, R. (2004). *Performance theory.* London and New York: Routledge.

Sluss, D. M., & Ashforth, B. E. (2007). Relational identity and identification: Defining ourselves through work relationships. *Academy of Management Review, 32*(1), 9–32. doi:10.5465/AMR.2007.23463672

Stanislavski, K. (1980). *An actor prepares* (1980 reprint ed.). London: Methuen.

Teo, T. (2018). Homo neoliberalus: From personality to forms of subjectivity. *Theory and Psychology, 28.* doi:10.1177/0959354318794899

Tesniere, L. (2015). *Elements of structural syntax* (T. Osborne & S. Kahane, Trans.). Amsterdam/Philadelphia: John Benjamins Publishing Company.

Twenge, J. M. (2006). *Generation me: Why today's young Americans are more confident, assertive, entitled – and more miserable than ever before.* New York: Free Press.

van der Kolk, B. (2005). Developmental trauma disorder: Towards a rational diagnosis for children with complex trauma histories. *APA PsycNet Psychiatric Annals, 35*(5), 401–408. doi:10.3928/00485713-20050501-06

Yam, S. (2018). Interrogating the 'deep story': Storytelling and narratives in the rhetoric classroom. *Composition Forum, 40.* ISSN-1522-7502

Zvelc, G. (2009). Between self and others: Relational schemas as an integrating construct in psychotherapy. *Transactional Analysis Journal, 39*(1), 22.

6 Functional-, Fictional-, and Relational-roles

This chapter explores and illustrates the ways the drama-processes explored in Chapter 5 work out for two individual students. On the one hand, there is a focus on the relationships that develop between the functional-, the relational-, and the fictional-roles, i.e., the real-life and fictional-roles that the students take on, and the themes appearing in the group drama on the other. There is exploration of the ways the identity-work that takes place in the classroom relates to my own journey as a teacher and as a person.

Peter First: Peter's work focussed on his relationship to rebellion and heroism.
Kelly Burk: Kelly's work focused on her identity as gendered and marginalised.

The work of these students illustrates the dynamics at play between functional-, relational-, and fictional-roles on the one hand and theme on the other. I take a snapshot look at the work of Peter First to illustrate the complex ways that the drama-processes co-arise and co-evoke. I found working with Peter difficult at first and I took a very personal journey through my own issues before I began to see his work as valuable. This was a salient lesson for me. I take a longitudinal look at the work of Kelly Burk which focusses on her identity as gendered and marginalised and shows change over time. At first, I worried that Kelly was not engaging with the drama. However, when I attended to what was going on using the four-part structure, I realised that she was working hard at exploring her own identity within the drama context and beyond.

Peter First

Peter had average academic achievement and formed part of the dominant groupings in school in terms of ethnic, cultural, gendered, and social presentation. Popular, and integrated in a friendship group, like many students in school, he was networked into the community through his family. He was interested in football and team-games and had experimented with a variety of identity-performances in school, including 'class clown' and 'bad-boy'. During lessons, he sometimes had difficulty regulating himself physically

DOI: 10.4324/9781003464532-6

Box 6.1 The terrorist gives a statement in court

Peter First: So, life as a terrorist did begin quite hard, I had to leave my family and stuff, and then, I had to worry about money, where to get guns, drugs, and stuff; so then, I worked with the local cartel, and then, you know, and then I got, paid big time for a drug heist. And then, Osama Bin Laden said that I could go do this big project he had planned, so, I agreed, and then, I only found out the day it happened, I have to be hijacking a plane and die. My friend is called Mohamed, and then Mohamed is like 'what are you doing?' and I'm like 'Daddy Bin Laden told me to do this, so I have to do it' ... then, well ... I went to heaven and it was actually just hell. ... which was heaven cos, you know ... I'm not religious.

No responsibility or agency. Encoded. Struggling to see any way of dignifying what is feeling to me like a recipe for chaos.	There are no helpful elements. Actually, this is what the terrorists were aiming for – utter chaos.

Figure 6.1 Excerpt from reflective journal: no helpful elements.

and depended on the interventions of his peers to temper this. In the transcript at Box 6.1, Peter has encoded in character-in-role as a terrorist who has been arrested for blowing up an aeroplane and is being questioned. As part of a devising process, the students were asked to 'find out more' about their characters by using a convention called 'hot-seating'. This is a technique where one student in a group encodes as a character-in-role and is asked questions by the others, which must be answered in role and on behalf of the character. The students were then asked to find a way of including the information they had learned about their characters-in-roles in their plays. Peter chose to be hot-seated as the character-in-role of a terrorist and his group chose to incorporate the new material they had made up or 'discovered' by having the terrorist character give a statement in a court of law to account for his crimes (Box 6.1).

I initially interpreted the work that Peter First and his group did as nihilistic and amoral. For example, in my reflective journal, I note my feeling that 'There are no helpful elements' in their story. I write about the lack of responsibility the students seem to have and how I struggle to find a way to dignify their work, which seemed chaotic (Figure 6.1).

Box 6.2 Excerpt from reflective journal: embodied senseless destruction and no emotional connection

Peter First/SoundBloke/Jent le Manx/Nulch Ap – tragedy that is beyond the control of the adults or the society. Embodied senseless destruction (there is no reflection on why the terrorists might have wanted to do that).

I refer to 'Embodied senseless destruction' and worry that there is 'No emotional connection' between Peter First and the human beings in his work (Box 6.2).

However, following a discourse analysis of the train of thoughts of the students (Adjei, 2013; Yousaf, 2017) (see Chapter 4), I re-evaluate.

I first determined the order of the train of thoughts presented by Peter First in the functional-role of actor, playing the fictional character-in-role of the terrorist, as follows:

1. Life as a terrorist was hard.
2. He had to leave his family 'and stuff'.
3. He had money worries.
4. He had to worry about where to get drugs and guns 'and stuff'.
5. Therefore, he got involved with the local cartel doing illegal jobs.
6. Osama Bin Laden offered him an opportunity.
7. The job was to blow up an aeroplane.
8. His friend Mohamed challenged him about what he was doing.
9. He questioned whether he was in heaven or hell, because apparently it was not clear.
10. He summed up his speech with the statement that he was not religious anyway.

At the start, Peter First, in the functional-role of actor, had the fictional-character of the terrorist make references to the hardships he had faced. In identifying these causal factors, both Peter First in the real and the character he had created could lessen their direct responsibility for what was done by invoking a story that placed social injustices at the heart of events (O'Malley, 2005). The drama referred to the culturally held belief that there are reasons why people behave as they do, including the impact of poverty on the young (Côté, 2014). There was cognitive and critical questioning. For example, what level of responsibility was Peter placing on the shoulders of the character-in-role? To what extent did Peter wish to distance from or identify with the actions of his character-in-role? To what extent does the final reference to heaven, hell, and religion, that his character claimed not to believe in, underline that this is a values negotiation. It seemed at this point that he did not quite know where his ethical allegiances lay.

The repeating 'and stuff' tag embedded in the first lines suggested that Peter was asking the audience to fill in missing details – maybe invoking an 'urban gangsta' shared discourse, including the idea that the 'urban gangsta' might treat other human beings as commodities. Asking the audience to supply missing information assumed a relationship with them and, by implication, a dialogue with their imagined positions relative to the discourse being invoked. Peter also appealed to other culturally shared discourses. One major way that such discourses, or scripts, are shared is through memes that are informed by the wider socio-political context via the globalised and globalising phenomenon of social media. For example, those whom we view as terrorists, from another values-perspective might be seen as 'freedom-fighters'. Yet, for the vast majority of the citizenry in the society in which Peter locates, that is not the case, so this is a shared discourse. Also, for the vast majority who subscribe to the idea of policing and governance by consent, which is a shared discourse, an 'urban gangsta' script might well include the idea that those who live in the criminal or extremist underworld, where it is believed that family support and connectivity is lacking – which is another shared discourse – subscribe to values that allow for the treating of other human beings as commodities. The idea of seeing people as commodities also links into the neoliberal discourse which makes it acceptable to employ free enterprise of almost any kind, and normal to value others only in terms of the commodification value they represent. Peter may not be able to label the value with the tag neoliberal, but that value, having replicated and infiltrated the shared discourse as a meme (Bear, 2020), became an active element in the students' values negotiations. My point is that through invoking a shared discourse by the expedient of saying 'and stuff', Peter opened-up a vista of possible multi-level overlapping and criss-crossing values-pathways, which, using the functional-role of actor, he was able to explore in his fictional-role, facilitated and supported by the relational-roles invoked by the drama-processes.

Placing the speech in the context of a judicial review gave an overall theme of justice being played out. Even had that not been Peter's plan, he was working in a group, and as a group, this was how the group positioned the terrorist. The group, who in terms of working process enjoyed devising their own content for which they happily took responsibility, made a values decision which manifested through the evolving plot of the play, to define what they considered to be acceptable actions and acceptable consequences. As Peter was swept along by the group's desire to bring the terrorist (Peter First?) to justice, Peter's attitude to his character began to shift. This became a challenging values exploration where the fictional terrorist was not the only person on trial. Also on trial were the values of each of the students in the group.

The nature of the group's encoding was mainly embodied and engaged; however, the overall performance genre was mainly ironic and distanced. Therefore, it was clear that multiple identity-working processes were being held in tension. One tension was that Peter, in the functional-role of director, had the material be delivered by Peter in the functional-role of actor encoded as an embodied human protagonist. This choice implied engagement with the character. This engagement was held in tension with the ironic mode of delivery, which distanced Peter from the horrific and dehumanising material. It was as if, in an intra-personal process, Peter packaged up the horrific content in an upbeat style, he could dis-associate from the emotional content of the material. At the same time, in an inter-personal relational process, he was able to signal to those around him his *intention* to be disassociated from the material. The concern to *communicate* his *relationship to the material* to his peers indicated that he was aware of the effect his choices might have on his audience. He was able to anticipate the possible responses of his audience and the nature of their feedback (Renfrew, 2015). It seems that the choices Peter made to deliver the fictional material in an ironic genre, which was a distancing technique, and to also encode in an embodied way, which was an engagement technique, were underpinned by embodied psychosocial and relational processes that ultimately facilitated ongoing engagement with the material, by allowing the material to be approached safely on multiple levels. He could approach the material secure from being overwhelmed by its emotional content, and he could also remain safe in his peer context by impression-managing his relationship to the material. Those elements of distance and safety may have felt necessary because Peter, on some level, felt that he might have become overwhelmed by the material which would imply an intra-personal process. Or it might have been because he did not connect to the material at all. That would also imply an intra-personal process, although one of a different nature. Furthermore, in choosing to deliver the lines in a way that did not imply shame, regret, or remorse, Peter added additional layers to a process that was to do with the exploration of values. In a three-way frame, Peter was able to observe himself encoded as a terrorist who was displaying disregard for human life. It was a 'hedge' frame where Peter could be himself and not himself at the same time, and where he could try out alternative values positionings without having to personally commit to them (Landy, 1992). By giving himself permission to play with this kind of forbidden discourse, he applied a 'shadow' scenario to his work (see Chapter 5). He could protect himself from being seen to be exploring his own attitudes because it was framed as not him but his character-in-role that was speaking. He could explore the interstices of his own values, the values he imagined belonged to the character-in-role, those of his immediate society, and those that may have felt more alien or culturally distant, with impunity. So, overall, there might be an argument to suggest that the evidence given by the discourse analysis of the speech is that this drama was not nihilistic at all and was not about glorifying or romanticising the 'bad boy' identity but rather about questioning it, in a process that involved the invocation and interplay of the functional-, fictional-, and relational-roles.

At the end of the project, Peter seemed less engaged with his character-in-role. When asked to tell the life story of his character, he short-handed the

Box 6.3 Excerpt from Peter First's reflections

Peter First: That he started out, as, he left his family to join a drug cartel, yarde yarde yarde, he got arrested, went to prison, bloke freed him, and sent him on a mission to crash into twin tower, yarde yarde yarde and then he went to prison and then he got shot and killed.

story to a bare-bones version. The text at Box 6.3 is an excerpt from a peer-led interview in which Peter First reflected on and talked about his work in the drama (Box 6.3).

There may have been a variety of contextual reasons why Peter was dismissive about his character's back-story during this interview. For example, he may have been reluctant to write, or he may have been distracted by the high-jinx of other students, or he may have been in a rush to leave the class because it was near the end of the lesson. However, I don't think any of those were the reasons that Peter foreshortened those sections of his narrative because: this interview formed the main part of the 'reflection' lesson; the work was peer led and the feedback was collected as recorded conversation; the students were given plenty of time to engage with the task; and there was a generally focussed atmosphere in the classroom. Therefore, I think it is appropriate to take Peter First's reflection at face value. Furthermore, I think it is important to note what it was that he chose to foreshorten, given that he could have made 'cuts' anywhere.

Not only was the content of the drama very summarised, Peter did not even invest enough in the story to tell it fully in words. Instead, he substituted the bored and dismissive 'yarde yarde yarde' and expected the listener to fill in the gaps. In terms of audience processes, not only did the 'yarde yarde yarde' invite the audience to fill in the missing gaps, it invited them to do so because the story was boring, and the audience were invited not only to understand that Peter thought that the story was boring but to also collaborate in understanding that Peter thought that the story would be boring to the audience as well. The meta communication was that there was an expectation that the audience and Peter would together construe the story as being of little interest. It was also of note that the sections that he chose to substitute with 'yarde yarde yarde' were the very episodes that had seemed to bring the danger and glamour to the character in the first place. They were also the aspects of the character's story that were the most challenged by the other students in his group. Therefore, it seems appropriate to conclude that to some extent Peter was anticipating the reaction of his audience to his story (Bakhtin, 2008). His expectations of the ways the story would be received were likely informed by the ways his peers had related to his character during the drama. When Peter was asked to tell a story where 'the character does something that you would do', in other words, where Peter First was being invited to find some common ground between himself and the character-in-role he had created so enthusiastically at first, he opined that 'There is nothing in this story that I would do'. In other words, in the way that this evaluative conversation was performed, the 'bad boy' identity had been explored and found unacceptable.

Overall, there was a complex negotiation to do with identifications and dis-identifications between Peter and his fictional character, mediated through the interplay of functional-, fictional-, and relational-roles, and reflecting dynamics to do with negotiations between shadow and idealised-self (Rogers, 1961). This kind of dialogy, sometimes written as diology, was in line with the work of McAdams, who suggested, after Hermans, that self-dialogue, played out in the context of a dramatic fiction, reflects the dialogical self where different internal voices or positions work together to provide coherence by 'participating in the same self-defining conversation' (McAdams, 2006, p. 119). The performed feedback revealed the fictional character's changing affiliations. Those affiliations changed in relationship to the changing affiliations of Peter First, in the context of his peers. His peers contextualised his work by both supporting and challenging his fictions. They were the very real audience and witnesses of his endeavours, whose responses Peter anticipated and accommodated (Bakhtin, 2008). All of the drama-processes, and all of the embodied psychosocial relational processes, are contained in the experience of encoding into a character-in-role, and, as soon as one aspect of the process is invoked, so are they all.

Kelly Burk

The work that Kelly Burk did illustrates not only the impact of multiple processes working together but also how those processes give rise to transformation over time. Kelly was a quiet young lady with low self-esteem and a questioning position regarding her sexual orientation. She self-presented ambiguously, embraced multiplicity (Josselson, 2012), and challenged dominant discourses, by wearing trousers in a school where girls typically wore skirts. She often covered her long hair with a hoodie (Brah & Phoenix, 2004; Burnes & Chen, 2012; Crane, 2000). Kelly did her identity-work in the overlap and interaction between the functional-roles of actor/director/technician, the relational-roles of audience/witness processes, and the fictional-roles, i.e., the characters-in-contexts. To establish the 'over time' nature of this process, I look first at an excerpt taken from the early stages of her work. I then put forward several excerpts taken from a four-month sequence of lessons through which it is possible to track Kelly's development from a non-binary gendered presentation that did, nevertheless, act into the traditional gender female role of shy and retiring, to a non-binary gendered presentation that seemed more assertive and self-consciously competent. Kelly's identity-work focussed on gender role and identity relative to her immediate and wider context (Josselson, 2012; Schiff, Toulemonde, & Porto, 2012; Szirom, 2017). Her growth in confidence and agency within the fiction did not disrupt her identity as marginalised. On the contrary, it helped her explore and discover new ways of doing marginality (Butler, 2006).

During the early-stages work, Kelly worked with three boys: Partygate and Spirp Heart, who strongly identified with masculine discourses to do with aggression and physical dominance, and Leven Baker, who was less interested in hypermasculine display. They created a fictional situation where Spirp Heart encoded as an axe murderer who came across Kelly, Partygate, and Leven Baker camping in the wood. In the excerpt below, Spirp Heart having dispatched Leven Baker is stalking Partygate. At this point in the drama, although the nature of her encoding is embodied, and her genre empathic, Kelly chooses to remain silently on the edges of the action creating an interesting relationship between her functional-role as actor and her fictional character-in-context. Her character-in-context was peripheral, and her relational style included a lot of observing. As audience within the drama, Kelly occupied a place of both being and not being. This establishes a baseline context for Kelly's work (Box 6.4).

Kelly's fictional-character avoided violent attack by enacting the gendered position of being overlooked/ignored and by retreating – or being pushed – to the edges of the action (Szirom, 2017). Despite having removed herself/been removed in both the fiction and the reality to the periphery of the action, Kelly did not opt out of the drama. She signalled that she remained part of the scene by *acting* as if to check that Partygate was OK and by moving round in a way that *signalled* to the audience that she was 'avoiding' the axe murderer. Kelly was positioned to occupy a marginal place in the group drama. She may have sought out that marginal role, or it may have been allocated to her. It may have been the result of an unequal negotiation. She was on the physical margins of the stage and in the fictional margins of the story. She watched. This positioning was done in relation to a gendered performance from Spirp Heart, who played the axe murderer and who acted into a 'larger culture' (Francis, 1997; Wharton, 2012, p. 68) story about men being more aggressive and dangerous than women (Richmond, Levant, & Ladhani, 2012) (see Chapter 3).

Box 6.4 Excerpt from the work of Kelly Burk

Leven Baker is lying, dead, on the floor. Kelly stands slightly up-stage of him, to the edge of the action and with her back up against the wall. Spirp Heart enters, making as if he is driving a vehicle, and 'drives' towards Partygate. He runs Partygate down and exits stage-right. Kelly shifts her position to a crouch and furtively moves further stage-left, making as if to see if Partygate is still alive. Spirp Heart re-enters from stage-right. He strides over to Partygate and then makes a stage-left exit, disregarding Kelly. Kelly moves to stage-right and waits there.

Box 6.5 Excerpt from reflections of Kelly Burk

Kelly Burk: My struggles with my mental health. But in general, ever since the start of year seven, I haven't fit in, and, like when I was younger, we didn't really have much money.

Box 6.6 Kelly gets support from home

Kelly Burk: I identify as queer and I, I, it's taken a lot of years to accept myself. My mum's pretty supportive.

This gendered performance may have reinforced Kelly's position as marginal and helpless and only able to survive by becoming invisible. It repeated and imposed the 'disregard' story that women often feel pertains to them (Szirom, 2017). Spirp Heart gave what could have been read as a stereotypically gendered performance that left little space for Kelly to do anything other than to go along with the way she was being positioned (Brah & Phoenix, 2004). It may have been that the coincidence of Spirp Heart's aggressive performance and Kelly's personal style reinforced her self-identification as a marginalised person as follows: as a person with no voice because she did not speak; as a person with few competencies because she watched but did not intervene; as a person with low self-esteem because she allowed herself/chose to occupy the periphery of the work; and as a person marginal to the dominant discourses in society. This interpretation was subsequently confirmed by Kelly in a follow-up interview (Box 6.5).

Additionally, when she was young, her father had been absent and she felt that as a consequence she had grown up 'fast'. Furthermore, she had questions regarding her sexual orientation that took her 'many years' to 'accept' despite support from home (Brah & Phoenix, 2004; Burnes & Chen, 2012; Josselson & Harway, 2012; Ndlovu, 2012; Ouellette, 2012; Schiff et al., 2012; Wharton, 2012) (Box 6.6).

Given the well-established links between how people perform in fictions and how they perform in real-life situations (Teglasi, 2010), it was not surprising that the same patterns of identity framing were observable in both the frame of the real and the frame of the fiction. What is more interesting for this chapter, however, is how over time Kelly was able to use the drama to explore her own relationships to her marginalised position, and how she managed to create different stories for herself that both challenged and clarified her identity-positioning.

Having established the starting point and context of Kelly's work, it is appropriate to move on several weeks. Students developed new plays. Kelly's group developed an alien invasion story. The gender context of her group had now changed, and so, the dynamic and the relational context of the group had also changed. Partygate and Spirp Art had both left the group. Kelly's group now comprised: Bright Spark who was a boy of mixed East-Asian ethnicity and new to the school; Leven Baker who did not perform male gender in a stereotypical way and, although being an army cadet trained first-aider, was also anti-aggression, anti-weapons, anti-alcohol, and anti-risky-behaviours in general; and Kelly. This group now comprised three students who existed on the margins of dominant discourses each in their own way. In the excerpt below, Kelly and her group hot-seat each other (Box 6.7).

What is of interest is the play between the frames of the real and the frames of the fiction. At times, it is not clear to what extent Kelly speaks for herself, and to what extent she speaks for her character. Her self-positioning as marginal, as 'shy and awkward', recapitulates her earlier work.

Box 6.7 Hot-seating Kelly Burk

Leven Baker:	So … what is your personality like?
Kelly Burk:	Erm … quite shy and awkward, not really knowing what to do so kind of dumb (*Laughs a little*).
Leven Baker:	No no … Erm. Do you … is there any more to your character than meets the eye?
Kelly Burk:	Possibly I support crows.
Leven Baker:	Ooh …
Bright Spark:	Is there any improvements that you want to add to your character?
Kelly Burk:	Erm, not really. Because I'm extremely awkward and I can't act anyone.
Leven Baker:	What do you think your character will do if it was left on its own devices with the aliens?
Kelly Burk:	Probably get killed.
Leven Baker:	'K … Erm … let's say we walked into a mine, what's the first thing you would be looking for?
Kelly Burk:	Erm, food, water, breathing air possibly.
Leven Baker:	'K
Bright Spark:	If you had a choice of water or champagne which would you choose?
Kelly Burk:	Champagne
Leven Baker:	Survival or being rescued?
Kelly Burk:	Erm, probably being rescued. Because I'd probably end up dying if I had to fend for myself.

However, this group, peopled by other marginalised students, enables Kelly to work with and challenge her 'self-stereotyping' (Wharton, 2012, p. 76) tendencies. Her claim to be 'dumb' could be interpreted in both meanings of the word, i.e., dumb as in stupid and dumb as in silent. She stated that she would need 'rescue' because she would 'end up dying' if she had to fend for herself. These statements, which could be construed as identity construction references or 'self-construction' (Gregg, 2012, p. 10), acted into a gendered positioning where women are seen as less capable and in need of paternalistic protection (Krumer-Nevo & Malka, 2012; Wharton, 2012). However, Leven Baker asked her if there was 'more to your character than meets the eye?' and in so doing introduced the possibility of change and growth and something new in the fiction. Kelly's 'self-stereotyping behaviour' also stood in contrast to her other statement in the drama that she would search for 'food, water, breathing air possibly' which was very practical. So, my first point is that a co-member of the group introduced the idea of change and growth within the fiction. My second point is that this happened in the three-way interface between student in the frame of the real, and character-in-context which is the frame of the fiction, and audience/witness processes. The identity-work happened in Kelly's relationship with, on the one hand, Leven Baker who had a gender presentation that limited Kelly less than had that of Spirp Heart in her earlier work, and, on the other, the developments that might be possible in the fiction (Ernst, 2012; Bakhtin, in Renfrew, 2015).

As time went on, in the context of the working processes of this group, Kelly was able to challenge her own self-stereotyping behaviours (Eagly & Wood, 2017). Using the vehicle of the fiction, she began to envision a scenario where she would survive. Kelly introduced the gendered item of a gun into the drama, and later, she armed herself with an axe (Box 6.8).

The point is that Kelly was able to explore alternatives to her self-stereotyping behaviours within the drama both because it had been established that there was the possibility of growth within the fiction and because the context of the group in terms of interpersonal dynamics, in particular those pertaining to gender dynamics (Francis, 1998), allowed that to happen.

As time went on, there were an increasing number of moments when Kelly's character functioned as the crucial character in this fiction, and, as time went on, her gender positioning took on different nuances. Her values orientation focused on helping the others to survive. This reflected on the one hand the concern with nurturing and the welfare of others that is traditionally associated with female gendering (Eagly, 1987, in Eagly & Wood, 2017; Francis, 1998; Gove & Watt, 2004; Wharton, 2012). For instance, she found the food, she did the emotional labour that kept the unit together, she mediated between the two boys in the group. On the other hand, she became more agentic and physically active and assertive in ways that are more traditionally associated with male gendering (Eagly & Wood, 2017; Francis, 1998; Szirom, 2017). This accorded with the findings of Francis, noted in Chapter 3, that suggests that stereotyped gender roles can be ignored or challenged (Francis, 1998).

Box 6.8 Expanded excerpt from the work of Kelly

(*At this moment,* Bright Spark *returns with something to drink that he shares with the others*).

Leven Baker: Thank you.

Bright Spark: There you go. (*He drinks enthusiastically*).

Leven Baker: Don't drink it all.

(Leven Baker *starts briefing the others*).

Leven Baker: OK, do you recommend that exploring here is a good idea? I was having a look at the maintenance ports and there's a computer in this bunker and I can find out about the air filters. I'm going to go see if I can work out how long they will hold out for.

Kelly Burk: Shall I try and go look for supplies?

Leven Baker: Good idea.

Bright Spark: I'll also go look for supplies as well.

Leven Baker: Yeah.

(Kelly Burk *moves off camera, casting one eye to the camera, followed by* Bright Spark. Leven Baker *moves off camera. After a moment, it appears that* Kelly Burk *has found something*).

Kelly Burk: A backpack! Face masks!

Bright Spark: Flashbulbs.

(Leven Baker *returns*).

The backpack has got things in it – a jumper?

Kelly Burk: Warm clothes. Shot gun.

Leven Baker: Found anything you guys?

Kelly Burk: There's also a gun.

Bright Spark: A whole bottle of water. I just guzzled the water.

Bright Spark: We found a backpack.

Kelly Burk: Maybe? we're going to be able to run away from the zombies.

Leven Baker: Maybe.

Kelly was adventurous and explored, she used a pickaxe to dig the group out of the mine, she behaved in aggressive ways towards the aliens, she was loud, she stated that she wanted to assert dominance, and she demanded credit for her contributions. In so doing, she challenged both traditional gender norms and her own self-stereotyping. She embodied her gender in a different way through these social interactions (Wharton, 2012) and explored using an exploratory/emancipatory scenario (see Chapter 5). The work did not move her from a marginalised identity to one that was less marginalised, but it represented a nuanced exploration and re-positioning of her own identity and the way she performed it. I took the following transcript from a moment ten weeks into the project. In the story, Kelly decided to take the lead. To escape the aliens, she used a pickaxe to dig a tunnel under the sea. In the transcript, Kelly engaged in activities that are more stereotypically associated with the male gender: she dug a tunnel, took the lead, and was physically aggressive (Box 6.9).

Kelly could embody gender alternatively because she was working in the frame of a fiction, in an empathic genre, and because the gendered balance and working practices of the group she was in supported her explorations; in other words, because of her in-context embodied psychosocial and relational situatedness. It was Kelly who led the way, and in doing so, she took on a more masculine role. Leven Baker on the other hand, who followed behind telling people to be careful, took on a more feminised role. It was Kelly who kicked at the carcass of the Alien and Leven Baker who 'taps the carcass with his toe' and makes a disgusted sound and comment. Kelly was

Box 6.9 Further excerpt from Kelly's work

(Kelly Burk *turns and starts to dig with her axe, leading the way*).
Kelly Burk: We'll start here.
(Kelly Burk *leads the way, digging under the sea. They go from stage-left across to stage-right, then all the way back from stage-right to stage-left, then all the way back again to stage-right. They mime stepping up. Their attention is grabbed by something on the floor in front of them*).
Leven Baker: Um, careful of that.
(Bright Spark *steps forward and puts several bullets into whatever it is on the floor.* Kelly Burk *takes several vicious swipes at it with her pickaxe and starts to attack an alien that is on the floor with her pickaxe*).
Leven Baker: OK, OK, guys, guys, guys, I think it's dead.
(Bright Spark *starts to shoot at it*).
Kelly Burk: I wanted to assert dominance.
Leven Baker: I think it's dead.
Kelly Burk: Oh (*she kicks it with her foot*).
Leven Baker: (*Taps the carcass with his toe*). Oooh *(disgust),* it's gooey. I think it might have been=
Kelly Burk: =Oooh (*delight*), it's slimy.
(Kelly Burk *turns and sees one in yet a different place, screams and goes to attack it with her pickaxe*).
Leven Baker: OK, calm down, calm down, calm down. They're already dead. They're already dead. Riga mortis has already set in.

repeatedly and unnecessarily aggressive and Leven Baker petitioned for calm. The gender roles had reversed. Kelly may not have been able to step into this more masculinised role had one of the boys in the group made a strong bid to occupy it (Bateson, 2000). The exploration of and challenge to stereotyped gender presentations (Francis, 1998), which some young people might fall back on at some times and might ignore or challenge at others (Eagly & Wood, 2017; Francis, 1997; Gove & Watt, 2004), were made possible in the interactions including: in the particular ways the individuals in the group positioned their gender presentations relative to dominant discourses; and in the group fictional context which acted as a container for their explorations (Josselson & Harway, 2012; Woodward, 2004). The point is that Kelly started to act beyond her self-stereotyping behaviours. She used the functional-, fictional-, and relational-roles, and the drama-processes as a vehicle for doing this, and was further facilitated by the gender presentations of the others in the group. What was startling about the work of Kelly Burk was that the characters she encoded became progressively more empowered and assertive over time and moved from a role in the fiction that might be considered traditionally female and which may have been imposed on her, to a role in the fiction that was more assertive and dominant (Szirom, 2017).

When asked about her own work, Kelly opined that what had been different for her in the frame of the fiction was that she had taken the leadership-role, which was a role that she would not ordinarily have taken in the frame of the real (Box 6.10).

One possible reading of her work is that over time Kelly experienced a challenge to her self-stereotyping. She recognised that within the drama, she had taken the leadership-role. She also stated that she would not 'usually' do that which left the possibility that sometimes, moving forwards, she might. The intonational and implicational context that accompanied this comment (Bakhtin, 1994; Holquist, 2008; Renfrew, 2015) carried connotations of this being something new but also something that could provide a template for the future. Moving on, in the frame of the real, towards the end of the process, she took a leadership-role in directing the play as well as taking a lead within the fiction. The next stage for her would be to begin to challenge her own self-stereotyping positioning within the frame of the real as well as within the

Box 6.10 Excerpt from Kelly Burk's reflections

Bright Spark: Please tell me a story where the character does something different to what you would do.

Kelly Burk: Erm, probably going in lead. Because I usually wouldn't do that.

fiction. Her behaviour and her beliefs about herself did not entirely match up, leaving room for re-definition and further identity-work.

The context for Kelly's work was the combination of situated functional-role, fictional-role, and audience/witness-roles. In other words, the context of her work was the relationship between: her explorations of being an actor, a director, and a technician within her working group; the leadership-role her character-in-role took; and her relationships with the others in the group. An important part of the dynamic was the ways her friends positioned themselves relative to prevailing discourses to do with gender and marginality. It would be easy to suggest that in the course of the drama Kelly moved from a shy and retiring position gendered traditionally female (Francis, 1997; Gove & Watt, 2004) to a more confident and assertive masculine positioning (Francis, 1997; Gove & Watt, 2004). On one level, she did do this. However, the processes involved were, in addition, more subtle than that. For example, in facilitating a less traditionally gendered presentation for herself which might on the one hand suggest that she was moving towards challenging dominant social scripts about the place and role of women and girls, she also consolidated her marginality. By moving into a more marginal presentation of gender, she also reinforced her marginal status. Important identity-work was pursued and achieved through the drama-process, but as with Peter First, the push-me-pull-me of positioning was nuanced and complex. In a social context where it is recognised that 'some forms of masculinity or femininity are more socially valued than others' (Wharton, 2012, p. 6), Kelly Burk explored through the drama some of the values associated with some of those masculinities and femininities. She explored the relationships between the dominations and subordinations within both masculinity and femininity (Francis, 1997; Wharton, 2012). It appeared that ultimately she derived much of her identity from her liminality (Krumer-Nevo & Malka, 2012), and it was this that she explored through the drama. At the start of the process, she performed her marginalised identity in a way that had her silenced and almost invisible. By the end of the work, she still occupied the margins, but in a more assertive, empowered, and visible way, having embraced some of the traits that are considered more highly valued and more masculine in this culture (Francis, 1997; Gove & Watt, 2004). It was as if she felt that she now had a right to be heard and seen (Hatton, 2013) and was no longer required to be 'dumb' (Oakley, 1986). In line with the idea that gender is a 'process', and that it is 'done' and not just expressed (Wharton, 2012, p. 9), I suggest that Kelly Burk was doing gender differently by the end of the project. In fact, she was doing identity differently by the end of the project. This change represented a fundamental change in the way she related to her context that went beyond an increase in confidence and reflected a nuanced but profound re-positioning (Josselson & Harway, 2012).

Conclusion

The drama-processes illustrated above cannot happen in independence of each other, nor in isolation from each other. They are co-dependent, interrelated, and co-evoking of each other. The processes to do with 'functional-roles: actor/director/technician', 'relational-roles: audience/witness', and 'fictional-roles: character-in-context' arise concurrently and cannot be separated. As explained in Chapter 3, the object relations theory of Klein and attachment theory of Bowlby also presuppose a co-emergence of individual context-based and personal identities because according to their theories human identity arises as a result of a dialectical relationship between audience, i.e., the significant other, and emerging self. Our perceptions of how we are being received by our significant others impact on the ways we see ourselves and therefore impact on how we relate to the world. The co-arising processes are manifest in the multi-dimensional relationships that link and separate the fictional and real-roles and themes played out by the students. They arise in the multiplicity of overlapping framings, including the negotiation between shades of fictional self and fictional other, between shades of real self and real other, between shades of fictional self and real other, and between shades of real self and fictional other. Therefore, it is not only that the processes of functional-role: actor/director/technician, relational-role: audience/witness, and fictional-role: character-in-context, that are contained within the drama crucible of role, performance, and story, are drawn-into-being in those liminal places. It is that those processes enable such negotiations to arise. The processes can be observed via an exploration of the roles and themes that the students inhabit, but they are not in themselves the roles or themes.

References

Adjei, S. B. (2013). Discourse analysis: Examining language use in context. *The Qualitative Report, 18*(25), 1–10.

Bakhtin, M. (1994). *The Bakhtin reader: Selected writings of Bakhtin, Medvedev, and Voloshinov*. London and New York: E. Arnold.

Bakhtin, M. (2008). *The diologic imagination: Four essays by M.M. Bakhtin*. Austin: University of Texas Press.

Bateson, G. (2000). *Steps to an ecology of mind*. Chicago and London: University of Chicago Press.

Bear, E. (2020). *Machine*. New York: Saga Press.

Brah, A., & Phoenix, A. (2004). Ain't I a woman? Revisiting intersectionality. *Journal of International Women's Studies, 5*, 75.

Burnes, T. R., & Chen, M. M. (2012). The multiple identities of transgender individuals: Incorporating a framework of intersectionality to gender crossing. In R. Josselson & M. Harway (Eds.), *Navigating multiple identities: Race, gender, culture, nationality, and roles* (pp. 113–132): Oxford Scholarship Online.

Butler, J. (2006). *Gender trouble* (1st ed.). New York and London: Routledge.

Côté, J. E. (2014). Towards a new political economy of youth. *Journal of Youth Studies, 17*(4), 527–543. doi:10.1080/13676261.2013.836592

Crane, D. (2000). *Fashion and its social agendas: Class, gender, and identity in clothing.* Chicago and London: University of Chicago Press.

Eagly, A., & Wood, W. (2017). Gender identity: Nature and nurture working together. *Evolutionary Studies in Imaginative Culture, 1*, 59. doi:10.26613/esic/1.1.10

Ernst, S. (2012). Evaluation of cultural and linguistic practices: Constructing Finnish-German identities in narrative research interviews. In R. Josselson & M. Harway (Eds.), *Navigating multiple identities: Race, gender, culture, nationality, and roles* (pp. 207–226). Oxford and New York: Oxford University Press.

Francis, B. (1997). Power plays: Children's constructions of gender and power in role plays. *Gender and Education,* 2, 179. doi:10.1080/09540259721358

Francis, B. (1998). Oppositional positions: Children's construction of gender in talk and role plays based on adult occupation. *Educational Researcher, 40*, 31–43. doi:10.1080/0013188980400103

Gove, J., & Watt, S. (2004). Identity and gender. In K. Woodward (Ed.), *Questioning identity: Gender, class, ethnicity* (2nd ed., pp. 44–77). London: Routledge.

Gregg, G. (2012). Multiple identities and their organisation. In R. Josselson & M. Harway (Eds.), *Navigating multiple identities: Race, gender, culture, nationality, and roles* (pp. 13–51). Oxford and New York: Oxford University Press.

Hatton, C. (2013). Educating Rita and her sisters: Using drama to reimagine femininities in schools. *Research in Drama Education: The Journal of Applied Theatre and Performance, 18*(2), 155–167. doi:10.1080/13569783.2013.787254

Holquist, M. (2008). Introduction to the diologic imagination: Four essays by M.M. Bakhtin (M. H. a. C. Emerson, Trans.). In M. Holquist (Ed.), *The diologic imagination: Four essays by M.M. Bakhtin* (pp. 1%–5%). Austin: University of Texas Press.

Josselson, R. (2012). The 'we of me': Barack Obama's search for identity. In R. Josselson (Ed.), *Navigating multiple identities: Race, gender, culture, nationality, and roles* (pp. 39–59). Oxford and New York: Oxford University Press.

Josselson, R., & Harway, M. (2012). The challenges of multiple identity. In R. Josselson & M. Harway (Eds.), *Navigating multiple identities: Race, gender, culture, nationality, and roles* (pp. 3–14). Oxford and New York: Oxford University Press.

Krumer-Nevo, M., & Malka, M. (2012). Identity wounds: Multiple identities and intersectional theory in the context of multiculturalism. In R. Josselson & M. Harway (Eds.), *Navigating multiple identities: Race, gender, culture, nationality, and roles* (pp. 187–210). Oxford and New York: Oxford University Press.

Landy, R. (1992). The drama therapy role method. *Dramatherapy, 14*, 7–15. doi:10.1080/02630672.1992.9689810

McAdams, D. P. (2006). The problem of narrative coherence. *Journal of Constructivist Psychology, 19*(2), 109. doi:10.1080/10720530500508720

Ndlovu, S. (2012). 'I am more (than just) black': Contesting multiplicity through conferring and asserting singularity in narratives of blackness. In R. Josselson & M. Harway (Eds.), *Navigating multiple identities: Race, gender, culture, nationality, and roles* (pp. 143–170). Oxford and New York: Oxford University Press.

Oakley, A. (1986). *Taking it like a woman.* London: Collins Publishing Group.

O'Malley, P. (2005). Risk and responsibility. In A. Barry, T. Osborne, & N. Rose (Eds.), *Foucault and political reason: Liberalism, neo-liberalism and rationalities of government* (pp. 189–208). London and New York: Routledge.

Ouellette, S. C. (2012). A garden for many identities. In R. Josselson & M. Harway (Eds.), *Navigating multiple identities: Race, gender, culture, nationality, and roles* (pp. 129–142). Oxford and New York: Oxford University Press.

Renfrew, A. (2015). *Mikhail Bakhtin*. London and New York: Routledge.

Richmond, K., Levant, R., & Ladhani, S. (2012). The varieties of the masculine experience. In R. Josselson & M. Harway (Eds.), *Navigating multiple identities: Race, gender, culture, nationality, and roles* (pp. 59–74). Oxford and New York: Oxford University Press.

Rogers, C. (1961). *On becoming a person: A therapist's view of psychotherapy*. Boston: Houghton Mifflin Company.

Schiff, B., Toulemonde, M., & Porto, C. (2012). Identities in the first person plural: Muslim-Jewish couples in France. In R. Josselson & M. Harway (Eds.), *Navigating multiple identities: Race, gender, culture, nationality, and roles* (pp. 167–191). Oxford and New York: Oxford University Press.

Szirom, T. (2017). *Teaching gender? Sex education and sexual stereotypes* (Vol. 21). London and New York: Routledge.

Teglasi, H. (2010). *Essentials of TAT and other storytelling assessments* (2nd ed.). New Jersey, Canada: John Wiley and Sons, Inc.

Wharton, A. (2012). *The sociology of gender: An introduction to theory and research* (2nd ed.). Chichester, West Sussex: Wiley-Blackwell.

Woodward, K. (2004). *Questioning identity: Gender, class, nation* (2nd ed.). London: Routledge.

Yousaf, N. (2017). Gestalt communication experience and its implications for a mutual relationship in organizations. *Organizational Dynamics, 46*(4), 227–232. doi:10.1016/j.orgdyn.2017.05.003

7 The Choices I Make as Teacher

Facilitating Identity-work That Is Not Always Possible in Models of School Drama Preferred by Market-oriented Curricula

This chapter looks at the impact the teachers' choices have on student identity-work as negotiated in the classroom. It identifies four dimensions of teacher use-of-self behaviour and four relational drama approaches and places those dimensions and approaches in the context of current policy and managerial practice. The chapter begins by establishing what is meant in this book by 'use-of-self'. 'Use-of-self' refers to choices made and influences on the classroom that arise from the intersection of professional role and personal identity. In my case, this includes my role as drama teacher with a dramatherapy sensibility (see Chapter 1). Drama is a relational activity, and all facilitating participants influence both the processes and the products of drama (Sajnani, 2012). In schools, the teachers' choices and actions impact the 'foundation' of the classroom environment (Zolkoski, 2019, p. 240). In its therapeutic form, use-of-self refers to the developing capacity of the practitioner to 'attune to the client' (Wosket, 2017, loc.130). I then present a snapshot moment from one group, and from it, I distil four dimensions of teacher 'use-of-self', which are structural, relational, technical, and interpretational. These dimensions co-arise; therefore, when discussing any one of those dimensions, the other dimensions must also be included. I then consider the students' work *over time* and identify four approaches, which are a relational approach, moving from heightened play to a theatre-based mode, use of ritual, and slowing down the drama. Each approach brings together the four teacher use-of-self dimensions. The chapter concludes by suggesting that this co-arising combination of structural, relational, technical, and interpretational choices resulted in students conducting a kind of witnessed identity-work that is not always possible in models of drama preferred by pre-determined-outcomes or audience/market-oriented curricula such as are described in Chapter 2.

DOI: 10.4324/9781003464532-7

Illustrative Material – A Snapshot

The boys chose a script and started rehearsing. They chose a script that was 'easy' but quickly decided that it was 'boring' and decided to make up a play of their own. The excerpt at Box 7.1 shows the boys encoding as naughty children in a school bus. The enraged teacher pulls the bus over and attacks the children (Box 7.1).

Making Structural Choices – Maintaining a Boundary Round the Lesson

How is it possible to maintain a structural boundary round lesson structure and content, and at the same time maintain positive relationships with participants, and validate their choices (Jang, Reeve, & Deci, 2010)? How is it possible to meet the needs of the young people and the demands of the curriculum, and the demands of the school for constant linear progression? As a teacher sitting in the midst of these competing pressures, I face an ethical conundrum. This irresolvable dilemma leads to stress and dis-ease. My initial strategy towards resolving this irresolvable tension was a relationally oriented appeal to the students' goodwill. As you read, I invite you to reflect on what competing pressures you are navigating, and how you choose to resolve those pressures in the classroom.

Box 7.1 The students want to make up a play of their own

Partygate: (*To* Jent le Manx). And I'll keep kicking your seat, and you turn round and say STOP DOING THAT and then you hit the guy and then the bus stops.

(*Real-life teacher enters room*).

SoundBloke: (*Stands up and picks up his script*). We actually have to do the script.

(*The boys all turn to look at* SoundBloke, *then to the real-life teacher*).

Real-life teacher: You need a script for this bit, because this bit you are doing from the script.

(*Pause*).

Real-life teacher: You do realise that I am asking you to work on THIS bit of script today....

(*Later...*).

Partygate: (*To* Peter First). This is the point when you grab me.

(*Real-life teacher arrives with police helmets for* Partygate *and* SoundBloke).

Peter First: (*To the real-life teacher*). And I have to get hit by a bus TEN TIMES!

(*Real-life teacher nods encouragingly*).

Consider the excerpt above. The boys were arguing amongst themselves about how much if at all they needed to refer to the actual script. They ultimately looked to me to make that call, and I reiterated my position, which was the position that I had negotiated with them in their previous lesson. I told them 'You need a script for this bit, because *this bit* you are doing from the script'. I tried to position myself relationally alongside the students, by framing my statement in terms of what they 'need[ed]' to do because of the task. In saying 'need', I tried to distance myself from the task and to ally or affiliate myself with the students (Bondy, Ross, Gallingane, & Hambacher, 2007). I strove to use relationality to persuade the boys to stick to the structure of the lesson as set. I repeated the phrase 'this bit' to remind them that there were other 'bits' of the work that they would be making up themselves.

However, the boys still grumbled about having to use a script, and so I had to work harder to maintain the structure established by the text-based focus of the lesson. Therefore, I said, 'You do realise that I am asking you to work on THIS bit of script today'. In other words, I shifted my approach a little. I jettisoned the strategy of distancing myself from the task and used a direct appeal to our relationship. It was 'I' that was asking. I also presented the task as a request. I hoped that this framing (see Chapter 5) would appeal to their desire to please. The use of the phrase 'you do realise', was a face-saving 'get-out', as it offered the boys an 'opt-in' of suddenly 'realising' what I was trying to say. My aim was still to maintain the structural boundary in the classroom by holding the students to the task as set, but I was trying to do it in a positive and non-confrontational manner. By making the statement, 'You do realise that I am asking you to work on THIS bit of script today', I also made clear what I wanted (Cheon, Reeve, & Song, 2018). My readings of this moment as I lived through it in the classroom, and my readings of it later as I reflected, were based on an embodied psychosocial relational conceptualisation of identity. My strategies included: an embodied appeal to relationality and a sense of allegiance; justifying my position not simply insisting on it; being clear in my expectations; and reminding the boys that they had actively participated in making this compromise and that we had an agreement. My choices were framed by having to negotiate a range of tensions including: the tension between wanting the boys to work within a containing structure and wanting to maintain a good relationship with the students; and keeping them engaged with the work in the situated context of the lesson. These elements of tension are often present in the classroom. However, in this particular case, the tensions were heightened because the boys were particularly strident in their unwillingness to work with their text (Brant & Castro, 2019). At the same time, in the context of the school environment, I found them embarrassingly loud and physically unbounded.

A further influencing factor was that I felt that I should allow students the autonomy to explore their own material if they wanted to (Cheon, Reeve, & Vansteenkiste, 2020) and was conflicted because I felt pressure to implement the pre-determined scheme of work that satisfied the school policy of providing clear progression from KS3 curriculum to KS4 curriculum. I felt that this was a particularly challenging negotiation for me to navigate because of the meta context which included: an educational model premised on the need to pre-determine outcomes; the primacy of the requirement to evidence linear progression; and the pressures of performativity. Furthermore, another interpretational tension emerged, which was that even as I encouraged the students along in the direction of their exploratory work, I was aware that I might not be able to award them a 'high grade' at the end of the process because they were not working towards the pre-determined outcome-measures. I found that this placed me in a position that was hard and ethically dubious. Yet, I also found that to not encourage the students in their enthusiasm to create their own material, also placed me in a position that was hard and ethically dubious. The simple act of making choices to do with maintaining the structural boundary of the task in the classroom invoked many other aspects of teacher use-of-self. It invoked interpretational, relational, and technical dimensions of teacher use-of-self that raised questions for me that were to do with how that structural boundary should or could be maintained and why. My identity as person, my identity as teacher-as-defined-by-this-context, and my identity as a teacher concerned with giving attention to the developing child were in conflict. Furthermore, they were in conflict in a context where impression management was important. All those aspects of teacher use-of-self were cast in and arose from the tensions between discourses emerging from the social, economic, and political shadow of the neoliberal marketplace, and those informed by a more human-centred pedagogy.

Making Relational Choices – Witnessing and Audience

Audience/witness processes are considered a dramatherapy core process (Jones, 1991) and a recognised part of identity development as people learn who they are and who it might be possible to be, in embodied psychosocial relationship to others who are audience/witness to self. Those people include but are not limited to primary carers (Klein, 1932; Lacan, 2004; Mitchell, 2014). Yet, as explained in Chapter 2, in the neoliberal market of current educational practice, this process is becoming commodified. This represents a marketisation of the fundamental human developmental process. In the classroom, how do I use on the one hand, and resist on the other, the commodification of relationship? Furthermore, 'witnessing' and 'being an audience' are separate processes. As you read, I invite you to reflect on your own use of the audience and witnessing processes.

I noted the ways the students 'performed' themselves for those around, who sometimes were required to be primarily an audience, and sometimes, primarily a witness. A distinction can be made between the mode of audience and the mode of witness that hinges on where the primary benefit lies. When the benefit of student presentation appears to be primarily for the observer, then the observer functions mostly as audience. When the benefit of the student presentation appears to be primarily for the student, the observer functions mainly as witness. The distinction between audience and witness is not a simple or absolute binary. The words 'primarily' and 'mostly' are important because there is inevitably a shifting balance between both modes in each performance. For example, in the above excerpt, when SoundBloke took his script and said, 'We actually have to do the script', I was being related to primarily as audience because, in this case, SoundBloke was putting on a performance for my benefit. He responded to my unexpected proximity by 'making a show' of getting on with the work.

However, there were also times when I was invited to act primarily as witness to the students. This happened when the students positioned themselves in such a way as to imply that they were seeking personal validation. An example of this was when Peter First said to me in excited tones 'And I have to get hit by a bus TEN TIMES!'. In contrast to the former audience interaction which was on balance somewhat more staged, in this latter interaction, there was something approaching a more personal presentation of self. This request for human validation which suggested a relational moment between a witnessing adult and an open child, of the kind that is so crucial for healthy development, is what is, as I explained in Chapter 2, being squeezed out of the curriculum-for-the-commodification-of-subjects (Ailwood, 2008; Lister, 2003). There are clearly aspects of school where students receive this kind of recognition from staff such as in out-of-lesson interactions. However, if students do not receive this as an embedded part of their learning, this dislocates their learning from their selfhood. Or, their selfhood becomes formed in the image of commodification because the whole learning experience, which is formative of self, has become the instrument of marketization (Burman, 2008). This is a serious matter to do with the reduction to a commodity not only of the educational experience but also of the child that grows and is affected by that experience. For these students, I felt that Peter First was sharing something relational with me that he felt excited by. He expected me, and invited me, to be excited with him. Therefore, I chose to act into his expectation and nodded encouragingly. In accepting his invitation to witness his excitement, I was given a valuable opportunity to build relationship and promote further engagement with the work (Lumpkin, 2007; Sajnani, 2012).

There are inevitably elements of both audience and witness processes in a performance. The boundary between audience and witness can become blurry (Emunah, 2020). For example, SoundBloke 'put on a show' of getting on with the work but, as explained in Chapter 3, 'active witnessing' can help to consolidate latent competencies (Mayor & Frydman, 2021, p. 6). Therefore, I made a 'use-of-self' choice to behave *as if* (Stanislavski, 1980) I had been witnessing SoundBloke actually moving on with work. I instrumentalised the audience/witness dynamic. I colluded with his micro-fiction and mirrored competency and motivation back to him. This strengthened and reconfigured those aspects of his identity and role competency (Emunah, 2020), and he began to take on the role of director and organiser more and more even when I was not in the room.

Making Technical Choices – Convention and Equipment

These students adapted the lesson task to suit their preferences. Given the structural and relational dilemmas that resulted, what technical tools did I have in my skills portfolio to support their decision despite the competing pressures on me to move the young people from a developmental and exploratory play space, into an audience-oriented 'performance' of 'good student'. As you read, I invite you to reflect on the ways you support students whose interests develop not according to pre-determined outcome-measures.

I chose to offer the students some equipment to support their dramatic choices, even though they had moved a long way 'off script'. The moment of transaction, i.e., the moment when I gave the students the equipment, was a relational moment. It was at this moment that Peter First excitedly told me about being hit by a bus 'TEN TIMES!'. In making a choice about what equipment to make available, I had acted as a quartermaster, and this in turn facilitated a relational moment. By choosing to support the students' play, which was their direction of work, and by accepting that for the time being, this moved them away from an outcomes/product-oriented theatre-model of practice into an exploratory developmental-play-model of practice, I was making teacher use-of-self technical choices that built the teacher/student relationships that went on to facilitate the identity-work of the students.

I held the tension between competing educational agendas in the belief that what would ultimately result would be worthwhile. I put to the side my awareness of what the boys' work might look like to other staff. I resisted the current direction of the marketisation of human relationship, which in school is engineered by the imposition of pre-determined and easily measured and therefore superficial outcomes which require students to give audience-oriented performances in both the dramatic sense and in the more technical performative sense. The work in the classroom was facilitated and supported by technical choices regarding what equipment to make available to the students, supported by technical skills to do with practitioner capacity to manage student play space, and predicated on my ability and willingness to ignore the pressures of performativity.

Interpretational Choices – Navigating the Tensions

The need to navigate between competing policy agendas gives rise to professional and personal tension. In my case, one policy agenda was promoted by a managerial and performative approach that demanded specific pre-determined learning outcomes. In tension with this, a second agenda afforded greater value to the moral and identity-work that arose as the children were allowed to use play to position and re-position themselves relative to the 'memes' that informed their work (Hess, 2015, p. 326), and to their peers, and to experience genuine non-commodified relationality. The interpretational choices I made whilst manoeuvring within this tension gave rise to the flavour of the classroom environment. As you read, I invite you to reflect on what interpretational and balancing choices you make in your own practice and policy environment.

The classroom environment influenced the kinds of work that the students were able to do, such as being able to negotiate for a greater say in the content and direction of their drama by being invited to become active partners in their learning journey (Mihalas, Morse, Allsopp, & McHatton, 2009; Zolkoski, 2019). This meant that students had some latitude in the contexts that they were able to explore through the drama, and the identity-positionings that they were able to try out, which at some points were fairly extreme. As explained in Chapters 1 and 4, my pedagogical orientation maintains: that students flourish best in environments where the teacher is working towards establishing and sustaining a positive relationship with the students, ***and*** setting effective boundaries (Cothran, Kulinna, & Garrahy, 2003); and that students are more interested in their work when their initiatives can be supported (Cheon et al., 2020; Patall et al., 2018). Therefore, I tried to structure the lessons with firmly held boundaries in terms of behaviour and the form of the lesson. At the same time, I tried to offer freedom within the fiction for the students to be creative and drive the drama where they wanted it to go. The result was that students were able to experience feeling validated in their creative choices. Students were able to explore issues that were exciting to them. They were able to move towards preferred behavioural outcomes. They remained engaged with the work.

Effect over Time

The next section explores the ways teacher use-of-self can impact the work of the students over time. I use the excerpt at Box 7.2 as an illustration, and it reproduces scenes one and four out of four scenes the students created. Scene 1 sets up the dramatic situation by showing the abusive nature of the father, and scene 4 resolves the situation by bringing the father to justice. The two scenes not reproduced here were a scene that showed the father attacking some school children on a bus; and a scene that showed the police making a statement to the public about what had happened.

I identify four approaches which are: a relational approach, moving students from heightened play to a theatre-based mode, use of ritual, and slowing down the drama. Each of those approaches brings together the four teacher-behaviour categories identified in the first part of this chapter which are structural, technical, relational, and interpretational behaviours. None of the approaches work in isolation but in relationship to each other. The identity-work and ethical exploration could have gone in any direction and was not under my control. As explained in Chapter 2, the impossibility of being

Box 7.2 Scenes 1 and 4 from Peter First's group's play

Scene 1:

Characters:

Mother: Jent le Manx
Father: Peter First
Son 1: SoundBloke
Son 2: Partygate

Father: So Honey, how was work? (*Suddenly angry*). Answer me woman! How was work!
Mother: Fabulous darling.
Father: How was Kyle, your boss?
Mother: How do you know Kyle?
Father: I know lots of things.
Mother: How did you find him out?
Father: I have my sources. And Mark ...
Mother: How did you find out?
Father: I know about all of it.
(*Enter the* sons, *late home from school*).
Son 1: Hi mum, hi dad.
Father: (*Angry*). Why are you late? I got a message on my phone from school today. Go on. What happened? WHAT HAPPENED?
Mother: Come on, spit it out!
Son 1: We had a detention at school.
Father: (*Shouting*). You What! (*Points at* Son 2). What happened?
Son 2: A kid was bullying SoundBloke (*Points to* Son 1), and so he punched him back. It wasn't very nice, but it wasn't his fault.
Son 1: Listen to him, he was there!
Father: And why did you hit him?
Son 1: He was bullying me! Ask him!
Son 2: He kept punching him, and it wasn't fair.
Son 1: He's been bullying me for ages!
Father: (*To* Son 1). Tell me the truth. Tell me the truth!
(*Silence*).
Father: (*To* Son 1). I won't hurt you.
(*Silence*).
Father: (*To* Son 1). I won't hurt you. Tell me the truth.
Son 1: It's the truth.
(Father *backhands* Son 1).
Son 2: What are you doing, dad?
Mother: Hey, that's my son!
(Father *knocks out* Son 2, *and starts to throttle* Mother).
Mother: Noooooo!

Son 1: Don't hurt mum!

(Son 1 *tries to protect his* mother *but is overpowered by his* father).

Scene 4:

Characters:

The Judge: Partygate

The Defendant: Peter First

Portrite Wrigley, the Witness, who is the wife of the Defendant: Jent le Manx

Police Officer: SoundBloke

(*The stage is set for the trial scene. The actors are waiting off stage in the stage-right wing*).

SoundBloke: (*Voice off*). All rise.

(*Enter the* Judge. *He walks formally across the stage, takes his place behind the* Judge's *bench, and pauses before he sits*).

(Police Officer *escorts the handcuffed* Defendant *to the stand down-stage-left then takes a position stage-left of the* Judge).

Judge: Defendant, take the stand. State your name.

Defendant: Fabric Wrigley

Judge: Will the first witness please come to the stand.

(Portrite Wrigley *enters and takes the Witness stand, down-stage-right*).

Defendant: I thought you were dead!

Judge: State your name please, madam.

Witness: Portrite Wrigley.

Judge: This session will be recorded for future use. The date is July 13th. Sir, can you recall what happened on June 13th?

Defendant: On June 13th, my wife attacked me, so I defended myself. My kids attacked me as well.

Judge: Please can you stop there.

Defendant: And then, later, because I'm a school teacher, I took my school children on the bus, on a school trip. Then, they attacked me, so I attacked them, and so then I tried to …

Judge: Stop there please.

Judge: Neighbours claimed that they heard shouting.

Defendant: Well, they're stupid.

Judge: Witness one, what is your statement please.

Witness: Well, he, he got very angry at me and my children.

Judge: What happened when your children entered the home.

Witness: He killed them.

Defendant: (*Shouting*). No, that's lies! I would never! She's lying! She's lying!

(*The* Defendant *becomes agitated and lunges towards the* Judge. *He is intercepted by* Police Officer).

Judge: Order! Order in the court! Order in the court! Order! Order!

(*The* Police Officer *removes the* Defendant *from the court*).

able to pre-plan for the issues that students will bring to and take from any given material is one key reason why this kind of drama is difficult to maintain in the curriculum. That is, for this kind of work it has to be up to the students to discover their own way through the material. Otherwise, the learning is not a process of growth but a process of imposition (Freire, 2013).

Approach: A Relational Approach

A relationally negotiated and co-created text became the basis for, and the result of, the work of this group. My work as the professional in the room and the work of the young people visibly and tangibly intersected in this work. Drama practitioners and teachers will recognise this kind of negotiation, and as you read, you are invited to reflect on your own experiences.

The main structuring mechanism that I fostered with the group was the continuing use of a text, but in this case, the work focussed on a new home-grown text that they and I co-created over 12 weeks, with only some of the original published text incorporated within it. In order for me to be ready to relate to the work of these students culturally as well as in terms of providing lesson materials, I needed to prepare (Zolkoski, 2019), so each week after their practical rehearsal, I transcribed their interactions and reflected on them. At the same time, it became my job to extract the additions and developments the students had made to their text throughout the lesson and to write them verbatim into their text. Over time, this built into a comprehensive record, in the form of a script, of their devised work. This provided for students both help (Jang et al., 2010; Zolkoski, 2019) and scaffolding (Vygotsky, 1978). Each lesson I invited the students to work from their growing text. The co-created text, developed relationally between us, became the foundation for their work and the container of their identity-work.

Approach: From Heightened Play to Theatre

The growing text provided a strong structure that helped the young people in this group move from a heightened play space to a theatre space. This took time, and throughout, the students positioned and re-positioned themselves and each other ethically relative to the discourses they referenced in their play. As you read, you are invited to reflect on your own experiences of this approach.

Over several weeks, the students crafted into a final scripted form, a 'Court' ritual. Using embodied dramatic form, they were able to represent their understandings of the abstract concepts of law and justice in physical three-dimensions. For example, the judge took centre stage, and the witness and the accused were physically separated. This physical separation could be seen as both the result of and facilitative of a process by which the physical violence that characterised the initial scene was replaced by consideration of right and wrong, appropriate conduct, and consequences for action. In other words, the colocation of role, performance, and story had created a crucible in which the boys could critically explore ethical positioning using an embodied modality, and the teacher's choice to work with them to capture and then craft the work over several weeks helped them to transition it from heightened play to theatre: the students gradually transitioned from 'acting out', or sometimes acting at 'acting out', to 'acting in' (Blatner, 1997). Their drama stabilised, and it became possible to reflect on the meanings that emerged from their now-crafted work.

For example, the students, when encoded into the characters-in-roles of 'sons', played out a scenario that invoked moral and ethical positioning to do with what they saw as right and wrong on multiple levels, and it was clear that their drama interrogated several dominant discourses associated with neoliberalism. For example, neoliberal policy and ideology has turned away from the ideal of egalitarian welfare provision and tends to favour a system where the provision of services and the management of public sector institutions is governed by market-regulation. In systems that are steeped in neoliberal discourse and ideology, public sector organisations and social institutions have become less respected and less trusted (Brown, 2019). As the students crafted their work and the drama stabilised, it became apparent that the fictional context created by the students reflected this discourse. For example, instead of resolving a bullying situation, the school put the boys into harm's way by contacting home where their father was violently angry at them for being in trouble at school. Wrapped around this kernel of a moral knot was a meta story that reflected traditional narratives about white male dominance (Brown, 2019) which was to do with the father being angry, unreasonable, and controlling, and which was expressed in the crafted build-up of tension created by the father's ominous silences, and which was further enhanced by his obviously fallacious promise, 'I won't hurt you... Tell me the truth', which, along with other lines in that sequence, Peter First delivered in a quiet voice which further added to the sense of menace and control. In line with the idea that neoliberalism responsibilises individuals and families (Brown, 2019), the boys set up a scene where family members took responsibility for sorting out a situation that the social institutional structure of the school had failed to address (Wells, 2015). It is important to create and hold open a space structured so as to enable genuine identity-work to occur, in which the content and the ethical and the identity-positionings that the students adopt and explore can be determined by the students themselves in the relational classroom context.

Approach: Use of Ritual

Introducing ritual gave the young people a chance to act into stereotyped roles that confirmed their identities as white males in this culture. But those same rituals also facilitated new learning and new relational possibilities. This takes time. As you read, you are invited to reflect on how time for this kind of work is created in your own practice.

I made the choice to invite students to invoke and dramatise a social ritual where hierarchy and order are closely woven and strongly upheld (Emunah, 2020). The court ritual provided strong framing, and this strong framing combined with the strong sense of ownership the students now felt for their play meant that Peter First, who often found it difficult to remain within the boundaries that had been established, could be contained not only within but by the drama. Whereas in a robust enactment of hegemonies about boys' entitlements to physical space and attention, Peter First's usual pattern of behaviour was to turn every interaction into a playfight, in this case, Peter First allowed his character-in-role to use words to express himself, for example, by shouting, 'No, that's lies!… I would never!… She's lying!', when his character-in-role's wife accused his character-in-role of violence. Furthermore, when Peter First did eventually have his character-in-role make a physical move, and the Judge called for, 'Order!… Order in the court!… Order! Order!', and the Police Officer moved forward to apprehend him, Peter First chose to allow his character-in-role to go along with the sequence of events and remained contained within the behavioural parameters set by the fictional context. A further benefit of this strong ritual framing was that the Judge's role was empowering for Partygate whose voice was sometimes overlooked within the group. By working in and on this ritual, the students rehearsed new behaviours and discovered new and alternative 'possible encounters' (Sajnani, 2012, p. 17), within their relationships, within their own drama, in the classroom context, facilitated and mediated by teacher interpretational and relational choices.

Approach: Slowing Down the Drama

The slowdown process facilitated ethical engagement and exploratory spaces as the drama opened-up and the young people could get a 'better look' at what was going on for them in their drama. As you read, you are invited to reflect on the effects that slowing down the pace of work has on student engagement, in your own experience.

Slowing down kept open the exploratory spaces that allowed students to explore a variety of values and identity positions. To this end, students were invited to create a back-story that might go some way to explaining the violence of the father. The back-story they created was fairly extreme and could be read as the students playing with values associated with the 'alt-right' (see Chapter 2) (Dignam & Rohlinger, 2019). For example, the father used the patronising, 'Honey', when he spoke to his wife about work. He used the derogatory and objectifying, 'woman', when she did not answer quickly enough. He demanded and expected total obedience and submission from both his wife and his children. When he did not get them, when it transpired that his wife had a life of her own, and when his children brought inconvenience and loss of control home from school, he flew into a rage and became violent. Although the boys in the group were aware that it is possible for men to adopt this positioning, they did not endorse that behaviour and those attitudes. They set to work improvising a scene, and over time, week by week, the conversation between the mother and the father and the children developed into the scene as rendered in Box 7.2. What was interesting about this scene was the role played by Jent le Manx, who until this scene had remained peripheral to most of the action, preferring to allow others to take the main roles and speaking only minimally. However, he became animated in the moments at which he became ethically engaged, and those moments in the drama corresponded to the points where the drama had been slowed down.

For example, the way that Jent le Manx realised his character-in-role suggested that his sympathies lay with the mother. This was confirmed in the reflection work where he clarified that the mother was a nurse, i.e., a skilled and caring person who worked odd hours to get away from her husband. He considered her brave and sensed that she could stick up for herself. He opined that if he could have given her any advice, it would have been to get the police involved or move out. In other words, the way Jent le Manx encoded into the character-in-role of the mother presented the issue of the mother's infidelity as secondary to the problem of her husband's anger, and in relationally and dramatically supporting this presentation, the group also took this as their ethical and moral position.

The Four Dimensions of Teacher Use-of-self

The choices I make as teacher are influenced by my dual training as dramatherapist and drama teacher and my personal identity which includes my embodiment. Aspects of my embodied identity bring challenges to the classroom. I do not inspire students with the same hegemonic authority as do my white male counterparts. Instead, students sometimes use me to explore or re-enact unfortunate racialised and gendered discourses, including those discourses at the intersection of race and gender, including standing too close and deliberately looming over me in a way both physically and sexually threatening, and using names and gestures to racially mark me. This is about the students' embodied response to my embodiment as small, female, and East-Asian. Relationality is important. It is influenced by feedback loops and the influence of discourses. The embodiment of the child makes a difference to me, and my embodiment makes a difference to them. The choices I make when navigating those discourses, within the policy constrains of the teaching environment, fall into four dimensions, but those dimensions are not absolute categories. They have fuzzy boundaries, they overlap, and they inter-relate.

Structural: The ways I define the structure of the lesson, maintain clear boundaries, define the content of the lesson, and allow the students to define/negotiate the initial and developing content of the fiction.

Technical: The ways I use vocational skill and experience to offer structuring and exploratory drama conventions and interventions including use of feedback, and supplying or withholding resources.

Relational: The ways I choose to give students positive regard, bring to bear personal qualities, and act as both witness and audience.

Interpretational: The positions I take as I struggle to maintain a coherent axiological position within competing educational paradigms, balance the demands of competing administrative structures, and reflect on the material and meanings that the students and I generate.

Interpretationally I hold competing tensions in balance in order to understand what is going on in the classroom on a variety of different levels, including conscious, unconscious, and discourse levels. There are tensions to navigate which include the tension between structure and freedom, the tension between being a witness and being an audience, and the tension between student trajectory and school policy constraints. Within those tensions, the effects of my positioning regarding the *interpretational* choices about what to validate and what not to validate in the classroom, which are realised via my *structural, technical,* and *relational* choices, had several outcomes and effects which were that the young people moved from a play to a theatre space, they remained engaged, they engaged in moral and ethical work, and they found their voices. The four dimensions are not independent of each other but co-arise through embodied psychosocial processes. Taken together, they bring together negotiated inter- and intra-relationality in social/structural contexts (Figure 7.1).

Unsurprisingly, the boys' work was also steeped with unquestioned assumptions that reflected the discourses of the contemporary social order, including but not limited to discourses to do with gender (see Chapter 3). For example, although it was reported that the mother worked, we only saw her at home, whereas the father came in from work and also had a scene where he was out and about at work. The mother was tasked with doing the emotional work in the family, in dialogue with an enraged white male who was seeking to maintain or establish or reclaim his place as dominant but without exercising 'common civil norms or commitments' (Brown, 2019, p. 43). Nevertheless, there was some exploratory re-positioning. For example, Peter First and Partygate both discovered new ways of relating to each other, and Peter First experienced new behavioural repertoire. Jent le Manx discovered his voice, and SoundBloke consolidated his leadership-role. There was also

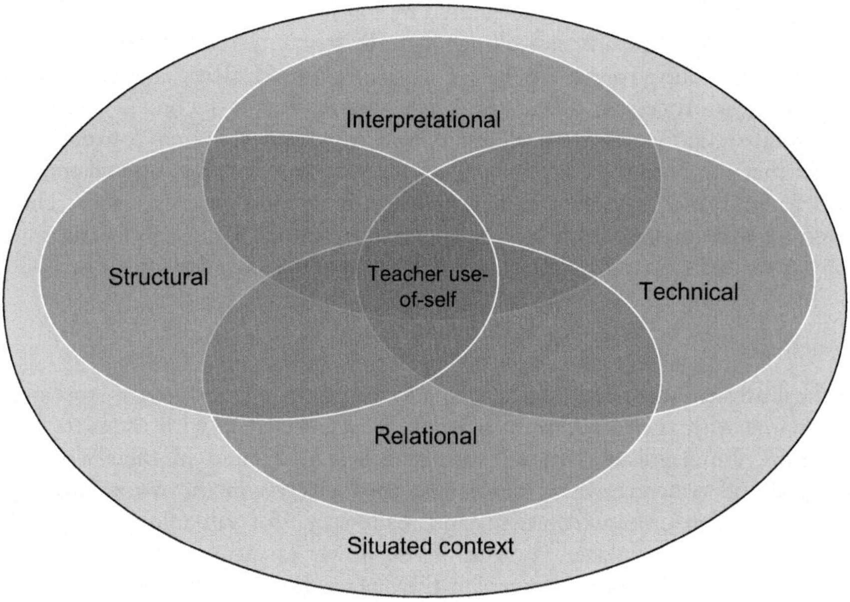

Figure 7.1 Four areas of teacher influence, situated in the wider social context.

some scrutiny of the contradictions inherent in a society replete with competing discourses, and the boys were able to give form to their own positions relative to those competing discourses. For example, although (as explained in Chapter 2) neoliberal cultures expect individuals to be able to function for themselves, ignoring any 'interlocking social processes' (Razack, Smith, & Thobani, 2010) that might make it hard for some people to do so, in the work of the boys the mother was seen as both vulnerable because a victim of domestic abuse and competent and able to be independent because a successfully employed nurse. There was a subtle positioning between understanding the woman's oppressed and powerless position on the one hand and an expectation that she had the ability to simply make the choice to be elsewhere – to move out – on the other. The mother was seen as a contributing member of society and therefore expected and entitled to have her own life and to make choices that benefited her (Brown, 2019), and there was no expectation that she should remain in a relationship that she was experiencing as not good for her, although this was still held in tension with her duty-of-care for her children which she had to maintain without recourse to social services or the understanding of the children's school and in the face of extreme violence from her husband.

The move from action to exploratory identity-work was facilitated by the introduction of contextualising elements that slowed down the drama.

Continued investment in the work despite that none of them were interested in pursuing drama at GCSE was facilitated by following the developmental need (Jennings, 2011) and interest (Jang, Kim, & Reeve, 2016) of the students, rather than sticking to the scheme of work as planned. Being aware of audience/witness processes, and at the same time deploying technical skill such as the introduction of ritual elements and exploratory drama conventions, meant that the boys were able to experience alternative and tempered modes of behaviour and experience different ways of relating to each other. They demonstrated increased role flexibility, explored ethical issues, and made and communicated clear ethical positioning choices. They did identity-work.

Conclusion

In the illustrative case described above, I followed the interests of the students, negotiated with them, compromised and problem solved with them to find solutions, communicated that I was genuinely interested in their work in practical and concrete ways, maintained their interest in the work, fostered a positive classroom environment, and made space for valuable identity and values work to take place. The use of the slowly growing text was a useful and concrete mechanism for keeping their play/drama space open, and providing it with a strong and therefore safe structure. The students were able to explore characters and issues and re-work their drama into a crafted piece of theatre. As part of this process, these boys were able to undertake valuable embodied psychosocial relational identity-work; explore ethical, moral, and values positioning in relationship to current values discourses; and experience alternative ways of behaving and relating to each other. In the centre of all the work the students do, and in the centre of the drama, sit the functional-, fictional-, and relational-roles, which overlap and have fuzzy boundaries. The functional-roles pertain to the actor-, director-, and technician-roles to which the students incline and to the trajectory of the developmental scenario and the working practice preferences of the groups. The fictional-roles pertain to the characters-in-roles the students create in the context of the stories and to the genre choices and nature of the encoding that the students prefer. The relational-roles relate to the use of audience and witness perspectives, and pertain to the performance element of the drama work, and to how the students manage their work by changing its framing. None of the processes are discrete. They all overlap and have fuzzy boundaries, and the relationships between them are mediated by the use of distancing and engagement strategies. The functional-, fictional-, and relational-roles, and their associated processes, are embedded within the classroom environment, which is mediated by teacher use-of-self choices. The classroom context sits within the socio-political context and is influenced by issues that include the environment and global warming, Brexit, a neo-conservative curriculum, a neoliberal administration, the demands of curriculum policy, the impact of COVID-19, and so on. This multiple layering of context can be framed by the four-part structure

(Chapter 5) which casts light on the classroom group-drama change-process that happens in the crucible of role, performance, and story that is drama.

References

Ailwood, J. (2008). Learning or earning in the 'smart state': Changing tactics for governing early childhood. *Childhood, 15*(4), 535–551. doi:10.1177/0907568208097206

Blatner, A. (1997). *Acting in: Practical applications of psychodramatic methods* (3rd ed.). London: Free Association Books.

Bondy, E., Ross, D. D., Gallingane, C., & Hambacher, E. (2007). Creating environments of success and resilience: Culturally responsive classroom management and more. *Urban Education, 42*(4), 326. doi:10.1177/0042085907303406

Brant, K. K., & Castro, S. L. (2019). You can't ignore millennials: Needed changes and a new way forward in entitlement research. *Human Resource Management Journal, 29*(4), 527–538. doi:10.1111/1748-8583.12262

Brown, W. (2019). *In the ruins of neoliberalism: The rise of antidemocractic politics in the West.* New York: Columbia University Press.

Burman, E. (2008). *Developments: Child, image, nation.* London and New York: Routledge.

Cheon, S. H., Reeve, J., & Song, Y.-G. (2018). Recommending goals and supporting needs: An intervention to help physical education teachers communicate their expectations while supporting students' psychological needs. *Psychology of Sport and Exercise, 41*(December 2018). doi:10.1016/j.psychsport.2018.12.008

Cheon, S. H., Reeve, J., & Vansteenkiste, M. (2020). When teachers learn how to provide classroom structure in an autonomy-supportive way: Benefits to teachers and their students. *Science Direct, 90.* doi:10.1016/j.tate.2019.103004

Cothran, D. J., Kulinna, P. H., & Garrahy, D. A. (2003). 'This is kind of giving a secret away...': Students' perspectives on effective class management. *Teaching and Teacher Education, 19*(4), 435. doi:10.1016/S0742-051X(03)00027-1

Dignam, P. A., & Rohlinger, D. A. (2019). Misogynistic men online: How the red pill helped elect Trump. *Signs: Journal of Women in Culture and Society, 44*(Spring 2019). doi:10.1086/701155

Emunah, R. (2020). *Acting for real: Drama therapy process, technique, and performance* (2nd ed.). New York and London: Routledge.

Freire, P. (2013). *Education for critical consciousness.* London: Bloomsbury.

Hess, K. (2015). Metaphors matter: Ethics and the memes of the market. *Georgetown Journal of Law and Public Policy, 13*, 321–336.

Jang, H., Kim, E. J., & Reeve, J. (2016). Why students become more engaged or more disengaged during the semester: A self-determination theory dual-process model. *Learning and Instruction, 43*, 27–38. doi:10.1016/j.learninstruc.2016.01.002

Jang, H., Reeve, J., & Deci, E. L. (2010). Engaging students in learning activities: It is not autonomy support or structure but autonomy support and structure. *Journal of Educational Psychology, 201*, 588–600. doi:10.1037/a0019682

Jennings, S. (2011). *Healthy attachments and neuro-dramatic play* (Kindle ed.). London: Jessica Kingsley.

Jones, P. (1991). Dramatherapy: Five core processes. *Dramatherapy, 14*(1), 8–15. doi:10.1080/02630672.1991.9689804

Klein, M. (1932). *The psycho-analysis of children* (A. Strachey, Trans.). London: Random House Vintage.

Lacan, J. (2004). *The four fundamental concepts of psycho-analysis* (A. Sheridan, Trans. J.-A. Miller Ed. Karnac Books Ltd. ed.). London and New York: Routledge.

Lister, R. (2003). Investing in the citizen-workers of the future: Transformations in citizenship and the state under New Labour. *Social Policy & Administration, 37*(5), 427. doi:10.1111/1467-9515.00350

Lumpkin, A. (2007). Caring teachers: The key to student learning. *Kappa Delta Pi Record, 43*(4), 158–160. doi:10.1080/00228958.2007.10516474

Mayor, C., & Frydman, J. S. (2021). Understanding school-based drama therapy through the core processes: An analysis of intervention vignettes. *The Arts in Psychotherapy, 73*. doi:10.1016/j.aip.2021.101766

Mihalas, S., Morse, W. C., Allsopp, D. H., & McHatton, P. (2009). Cultivating caring relationships between teachers and secondary students with emotional and behavioral disorders: Implications for research and practice. *Remedial and Special Education, 30*(2), 108–125. doi:10.1177/0741932508315950

Mitchell, S. A. (2014). *Relationality: From attachment to intersubjectivity* (Kindle ed. Vol. 20). New York and London: Psychology Press.

Patall, E. A., Steingut, R. R., Vasquez, A. C., Trimble, S. S., Pituch, K. A., & Freeman, J. L. (2018). Daily autonomy supporting or thwarting and students' motivation and engagement in the high school science classroom. *Journal of Educational Psychology, 110*(2), 269–288. doi:10.1037/edu0000214

Razack, S., Smith, M., & Thobani, S. (Eds.). (2010). *States of race: Critical race feminism for the 21st century*. Toronto: Between The Lines.

Sajnani, N. (2012). The implicated witness: Towards a relational aesthetic in dramatherapy. *Dramatherapy, 34*(March 2012), 6–21. doi:10.1080/02630672.2012.657944

Stanislavski, K. (1980). *An actor prepares* (1980 reprint ed.). London: Methuen.

Vygotsky, L. (1978). *Mind in society: The development of higher psychological processes.* Cambridge: Harvard University Press.

Wells, K. (2015). *Childhood in a global perspective* (nd ed.). Cambridge: Polity Press.

Wosket, V. (2017). *The therapeutic use of self: Counselling practice, research and supervision* (Classic ed.). London and New York: Routledge.

Zolkoski, S. M. (2019). The importance of teacher-student relationships for students with emotional and behavioral disorders. *Preventing School Failure, 63*(3), 236–241. doi:10.1080/1045988X.2019.1579165

8 Conclusions

Negotiating Change in the Overlaps and the Spaces In-between

This chapter summarises what the change-processes are and looks at how the practices and contexts that facilitate those change-processes can be created and maintained. Student participation in drama and student identity expression hinges on the dynamic between embodiment and psychosocial relationship. This is inflected by the classroom environment, contained by the drama, mediated by the drama-processes, and negotiated in the relational spaces that are created by the drama. Individual personal narratives, and narratives about who the young people feel they are as a group, are negotiated relative to the fictions that they create. Identities shift via a complex of nuanced identifications and dis-identifications that change over time. Identity-performances change as the result of group processes as summarised below. One of the implications for education is that this introduces the processes of embodied psychosocial relationality and positioning, and this sheds new light on the educational change-process. One of the implications for dramatherapy is that this brings dramatherapy back to mainstream education and offers a workable model of non-clinical practice.

Identity-work Is Done through Embodied Psychosocial Relationality for Which the Drama-process Is a Vector: The Four-part Structure

When students engage in drama, the four-part structure provides a way of seeing the embodied psychosocial relational processes that underpin the change that is facilitated by the drama. The four-part structure does not describe a linear or chronological journey through the story-making process. Instead, it is a way of looking at the different relational processes that co-arise as students create dramatic fiction. In other words, what the four-part structure contributes is a way of foregrounding the processes over the content of the fiction. When adapted to a school context, this focus on process rather than content rekindles debates about why we educate and about what education is, as well as about how we educate. This is useful because it draws the attention of educationalists to the central role of relationality in the educational journey, and it focuses the attention of classroom drama teachers onto the embodied

DOI: 10.4324/9781003464532-8

psychosocial relational nature of the drama-processes. The four-part structure demonstrates and explains, in embodied psychosocial relational terms, the efficacy of drama for facilitating and containing ethical and identity exploration. It makes visible the richness of experience that is possible in the drama classroom and validates the place of play. Furthermore, it adds weight to the idea that an approach other than an 'outcome-measured' approach can have outcomes that are of value. This has significant implications for policy and curriculum development and underlines the limitations of the drama curriculum as it currently stands, where teachers are allowed to judge the students only on a pseudo-professional performance-skills model. This raises the question of why pre-determined outcome-measures are being imposed on subjects such as drama, when the power of drama is to facilitate the self-actualisation of young people, and whereas this can be described, it cannot be pre-determined.

Co-arising Processes: Increase Access to Relational Spaces

The drama-processes, and the embodied psychosocial processes, co-arise and work in parallel. The drama-processes identified in this book include the embodied psychosocial relational work the students did in and between the functional-, fictional-, and relational-roles, using encoding, genre, distancing techniques, and audience and witnessing processes, as foregrounded by the four-part structure. Those drama-processes include group dynamics and the dialogic practice of exploring and rehearsing fictional material. This resonates with the work of Paquette, Carbonneau, Dubeau, Bigras, and Tremblay (2003), van der Kolk (1977, 2005), and Baker (2014), all of whom point to the importance of the synthetic co-arising of processes to do with identity-formation, including processes to do with audience or 'other' and processes to do with embodiment. However, in contrast to this, within the dramatherapy literature, it is usually acceptable for the core processes to be conceived of as separate and the intersecting nature of the processes is not emphasised, resulting in repeated calls for research into the individual core processes as if the potential to effect change inheres within the core processes *per se* (Armstrong et al., 2016). However, if the processes co-arise, and only exist in co-invoking tension, then at the heart of the drama change-process is a relational dynamic that happens over time and in three-dimensional space. The implication of this is that it is the relationality between the co-arising elements as worked out in the context of embodied time and space and the relationality between the students and the processes as worked out in the context of embodied time and space that is at the heart of the change-process. This is something that should be addressed, and I suggest that in the future, there is a need for research that takes as its focus the impact of relationality and dialogy, as worked out in the context of embodied time and space, between the core processes. In school terms, the significance of relationality to the self-actualisation process implies that to enable purposeful identity-work to be achieved, there is a need to increase, not restrict, relational spaces.

Encoding: Stop Learning About Drama and Theatre and Start Doing Drama and Theatre

Encoding is the fundamental embodied process by which a person takes a part of themselves into a role with them. It stands apart from projection, because projection implies a splitting off and putting over there. When first describing the process of encoding my understanding was that students hid themselves in their characters-in-roles (Brook, 1989). In considering the relationships between the self-narratives of individual students and the narratives the group held about individuals in the group, and the relationships between student group-fictions and the place of individual students in that fiction, I noted that aspects of the students' identities were foregrounded not hidden in the roles the students played.

Whereas multiple people can project onto a single character-in-role, only the performer can encode within that character-in-role. Encoding is a bodily experience: a physical as well as an emotional, psychological, imaginative, and cognitive relationship with a character-in-role. Some relationships are more tentative, some are more committed. Encoding is the process by which aspects of the students' identities emerge in the characters-in-roles they are playing and explains why, as Wilshire says: 'We are never aware merely of the character, as if it were an animated Platonic archetype viewed by the "eye" of the mind. We are always aware of Hamlet-played-by-this-actor, and often focally aware of this' (Wilshire, 1982, p. 275). In the drama lesson, aspects of self can be processed by encoding them into characters-in-roles where they are stored temporarily, thus invoking the safety of the 'one remove' of fiction, so that aspects of identity can be negotiated. The implication for the school drama classroom is that students should be encouraged to explore the spaces between being in and out of role. In other words, rather than being required to learn *about* drama and theatre, they should be encouraged to *do* drama and theatre.

Developmental Scenarios: Allowing Space for the Safe Exploration of Unpalatable Material

The work the students did suggested that in the relationships between the trajectory of the fictional story, the trajectory of any single character-in-role within that fictional story, and the self-narratives of the students and groups of students as mediated by embodied psychosocial relational processes, identity-work takes on a form similar to a family 'script' (Byng-Hall, 1985, p.301, 2008). However, I conceptualised those trajectories as 'scenarios' rather than scripts because a scenario is conducted by way of an improvisation made up in situ. As explained in Chapter 5, I identified and observed four exploratory trajectories or 'developmental scenarios' that I termed: aspirational, shadow, consolidatory, and exploratory/emancipatory. In an aspirational scenario, students encoded into a character-in-role that foregrounded an idealised version of self. In a consolidatory scenario, students encoded into a character-in-role that reinforced their already established identity expression within the group. In a shadow scenario, students encoded into a character-in-role and then used the drama to explore a forbidden or unpleasant aspect of self. In an exploratory/emancipatory scenario, students encoded into a character-in-role and then used the drama to explore possibilities for identity expression that had up to that point, for them, been in abeyance within the group. Looking forwards, it would be interesting to do more research into these developmental scenarios. It would be useful to know how the scenarios relate to family scripts and how they relate to dominant discourses. It would be interesting to discover what other scenarios can be identified and how the scenarios relate to experience/expression of identity. It would also be of value to find out more about how different scenarios inter-relate, both for one person exploring more than one scenario and between people in the same working group who might be on different or similar trajectories.

The implications for school drama classrooms are wide ranging. Firstly, it should be acknowledged that there is a benefit in allowing students to spend some time exploring material that is of relevance to them, even when that requires the adults in the room to let go temporarily of their own agendas. In turn, this means that there must be place and space on the curriculum to allow this to happen, and an understanding that sometimes young people will benefit from being able to explore unpalatable material, to individually and collectively position and then re-position themselves relative to the material. This implies that to facilitate ongoing safe practice, drama teachers should understand more fully the processes that are taking place inside the drama, and one way of doing this would be to become more aware of dramatherapy theory and practice. Therefore, drama teacher training courses should include modules on dramatherapy theory and practice. The converse holds. Dramatherapists could deliver classroom drama if they were offered, as standard, modules that qualified them to teach drama as well as to practice dramatherapy.

Functional, Fictional, and Relational-roles: Time 'Off Task' should be Built into Lesson Planning and Considered an Essential Part of Classroom-based Identity-work

As explained in Chapter 3, I observed three kinds of roles that contributed to the dramatic process: the drama functional-roles of actor/director/technician, the relational-roles of audience/witness, and the fictional-roles which are the characters-in-contexts. As a result of the drama they took part in, students enjoyed greater role flexibility at the end of the process than they did at the start (Crawford, 2018; Newman, 2017). For example, students became more willing to take on central and agentic roles and enjoyed greater role flexibility as the work progressed (Chris Hatton, 2003; Christine Hatton, 2012, 2013; Emunah, in Landy, 1990, p. 225). This is of interest to drama-teachers and dramatherapists, educationalists in the wider sense, policy makers and administrators, teacher-trainers, and anyone who purports to advocate for an education that will fit students for a role-flexible future. Reflection in and between the functional-, fictional-, and relational-roles is an ongoing process and inherent in the rehearsal process. This implies that in the drama classroom, allowing students to come in and out of role, rather than always pressing for skills such as 'staying in role' is an important part of the process of identity-work. This in turn suggests that constantly pushing towards skills improvement will not allow for the rearticulation of self that is the key to the ethical development of the students. Furthermore, group aspects of the work and the context of the work are key. It is in the dynamics between the group, the individual, and the material that the rearticulation of self is negotiated. This would indicate that, sometimes, time 'off task' is helpful because this gives students an opportunity to bring to the drama context aspects of their wider experience. Sadly, time for this kind of identity-work, and the flexibility required to accommodate it within the curriculum, is rarely available in neoliberal frameworks.

Aesthetic Relationality: Allow Time for Students to Work Through Defensive Positions

In group work, aesthetic choices are made relationally and are a constant negotiation. From the perspective of the aesthetic choices that are made in the classroom, the change mechanism inheres in the relationships between the person and the material as mediated by group choices to do with genre, working practices, framing the drama, and the nature of the encoding. Therefore, in group work, aesthetic distance should be thought of as a web of intrapersonal and interpersonal tensions and not as a continuum.

It is established within dramatherapy theory and practice that allowing participants to move away from challenging material enables them to move closer to it. This process holds true in the drama classroom. Several implications flow from this. Firstly, the process of allowing for attitudes to be relationally challenged by the group takes time, and although time is often not available within a neoliberal framework (Gilchrist, 2018), if that time were made available, the benefits would be significant. Secondly, the process of allowing students to navigate their ways to genuine engagement with challenging material takes different students different amounts of time, and takes different students and groups of students in different directions, so flexibility is important. Although it is not always easy to be flexible when working within a neoliberal framework, the curriculum would be more effective if it was rooted in flexibility rather than, as it is at present, in a pre-determined and pre-determining curriculum with specifically pre-defined outcome-measures. A further implication is that requiring students to engage with a mass of content in the interests of fulfilling the requirements of a knowledge-based exam, without sufficient time for students to synthesise, contextualise, reflect on, and process that material in relation to their own embodied psychosocial contexts, increases the possibility that defensive positions will be consolidated. In other words, in terms of the performance of identity and of ethical positioning, the cramming of mass content will do more harm than good.

Dialogue between Audience and Witness Processes: Use Audience and Witnessing Processes Knowingly

As explained in Chapter 2, the audience/witness process is one of the core processes of dramatherapy (Jones, 1991). It is also fundamental to the ways our identities are developed (for example, Bowlby, 1988; Klein, 1932). However, some dramatherapy research has suggested that the audience/witness process is the least likely to be referenced in school-based dramatherapy write-ups (Mayor & Frydman, 2021). My own findings support the suggestion of Mayor and Frydman that the audience/witness process is crucial. Mayor and Frydman suggest that one reason for the under-reporting of the audience/witness process may be that the audience/witness process has not as yet been sufficiently clearly defined to be useful (Armstrong et al., 2016). With that in mind, I found it helpful to introduce a defined difference between audience processes and witness processes (see Chapter 7). This introduced the possibility of a dialogic relationship between audience processes and witness processes. This goes some way to answering the call for more research on the core processes of dramatherapy, including refining the definitions of the processes (Mayor & Frydman, 2021). Future research should consider more deeply the differences between the audience and the witnessing processes, and how they dialogue. This implies that the teacher/facilitator needs to know that the audience and the witness processes are different, and to be prepared to engage both audience and witness modes as appropriate, and to be able to dialogue between them. This dialogue between audience and witness modes happens as an emergent property of the drama-process. However, being able to access these modes knowingly brings an extra level of nuance and understanding to the practitioner. It is also an important part of being able to see and manage the competing and interrelating pressures on participants when they are caught between different performative demands.

The Role of the Teacher: Become a Critically Aware and Reflective Practitioner

If identity-work is done relationally, then this implies that there is no neutral way of presenting information or material, because all information is encountered as part of a relational dynamic. Practitioners should ensure that they are aware of how their own intersections of embodied privileges and oppressions position them to the material that they are sharing and creating with group participants.

For example, the identities I enact in the classroom are a result of the combined influence of my personal social and embodied autobiography; my embodied ethical, conceptual, and procedural knowledges; my professional trainings as drama teacher and dramatherapist; and the socio-political context as worked out in school policy. The students also bring the legacy of their own embodied psychosocial relational contexts and cultures to the classroom. As explained in Chapter 6, in my role as teacher, I found the identity-performances and relational cultures of some of these students difficult to relate to but understood that in order to facilitate a culture of respectful interaction in the classroom, I needed to find a way to attune to the students (Sajnani, 2010). Therefore, I tried to tolerate and understand student working, exploratory, and relational styles even though they felt culturally removed from my own (Bondy, Ross, Gallingane, & Hambacher, 2007; Brown, 2003). To this end, I negotiated with students (Steingut, Patall, & Trimble, 2017), offered choices (Cheon, Reeve, & Vansteenkiste, 2020), and allowed time (Assor, Kaplan, & Roth, 2002). I also invoked a professional demeanour and professional competencies and observed that teacher competencies could be grouped into four categories which were structural, relational, interpretational, and technical.

However, the dynamic of the above was further nuanced by my identity as small, female, and racially marked. There has been a lot of research on culture, respect, and interactional style (Bondy et al., 2007; Brown, 2003) which highlights the issues that can arise when student cultures are not respected (see Chapter 7). However, that research took place in the context of a teacher from a dominant group and students from marginalised groups. On the other hand, my work was conducted in a context where the dynamic was between a teacher from a marginalised cultural and ethnic group and a mainly homogenous student body from a mainly dominant group. I would be interested to do further research into this dynamic. In particular, I would like to ask: how can a teacher 'insist' (Bondy et al., 2007, p. 326) on a respectful interactional style in the classroom if that teacher is a part of a marginalised cultural/ethnic group at risk of being subject to unpleasant and provoking social memes invoked by students in the classroom.

In short, teachers do not stand outside the processes that influence student attitudinal positioning and re-positioning. In their situated embodiment as people, teachers are also positioned by and to the discourses embedded in the material that is being explored, and the ways the teacher positions to or is positioned by that material become part of the influencing dynamic in the classroom. This implies that attitudinal learning cannot be facilitated by simply passing on information because there is no neutral way of doing that. Attitudinal learning always arises in the relationships between the students as situated and embodied people, and the teachers as situated and embodied people, and the materials, in the school and societal context. Understanding that there is no neutral way of presenting information will help teachers to become more reflective, and more critical in an analytical sense, of policy and materials and, if democracy is to maintain validity, these are sensibilities that need passing on to students. This has implications for teacher training, for the provision of continuing professional development, and for classroom practice and suggests that as part of initial and ongoing training, teachers should spend time formally reflecting on the ways they are positioned to and positioned by the materials they are asked to introduce to their students.

Looking to the Future

In the wider context, the work offers validation to myself as a classroom practitioner and to others who see the extended value of the work that is possible when students engage in drama. It offers encouragement to persist with the ongoing and ever-present struggle to straddle competing paradigms and to maintain a space of witnessing in the face of increasing pressure to focus on audience-oriented 'performative' work, both within the drama of the fiction and in the dramas that are the lived lives and relationships of students. The relevance of this work to policy makers, school leaders, teacher-trainers, and drama teachers in the broader context of the National Curriculum for England and Wales is the same. The drama curriculum already stands outside the rest of the school curriculum, having been marginalised now for several decades. That already differentiated place, which marks drama as a different kind of subject, affords dramatherapeutically sensitised practitioners the opportunity to facilitate something unique within the mainstream drama classroom and to contribute to the school's curriculum provision something profoundly different to the contributions made by other curriculum subjects. However, this can only happen if stakeholders understand the fundamental differences between what drama can offer, how, and why, and what is going on in the rest of the curriculum.

In practice, the work that went into the preparation of this book was possible because of my dual training and dual identity as dramatherapist and drama teacher. However, others could easily emulate much of what I do in the classroom. For example, at the heart of the approach is a regard for the students as people, a regard for their drama which goes beyond an appreciation of theatrical skills-development, and a grounding in a wide range of drama/theatre forms, including those that have been developed within therapeutic and applied theatre fields such as Theatre for Social Justice. A dramatherapeutically informed drama classroom is not created by the deployment of a specific range of alternative drama conventions but by a reorienting/re-balancing of the teacher-student-classroom experience. Specifically, it would mean a refocussing of the KS3 curriculum on to exploration and self-articulation.

The Crown Dependencies are not the only places where some community-held values, and some of the values of managerialism, are held in tension. Every community and organisation has its own patterns of assimilation, accommodation, and resistance. However, at time of writing, there are some organisations that appear to be promoting with notable success a relational and values-based, not commodity and value-based, orientation. In each case, the way that organisation's identity is inflected by its interface with and expression of neoliberal structures is different. In some cases, the promotion of values-based not value-based exploration seems to be being used performatively. In others, the commitment to being values-based appears to run more deeply and could be seen as providing a genuine alternative. In others, the turn to relationality is fundamental to the functioning of the processes at play within that organisation. In other words, there are supposedly a-political, political, and implicitly political responses.

UWC Atlantic

Established in the 1960s and originally based on the educational principles of Kurt Hahn, for many years, UWC Atlantic aimed intentionally to enable young people to experience the necessity and the benefit of service to the community and the character building effects of experiential learning (Godfrey, 1980). Past graduates of UWC Atlantic cite their rigorous outdoor and community service-based experience with the College as being fundamental to what they are doing now, and to how they are doing it (Baumgart-Turner, personal communication, 2023). At the time of writing, the college continues to develop its educational vision and seeks to establish a culture of service and compassion, and to encourage young people to consider their individual world-views, how those views have been curated, and how those views position them to others in the world (Bardai, 2023). Using their own bespoke Systems Transformations Pathway, the college offers a non-examined, competency-based route through the International Baccalaureate qualification (UWC Atlantic, 2023). The vision of the college is to create just leaders, who are working towards an internationally just and sustainable future.

SOL Center Hawaii

The SOL Center is based in Hawaii which is a place that despite its obvious geographical isolation is also an international centre for environmentally sustainable initiative (Chang, Winter, & Lincoln, 2019). SOL Center Hawaii was created to 'provide transformational experiences that inspire commitment to creating equitable, sustainable solutions for a more just and peaceful world' (SOL Center, 2023). Group collaborative working and relationships are central to the ways that the SOL Center teams work with participants. The commitment to working collaboratively and relationally extends to: enabling young people to work in groups in relationship to one another; supporting young people's exploration of the nature of their collaboration with the natural and cultivated environment; and working in partnership with allied organisations. There is a commitment to thinking critically and strategically across national and geographic boundaries, and to doing so with the intention of addressing social and climate injustices.

Phoenix Centre for Experiential Trauma Therapy

The work of Dr Scott Giacomucci, who is the founder of the Phoenix Centre for Experiential Trauma Therapy, is of interest. The work he does is relational and includes an acknowledgement of the connections that exist between body, soul, and mind (Giacomucci, 2023), the relational networks that arise between people, and the relationships that exist between disciplines (Giacomucci, 2021). Whereas the work I do brings knowledges and practices from drama-teaching and dramatherapy into one space, his work brings together knowledges and practices from the disciplines of sociometry, psychodrama, and social work (Giacomucci, 2019, 2021). He has also written about the integration of experiential education, sociometry, and psychodrama (Giacomucci, 2021) and is currently working on an edited book on the same topic. Some of the most useful things his practice brings to the classroom are the use of trauma-informed principles to guide the use of drama in the classroom, the use of sociometry as experiential teaching in the classroom, the importance of the warming-up process before using role play in the classroom, and the application of Moreno's spontaneity theory of learning (Giacomucci, 2021, 2023).

Final Comments

Several years have passed since the work described in this book was initiated. Some things have changed. For example, for the jurisdiction where the work took place, OFSTED has become an embedded part of the local educational landscape. However, what has remained constant has been the high level of contestation surrounding education. At the time of publication of this book, a new education law for the jurisdiction, that was proposed and which should have come into effect several years ago, is still to materialise. Plans to restructure the organisation of school sites across the jurisdiction have been resisted with some success. What collaboration across the community's school sites should look like continues to be debated, with some factions believing that their children will be best served by maintaining different schools with individual characters, and other factions believing that their children will be best served by removing as many differences between the schools as possible so that every child enjoys the same educational provision. The de-valuing of drama on the curriculum continues to be resisted by current staff who have been strident in their rejection of the 'one-size-fits-all' approach being imposed from above. There continue to be tensions that arise from the unfortunate mismatch between the developmental and collaborative pedagogy preferred by some teachers and which underpins the delivery of some creative subjects, versus the continuing pursuit of external validation by way of pre-determined outcome-measures preferred by managers and policy makers. As a result, teachers become sick, leave the profession, leave the school, leave the jurisdiction, express disquiet, and sometimes become unionised, and this represents significant resistance to what can feel like the relentless incursion of neoliberal managerialist culture.

For dramatherapists, I hope that this book rekindles interest in the idea of a kind of dramatherapy that returns an historic but now mostly elided non-clinical and pedagogic sensibility to schools-based dramatherapy. It builds on the current work of dramatherapists such as Holmwood (2016); Holmwood and Stavrou (2012), Jennings (2011), and Pendzik (2013) who challenge the idea that dramatherapy should be a purely clinical model of intervention. It offers a form by which dramatherapy can make an impact within the mainstream curriculum by highlighting the points of overlap between dramatherapy, developmental drama, and educational drama that were present at the genesis of both professional dramatherapy and professional drama-teaching and is a useful response to the call from Pendzik to move away from a purely clinical research orientation and to become more interested in what applied/social theatre forms, such as that of Boal (Boal, 1979, 1995), have to offer (see Chapter 3). There are some fundamental differences between classroom drama, including classroom drama informed by a dramatherapy sensibility, and Theatre for Social Justice. For example, classroom drama tends usually but not absolutely to focus on the creation and exploration of dramatic fictions whereas 'applied theatre' and Theatre for Social Justice is often but not exclusively based on the exploration of real-life stories deriving from the autobiographies of the participants. Nevertheless, this book presents a model that embraces a more diverse application of dramatherapy. It offers a developed conceptualisation of audience/witness processes: one which suggests that audience processes and witness processes, although related and overlapping, are in fact discrete. This conceptualisation goes some way to answering the call by Armstrong et al for further research into defining the dramatherapy core processes (see Chapter 3). Furthermore, it also goes some way to answering their call to relate dramatherapy change-processes to other models of psychotherapeutic change (see Chapter 3). In this case, the drama-processes of role, performance, and story, in which inhere the core processes of dramatherapy, are related to an embodied psychosocial relational conceptualisation of identity.

In resistance to technologies such as SISRA and other industry-based testing that accepts and delivers only a limited kind of data and that narrow the frame of reference, I believe that the material that forms the basis of this book indicates that there should be a move to broaden the educational knowledge and practice base, which should move away from a focus on the technologies and psychologies of information delivery and should include a consideration of relationality, positioning, and identity. In practice, this would mean more opportunities for policy informed by horizontal discursive practice and less subjection to policy implemented by top-down hierarchy. The current top-down management structure is monolithic and replicates the business model whereby a company is run by the directive of an executive who is entitled to determine the ethos of the business and to control everything that goes into and comes out of it (Walshaw, 2017). This is a deeply anti-democratic organisational model.

I hope that this book provides sufficient insight into the change-process at play in the drama classroom, to enable those practitioners and policy makers who are able to see the value of developmental and exploratory work to continue to resist the imposition of easy to measure and therefore superficial outcome-measures in the drama context; to justify why drama is important because it offers students and therefore the communities in which those students will become adults something unique and invaluable; to more clearly understand and articulate what actually is happening in the drama classroom; and to fight for the right of our children to develop into the ethically grounded, critically aware people they deserve to be allowed to be, and who are fit for leading our communities into the uncertain future as it unfolds.

References

Armstrong, C. R., Rozenberg, M., Powell, M. A., Honce, J., Bronstein, L., Gingras, G., & Han, E. (2016). A step toward empirical evidence: Operationalizing and uncovering drama therapy change processes. *The Arts in Psychotherapy, 49*, 27–33. doi:10.1016/j.aip.2016.05.007

Assor, A., Kaplan, H., & Roth, G. (2002). Choice is good, but relevance is excellent: Autonomy-enhancing and suppressing teacher behaviours predicting students' engagement in schoolwork. *British Journal of Educational Psychology, 72*(2), 261. doi:10.1348/000709902158883

Baker, E. S. (June 2014). *A therapist moving beyond therapy into applied theatre practice: A personal account by a Rogerian practitioner* (PhD). University of Exeter, England.

Bardai, N. (2023). Transformative Education for global impact: Welcome. Retrieved from www.atlanticcollege.org/userfiles/uwcacmvc/09%20Publications%20and%20Policies/10%20YEAR%20VISION.pdf

Boal, A. (1979). *The theatre of the oppressed*. London: Pluto Press.

Boal, A. (1995). *The rainbow of desire* (A. Jackson, Trans.). London: Routledge.

Bondy, E., Ross, D. D., Gallingane, C., & Hambacher, E. (2007). Creating environments of success and resilience: Culturally responsive classroom management and more *(4)*, 326. Retrieved from https://bit.ly/3xvJWiX

Bowlby, J. (1988). *A secure base: Clinical applications of attachment theory*. London: Routledge.

Brook, P. (1989). *The shifting point: 40 years of theatrical exploration 1946–1987*. London: Methuen Drama.

Brown, D. F. (2003). Urban teachers' use of culturally responsive management strategies. *Theory Into Practice, 42*(4), 277–282. doi:10.1177/0042085904263258

Byng-Hall, J. (1985). The family script: A useful bridge between theory and practice. *Journal of Family Therapy, 7*(3), 301–305. doi:10.1046/j..1985.00688.x

Byng-Hall, J. (2008). The significance of children fulfilling parental roles: Implications for family therapy. *Journal of Family Therapy, 30*(2), 147–162. doi:10.1111/j.1467-6427.2008.00423.x

Chang, K., Winter, K. B., & Lincoln, N. K. (2019). Hawai'i in Focus: Navigating pathways in global biocultural leadership. *Sustainability, 11*(2). doi:10.3390/su11010283

Cheon, S. H., Reeve, J., & Vansteenkiste, M. (2020). When teachers learn how to provide classroom structure in an autonomy-supportive way: Benefits to teachers and their students. *Science Direct, 90*. doi:10.1016/j.tate.2019.103004

Crawford, J. (2018). *The use of role theory to build identity in adolescents.* (Master of Arts). Lesley University Massachusetts, Lesley University Massachusetts Retrieved from https://digitalcommons.lesley.edu/expressive_theses/62/

Giacomucci, S. (2019). *Social group work in action: A socicometry, psychodrama, and experiential trauma group therapy curriculum* (PhD). Retrieved from https://repository.upenn.edu/entities/publication/66e1bb41-7e02-46d2-b54b-1e7bd6df71ba

Giacomucci, S. (2021). *Psychodrama in counselling, coaching and education: Experiential approaches for group therapists, community leaders, and social workers* (Vol. 1). Singapore: Springer.

Giacomucci, S. (2023). Specialised treatment for trauma, loss and addiction. Retrieved from www.phoenixtraumacenter.com

Gilchrist, G. (2018). *Practitioner enquiry: Professional development with impact for teachers, schools and systems.* London and New York: Taylor and Francis, Routledge.

Godfrey, R. (1980). *Outward bound: Schools of the possible.* Garden City, New York: Anchor Press.

Hatton, C. (2003). Backyards and borderlands: Some reflections on researching the travels of adolescent girls doing drama. *NJ, 27*(1), 33–44. doi:10.1080/14452294.2003.11649457

Hatton, C. (2012). Performing 'girl' in the Facebook era: Drama as a safe space for negotiating adolescent identities and agency. *NJ, 36*(1), 36–49. doi:10.1080/14452294.2012.11649553

Hatton, C. (2013). Educating Rita and her sisters: Using drama to reimagine femininities in schools. *Research in Drama Education: The Journal of Applied Theatre and Performance, 18*(2), 155–167. doi:10.1080/13569783.2013.787254

Holmwood, C. (2016). *Drama education and dramatherapy: Exploring the space between disciplines.* London: Routledge.

Holmwood, C., & Stavrou, C. (2012). Dramatherapy and drama teaching in school – a new perspective: Towards a working relationship. In L. Leigh, I. Gersch, A. Dix, & D. Haythorne (Eds.), *Dramatherapy with children, young people and schools: Enabling creativity, sociability, communication and learning* (pp. 30–38). London: Routledge.

Jennings, S. (2011). *Healthy attachments and neuro-dramatic play* (Kindle ed.). London: Jessica Kingsley.

Jones, P. (1991). Dramatherapy: Five core processes. *Dramatherapy, 14*(1), 8–15. doi:10.1080/02630672.1991.9689804

Klein, M. (1932). *The psycho-analysis of children* (A. Strachey, Trans.). London: Random House Vintage.

Landy, R. (1990). The concept of role in dramatherapy. *The Arts in Psychotherapy, 17*, 223–230. doi:10.1016/0197-4556(90)90005-B

Mayor, C., & Frydman, J. S. (2021). Understanding school-based drama therapy through the core processes: An analysis of intervention vignettes. *The Arts in Psychotherapy, 73*. doi:10.1016/j.aip.2021.101766

Newman, T. (2017). Creating the role: How dramatherapy can assist in re/creating an identity with recovering addicts. *Dramatherapy, 38*(2–3), 106–123. doi:10.1080/02630672.2017.1340492

Paquette, D., Carbonneau, R., Dubeau, D., Bigras, M., & Tremblay, R. E. (2003). Prevalence of father-child rough-and-tumble play and physical aggression in preschool children. *European Journal of Psychology of Education, 18*(2), 171–189. doi:10.1007/BF03173483

Pendzik, S. (2013). The 6-key model and the assessment of the aesthetic dimension in dramatherapy. *Dramatherapy, 35*(2), 90–98. doi:10.1080/02630672.2013.822524

Sajnani, N. (2010). Mind the gap: Facilitating transformative witnessing amongst audiences. In P. Jones (Ed.), *Drama as therapy: Clinical work and research into practice. Volume 2* (pp. 189–207). East Sussex: Routledge.

SOL Center. (2023). SOL Center: Cultivating climate justice and peace. Retrieved from www.solcenterhi.com

Steingut, R. R., Patall, E. A., & Trimble, S. S. (2017). The effect of rationale provision on motivation and performance outcomes: A meta-analysis. *Motivation Science, 3*(1), 19–50. doi:10.1037/mot0000039

UWC Atlantic. (2023). Inspiring changemakers: College prospectus. Llantwit Major: UWC Atlantic.org

van der Kolk, B. (1977). *The body keeps the score: Brain, mind, and body in the healing of trauma.* New York: Penguin.

van der Kolk, B. (2005). Developmental trauma disorder: Towards a rational diagnosis for children with complex trauma histories. *APA PsycNet Psychiatric Annals, 35*(5), 401–408. doi:10.3928/00485713-20050501-06

Walshaw, T. (2017). *Double entry bookkeeping: Or dear Cilla. The easy way to debit and credit all the way to trial balance.* (Kindle ed.). Canberra, Australia: Tim Walshaw.

Wilshire, B. (1982). *Role playing and identity: The limits of theatre as metaphor.* Bloomington: Indiana University Press.

Index

Note: Page numbers in *italic* refer to figures.